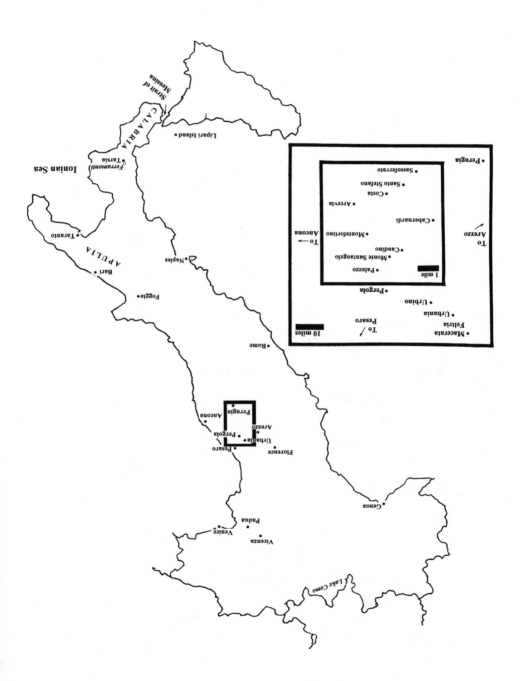

The Persistence of Hope

The Persistence of Hope

A True Story

Albert Alcalay

To our good neighbour?

Rex c Starder.

Albert

DELAWARE

Newark: University of Delaware Press

Associated University Presses
2010 Eastpark Boulevard
Cranbury, NJ 08512

The paper used in this publication meets the requirements of the American National Standard for Permanence of Paper for Printed Library Materials Z39.48-1984.

Library of Congress Cataloging-in-Publication Data

Alcalay, Albert, 1917–
    The persistence of hope : a true story / Albert Alcalay.
        p.   cm.
    Includes bibliographical references and index.
    ISBN-13: 978-0-87413-963-1 (alk. paper)
    ISBN-10: 0-87413-963-5 (alk. paper)
    1. Alcalay, Albert, 1917–   2. Jews—Serbia—Belgrade—Biography.   3. Holocaust,
Jewish (1939–1945)—Italy—Personal narratives.   4. Painters—Biography.   5.
Belgrade (Serbia)—Biography.   I. Title.
    DS135.Y83A733   2007
    940.53′18092—dc22
    [B]   2006037593

PRINTED IN THE UNITED STATES OF AMERICA

I offer this book to my sons and to their children, so that future generations will have the living memory of these events. I also dedicate this book to those good Italian people—and others—without whose help my family and I may not have survived, so that their courage, humanity, and resourcefulness be known.

—A.A.

Contents

Preface

THROUGHOUT MY LIFE, I HAVE WORKED AS AN ARTIST. VISUAL PROBLEMS of space, rather than temporal issues of narrative, have consequently honed my perceptions and shaped my mind. This does not mean that I have neglected the written word, although I have never actively been a writer. Since my early youth, I have been a voracious reader of literature and of scientific, philosophical, and technical works, and I owe to books—and the abstractions and realities and poetics of their authors—a lifetime of nourishment and learning.

In recent years, I have felt the approach of a time of renunciation. I have become more fully aware of the ultimate closing of the circle of life. Before the horizons of my memory grow dim in the twilight of advancing age, I have turned the light of my spirit to reflect upon the past. I have feared that even I may have forgotten the tragedy of the time in which I have lived and the force of what I have experienced. The past had receded in the succession of the many chapters of my life, and the sharp edges of my memories had dulled. Through meditation and reflection, their vividness has been restored to me, and from this I have drawn consolation.

I first began to transcribe these memories and reflections at the age of fifty-nine. Now, almost three decades later, I am at last gathering them into a coherent story. My experience of life has been filled with challenges, and the struggles to overcome them. My ideals have been tested against harsh realities, and my enthusiasms have been subjected to self-doubt. In the effort to recover the fullness of the most difficult period of my life—and the period that formed my character—and in the search for its ultimate meaning and consequences and value, I decided to record my memories of my experiences in a Europe shattered by war.

I escaped the eruption of Nazi evil in which six million Jews—my people—were horribly exterminated in an industrialized genocide un-

11

paralleled in human history. I feel compelled now to set my story into words, to leave it to my two sons, to their children, and to their children's children. My five-year odyssey during the years of the Second World War profoundly shaped my life and character. These experiences left their indelible mark on my entire career in art. I have dedicated myself to representing them through the symbolic forms and subconscious ideas of my paintings and drawings, where they remain as the testament of my creative process.

As an artist works, he registers his perceptions of the world around him. This world shapes his sensibility, and the artist absorbs it into his very identity and becomes part of it, but he reacts to the world through imagery of his own invention. The artist draws this imagery—uncanny, mysterious, sometimes unpredictable, and sometimes indecipherable—from the well of archetypes, from the deep and profound abyss of his being. I have always expressed myself through my painting. I have never mastered any tool as well as my brush. My expressive powers in painting are the standard against which I measure everything.

My strength has always been in doing things, not in writing about them, and I must struggle with a sense of self-consciousness and vulnerability in writing about my life. Yet it is with words and not my brush that I must paint this story, as truly as I can and with all the force of a time regained. I am a *deraciné* (an uprooted person). My mother tongue was Serbian. I was trained in French in my youth and, during the war and the critical years of my formation as an artist, I learned Italian. But I set this story down in English, the language of the land that has become my adopted home and the mother tongue of my posterity.

As I write from my beloved island home of Martha's Vineyard, I look across the Atlantic Ocean to the past. Sixty-five years ago, in 1940, when I was a young man and Europe was at war, this island did not exist for me. Now, as the sun hangs low on the western horizon of my life, I cast its light to the east across an ocean and a gulf of time, with the hope that it will illumine a past that is quickly receding but should never be forgotten. In the light of this illumination, I offer this account of my youth and trace the role of Europe's tragedy in the shaping of my talent, my view of the world, and my destiny. Yes, this

is a personal book. How else could I be honest with you? It is the
banner of my beliefs and all the passion for life that I have carried
within myself all the years of my journey from the east. I leave it with
love to you, my dear children, and to your children, and yes, to you,
gracious readers, with hope persevering that this passion may yet burn
within your hearts.

Albert Alcalay
West Tisbury, Mass.
June 2005

Acknowledgment

Special gratitude to my son Leor for his indefatigable efforts and his invaluable assistance from the inception of this project in his early recording of my stories to its conclusion in this publication. Thanks also to John Letterman for his editing help in restructuring the narrative presentation.

Pronunciation Table

aceite (Span.)	ah-**sey**-teh
aceto (Ital.)	ah-**cheh**-toh
Aegean (Sea)	eh-**jeeh**-ahn
Ancona	ahn-**koh**-nah
Ante Pavelic	anteh **pah**-veh-litch
Apulia	ah-**pooh**-leeh-yah
Arcevia	ahr-**cheh**-veeh-yah
Arezzo	ah-**reh**-tsoh
Arno (River)	**ahr**-noh
Bari	**bah**-reeh
Basilicata Taranto	bah-seeh-leeh-**kah**-tah tah-**rahn**-toh
Biennale di Venezia	beeh-yeh-**nah**-leh deeh veh-**neh**-tseeh-yah
Bregalnica (River)	breh-**gahl**-neeh-tsah
Cabernardi	kah-behr-**nahr**-deeh
Caen	kah-**ehn**
Calabria	kah-**lah**-bree-yah
Capella degli Scrovegni	kah-**peh**-lah deh-leeh skroh-**veh**-neeh
Carabinieri (Ital.)	kah-rah-bih-neeh-**yeh**-reeh
caravanserai (Turk.)	kah-rah-**vahn**-seh-rah-yeeh
(Lake) Como	**koh**-moh
contretemps	kohn-treh-**tohm**
Cosenza	koh-**sehn**-tsah
Crati (river valley)	**krah**-teeh
Dubrovnik	dooh-**brohv**-nihk
Durres	**dooh**-rehs
Ferramonti di Tarsia	feh-rah-**mohn**-teeh deeh **tahr**-sheeh-yah
(Michael) Fingesten	**feehn**-geh-stehn
Foggia	**foh**-jah
Frankfurt am Main	frahnk-foohrt ahm-**mah**-yin
Giotto	**joh**-toh

17

Gorizia	goh-**reeh**-tseeh-yah
gymnasium (Lat.)	geehm-**nah**-zeeh-oohm
(Bay of) Kotor	**koh**-tohr
halvah(Turk./Serb.)	**hahl**-vah
Herceg Novi	hehr-tsehg-**noh**-veeh
Jasenovac	yah-**sehn**-oh-vahts
Jude!	**yooh**-deh
(Island of) Kamilanisi.	kah-meeh-lah-**neeh**-seeh
Kavaja	kah-**vah**-yah
Kukes	**kooh**-kehs
Kumanovo	**kooh**-mahn-noh-voh
"Laku noć, gospodićna" (Croat.)	lah-kooh-**notch** goh-spoh-**deech**-nah
lasciapassare	lah-shah-pah-**sah**-reh
Langsam (Ger.)	**lahng**-sahm
lepinja(Serb.)	**leh**-peeh-nya
Lesbos	**lehz**-bohs
Lipari	**leeh**-pahr-eeh
Ljubljana	looh-beeh-**yah**-nah
"Los!" (Ger.)	**Lohws**
Lovcen (Mountain)	**lohv**-chen
lumpen	**lahm**-pehn
Macedonia	mah-keh-**doh**-nee-yah
(Sea of) Marmora	**mahr**-moh-rah
Macerata Feltria	mah-cheh-**rah**-tah **fehl**-treeh-yah
Marche	**mahr**-keh
mezzadria (Ital.)	meh-tsah-**dreeh**-yah
Mongrassano	mohn-grah-**sah**-noh
Monte Sant'Angelo	mont-sahn-**tahn**-jeh-loh
Montefortino	Mon-teh-for-**teeh**-noh
Montesecco	mohn-teh-**seh**-koh
Moshe Pijade	**moh**-sheh pee-**yah**-deh
Niš	**neesh**
numerus clausus (Lat.)	**nooh**-meh-roos **klauh**-zoos
Padua	.**pah**-dooh-ah
Paiki (Serb. name)	**pah**-yeeh-keeh
Palazzo	pah-**lah**-tsoh
Pančevo	**pahn**-cheh-voh
Panzerkampf-wagen	pahn-zehr-kampf **vah**-gehn
pasta asciuta (Ital.)	pah-stah-ah-**shooh**-tah

pecorino (Ital.)	peh-koh-**reeh**-noh
Pelivan	peh-leeh-**vahn**
Pensione (Fr./Ital.)	pahn-**syohn**
Pergola	**pehr**-goh-lah
Pesaro	**peh**-zah-roh
Piraeus	peeh-**rey**-oohs
poderi (Ital.)	poh-**deh**-reeh
polenta (Ital.)	poh-**len**-tah
Postumia	poh-**stooh**-meeh-yah
il prete (Ital.)	eel-**preh**-teh
Prizren	**preeh**-zrehn
Priština	**preesh**-tih-nah
Quattrocento (Ital.)	kwah-troh-**chen**-toh
rastrelamento (Ital.)	rah-streh-lah-**mehn**-toh
Šajmiste	**sah**-ye-meesh-teh
San Lorenzo	sahn loh-**ren**-zoh
Santo Stefano	sahn-toh-**steh**-fah-noh
Sassoferrato	sah-soh-feh-**rah**-toh
(Lake) Scutari	skooh-**tah**-reeh
"Sehr Wenig" (Ger.)	zehr **veh**-nik
Sibari	**seeh**-bahr-eeh
signori (Ital.)	seeh-**nyohr**-eeh
Skadar	**skah**-dahr
Shqiptar	**ship**-tahr
Spa	**spah**
Split	**split**
Šibenik	**sheeh**-beh-nihk
Štip	**shteep**
Sterletto	stehr-**leht**-toh
Stražin	**strah**-*zh*in (as in "s" in measure)
Stukas	**shtooh**-kahz
Skoplje	**skop**-lih-yeh
Tašmajdan	**tash**-mah-ye-dahn
Trecento (Ital.)	treh-**chen**-toh
Trieste	treeh-**yes**-teh
Tjustendil	choohs-ten-**deehl**
Tirana	teeh-**rah**-nah
Tomori (Mountain)	**toh**-moh-reeh
ufficio stranieri (Ital.)	ooh-**feeh**-choh strah-**nyeh**-reeh

Urbania	oohr-**bah**-neeh-yah
Urbino	oohr-**beeh**-noh
Uroševac	ooh-**roh**-sheh-vahts
Vicenza	veeh-**chen**-tsah
Volatica	voh-**lah**-teeh-kah

1

Thursday, March 27, 1941

I WOKE LAZILY THAT MARCH MORNING AT AROUND SEVEN THIRTY. Strong sunlight penetrated the closed shutters. Still in my night-clothes, not fully awake, I wandered through the apartment, slowly adjusting to the light of the bright day, another day of hope and expectations. The apartment was large with many rooms, some overlooking the street and others looking into an inner courtyard. Here I lived with my father, Samuel, my mother, Lepa (née Afar), and my sister, Buena. A housemaid also lived with us. I was restless at this time in my life. As a Jew, I had ample cause to feel anxious.

As it was my habit each morning, I turned on the radio for the news and then approached my bedroom window to open the shutters. Pushing the shutters wide, I stared in disbelief at a chilling sight. Diagonally across the intersection from the corner on which our building stood, three soldiers in full battle dress crouched beside a large machine gun. The gun was trained directly at me. At first I thought this was an apparition. But as my eyes adjusted to the light, I realized that the soldiers were very real. And this reality was confirmed when I heard the radio announcer solemnly report that the regent Prince Paul had abdicated and that young Prince Peter had been proclaimed king and commander of the armed forces. King Peter had assumed sole command of the army and had decreed emergency rule. I ran to wake my parents and sister to tell them the news. The announcer urged listeners to go into the streets to celebrate the event, but also to remain calm and maintain order. The news struck like a lightning bolt from a clear sky! It was March 27, 1941.

My father immediately became very anxious and agitated. He had lived through two previous wars, the Serbian–Bulgarian War of 1912 and the Great War of 1914, and he feared that yet another calamity

23

could strike the Balkan lands. My father was a student of world politics. He intensely followed news of the war that had engulfed Europe,
and the strategies of Hitler, Stalin, and Churchill. He sat by the radio
for hours, listening to news, speeches, and announcements in many
languages. He read many newspapers voraciously as well. Was this
the news that he had been dreading? Was this the prelude to war in
Yugoslavia?

Intensely excited, I explained to my family that I had to join my
friends to see what was happening. Was young King Peter's accession
to the throne an assertion of Yugoslavia's independence and an end to
German influence over the nation? I passionately wanted to resist the
Germans and to rid Yugoslavia of their presence. I loathed all that
Germany had come to represent. I was prepared to take almost any
action to vent my anger and seek revenge. I had studied the tragic
history and suffering of the Jewish people during two thousand years
of exile from our homeland. I knew many terrifying details of the latest
chapters of anti-Semitic persecution whose virulence had infected all
of Nazi Europe. I was fearful for our people. I wanted to join in any
expression of resistance to the brutal Nazi forces that threatened them.

Tearing myself from my parents and sister, I jumped into my
clothes and ran into the street. I was immediately caught up in the
motion of a great mass of people, all moving toward Monument
Square, from whose center arose a gigantic equestrian monument of
Knez Mihajlo. The verdigris-tarnished bronze statue of the great Serbian duke dominated the square from atop its pedestal, on which were
carved scenes of the duke's heroic life. Streetcar lines radiated from
the square to different parts of Belgrade. The austere gray building of
the national theater occupied one side of the square. Facing the theater across the vast space loomed the massive headquarters of the nation's Property Bank, built in the monumental architectural style of
nineteenth-century Europe. A tall, quite modern building occupied
the third side of the square. This building housed the Riunioni Insur-
ance Company, a great many offices, large luxury apartments, a row of
elegant stores, and a cinema. A wide avenue, flanked on both sides by
stores, cafés, and boutiques, opened onto the fourth side. The square
pulsed with activity. It was crowded with a constantly changing urban
kaleidoscope of busy humanity—shoppers, pedestrians, soldiers on

leave, and beggars. Its many kiosks were crammed with newspapers and magazines. Street vendors displayed and sold their wares on its wide sidewalks. People waited in line at its busy streetcar stops. And from all of this arose the music of the heart of the city: a symphony of shouts and the hum of thousands of voices commingled with the clanging of the streetcars and the horns and roaring of a dense traffic of cars and trucks and other vehicles.

People of all kinds—clerics in long black robes, students, mothers with their small children, office workers, soldiers, the young and the old, the rich and the poor—were crowding into the square when I breathlessly arrived there with my camera. The electrifying atmosphere was intensely charged with passion. Everyone was elated, excitedly speaking and gesturing, gathered in groups or simply on his or her own. Everyone was shouting *"Bolje rat, nego pakt!"* (Better war than the pact!). Many people menacingly raised their fists toward the Riunioni building from which the German Tourist Bureau, quartered on the third floor, provided materials and support for members of the Nazi fifth column.

The Nazi government had organized a fifth column in Yugoslavia, as it had among people of German extraction in all the countries of Europe. These Germans were deeply patriotic and loyal to Hitler's new Reich. Germany had organized many of them into networks of spies and agents to advance the interests of the Reich and, in many cases, to prepare the way for Nazi invasion. There were around one million *Volksdeutsche* in Yugoslavia, many of whom were susceptible to Nazi indoctrination and were willing to act as spies and agents for Germany. The German Embassy set up "tourist bureaus" and other offices to encourage and support these treasonous activities and to facilitate the gathering of all kinds of intelligence, from the identification of wealthy Jews and politically progressive leaders to the locations of supply and munitions dumps and the deployments of troops and fortifications.

The late March weather was beautiful, almost balmy, and the passionate atmosphere in the square was strangely festive. Everyone in the crowd focused on the third-floor windows of the German Tourist Bureau. They had all somehow simultaneously understood that something dramatic was about to happen. Constantly observing the faces, the expressions, the gestures, and dress of everyone around me, and always aware of the cries and shouts that were rising from the crowd, I searched for a vantage point from which I could take good photographs. Suddenly, the plate glass windows of the German Tourist Bureau shattered into fragments, and file cabinets, chairs, desks, and tables crashed to the pavement three floors below. The crowd roared enthusiastically as pillows, posters, photographs, bundles of documents, and great rafts of papers were tossed through the gaping windows. Several minutes later, a German flag and a huge portrait of Hitler were thrown onto the pile of wreckage below. The crowd shrieked with delight. People frantically screamed and gestured, shook hands, and embraced, as if a great victory had been won.

I wanted to photograph the entire scene. I first tried to lift my camera above the heads of the crowd, to take chance shots without viewing and focusing. But I wasn't sure that my camera was catching anything, so I looked around and made a quick decision to climb the equestrian monument to have a view of everything. Pleased with my decision, I clambered onto the pedestal and was taking pictures when a man in the crowd suddenly fought his way toward me, pointing and yelling, "There's a Nazi spy photographing for the German press." At this very moment, the pile of goods thrown from the German Tourist Bureau burst into flames. The crowd was extremely charged with pent-up emotion. This was the first time since the Nazis had seized power in Germany in 1932 that the people of Yugoslavia had dared to express their hatred for the odious German regime. I had been accused of being a Nazi and the crowd had no ears to hear my desperate denials. Angry men pulled me off the pedestal and beat me, tearing at my clothes, grabbing at my camera, cursing me and spitting at me. I tried to reach for my wallet to pull out my identification card. I tried to raise my voice over their shouts to tell them that I was Jewish and that I was taking pictures for the student newspapers. But everything was futile.

I was terrified. A huge, enraged crowd, a microcosm of the entire society, encircled me. A thousand thoughts raced through my mind. I was afraid that the crowd was going to hang me. Still unable to make my explanations heard, I instinctively gripped my camera tightly, not wanting to give anything away and aggravate the extreme danger of the situation. The crowd screamed, "Grab the camera! Grab the camera! Destroy the film!" At that moment, a single policeman, truncheon in hand, forced his way toward me through the crowd. He had already understood from the screams of the crowd that the camera was the cause of the trouble. When he finally reached me, he grabbed me by the arm, tore my camera away from me, threw it on the ground, and crushed it flat with one stomp of his heavy boot. I was in shock, but at least I was now under the protection of the authorities. The policeman started to spit questions into my face. He then shoved me away and told me to go home. He didn't bother to listen to anything that I had to say. He told me that he had his orders and that he had no use for my explanations. The people around me dispersed and drifted back toward the bonfire. They somehow understood that they had made a mistake. I was left alone, bruised, filthy, exhausted, in utter despair.

The excitement of the day was too great. I could not surrender to fear or depression, even after the trauma I had suffered in the square. I was trembling, but I recognized that history was being made before my eyes. I was witnessing the rising of the entire nation. The people of Yugoslavia would resist Nazi domination and political oppression. As I walked home, I reflected on the events of the day and understood why the people in the square had reacted as they had. Gradually, I collected myself. I did not linger at home. I changed out of my torn clothes, washed and refreshed myself, and then returned to the streets to join my friends.

Everywhere the people were celebrating. Flags and banners were held high and swirled in the air. Throngs gathered spontaneously and marched throughout the city. Patriotic songs and music filled the streets. Schoolchildren and parents, soldiers, priests, peasants, workers, and shopkeepers—everyone—was joyously participating in the festive scene. Everyone was proud and optimistic. Everyone had something to say. The dark tensions that had oppressed the city for so many months had suddenly burst into a bright rainbow of hope. I witnessed acts of violence as well, which, in the excitement of the moment, seemed curiously amusing. A couple of young men hurled bricks through the plate glass window of an elegant café as they exultantly shouted, "Germans drank coffee here!" They felt no concern or respect for the Serbian owner of the café. The latest declarations of the newly named King Peter blasted from megaphones, handheld or mounted on cars, assuring the crowds that the new Yugoslav government had rescinded the Nazi pact, and that the army stood with the people and the new king.

By evening of this fateful day of March 27, 1941, the crowds had calmed and dispersed to their homes and cafés. Prince Paul and his cabinet had fled Belgrade. Of course, not everyone, certainly not the *Volksdeutsche* who were streaming away from the city, was pleased with the turn of events. I returned home, utterly exhausted and so hoarse that I could hardly speak. After the excitement and celebration of the day, the gravity of the situation began to sink in. I was very worried, as was my entire family. No people had ever dared to treat the Germans as we had done that day. We had expelled many of them from their offices and homes. We had burned their symbols and their flags, their photos of Hitler, Göering, and Goebbels. Our pride had had its day, but the fury of our pride had subsided as sober assessments of the peril that Yugoslavia now faced became the topic of tens of thousands of intense conversations. For more than eighteen months since the outbreak of the war in the autumn of 1939, Yugoslavia had remained outside the war. We knew that the Germans would now attack Yugoslavia and that Belgrade, our beautiful capital, would be a primary target, not least because of the events of this fateful day in March when the people rose in joy with shouts of freedom. We knew that we could no longer remain neutral. We knew that war was at hand.

2

A Proud and Fearful Nation

Yugoslavia was artificially created at the Versailles conference at the end of World War I. The Treaty of Versailles joined into
one state many different nationalities, attaching to Serbia administrative regions that had been torn from the corpse of the Austro-Hungarian Empire after the war. France had insisted upon this at the
Versailles peace conference. But the bequest of these regions to her
Serbian ally was a poisoned gift. It was not a true nation, and its people were never united. The dominant Serbs were not only set apart by
their Orthodox Christianity, they also used the Cyrillic alphabet. Their
Slavic blood was the only element they held in common with some of
the peoples over whom they had been set to rule. The peoples of Slovenia, Croatia, and Bosnia had all long-been governed as separate
provinces under the Austro-Hungarian Empire, and tiny Montenegro
had been an independent kingdom. The Slovenes and the Croats were
Catholics and used the Latin alphabet. The population of Bosnia was
a complex mix of Moslems, Jews, and Christians. The population of
Kosovo, within the borders of pre-World War I Serbia, was mostly ethnic Albanian, and Moslem.

King Alexander had assumed the throne of the Kingdom of Serbs,
Croats, and Slovenes, as it was called at the time of his accession, in
1921. Son and heir of King Peter of Serbia, Alexander was an Orthodox Christian, like almost all of his Serb subjects, the dominant group
in the new nation he ruled. King Alexander was a mediocre sovereign
burdened with the nearly impossible task of holding together an ethni-
cally divided kingdom. In 1929, he abrogated the constitution and re-
named the country Yugoslavia. Yugoslavia gradually became an
authoritarian police state. When Alexander was assassinated in 1934,
his son Peter was too young to become king. Prince Paul, a cousin of

29

the assassinated king, was appointed to serve as regent until Peter came of age to assume the throne. Prince Paul had great difficulty maintaining both the internal stability and the external neutrality of the nation. Some people reassured themselves by thinking that Yugoslavia was a small unimportant country that would survive undisturbed. It was isolated, they argued, from the monstrous events that were tearing Europe apart. But Yugoslavia was spinning within a vortex of war that would engulf it.

I had completed my studies at the secondary school in the eventful year of 1936. The tragic Spanish Civil War had electrified all of Europe. This brutal war had merely been a prelude to the conflagration of 1939 that would rapidly engulf all of Europe. In 1938, the brutal Nazi persecution of the Jews had begun in earnest. It was the year of the *Kristallnacht* (the Night of Broken Glass). That year, as the specter of approaching war cast its shadow across Europe, all the nations of the Continent looked uneasily to their alliances, the imperial democracies grouped on one side, the Fascist states on the other. Almost every nation was forced to cast its lot with one camp or the other. The great exception seemed to be the Soviet Union, which stood alone until August 1939, when Hitler and Stalin shocked the world by signing a nonaggression pact on the eve of their dismemberment of Poland.

After graduating from *gymnasium* in 1936, I worked with a Zionist organization, educating young people in the ideals of Zionism and participating in public affairs. Through my work, I met innumerable Jewish refugees—from Germany, later from Austria, still later from Czechoslovakia, and then even more, an unending, anguished stream in flight from terror. I was intensely aware of anti-Semitism. I had studied its history. But it was through the accounts of these refugees that I was first exposed to its actual practice. My consciousness darkened with a growing understanding of the real situation and the imminent danger that we were facing even in Yugoslavia. And it was from this time on that I began urgently preparing to face this danger.

The persecution of Jews in Germany began almost immediately after Hitler had become chancellor and the Nazis had seized total power. Many Jews, individually or in family groups, passed through Yugoslavia on their way to Palestine. Some of these Jews obtained permits to reside permanently in Yugoslavia, where they felt safe from persecution. Because I was active in the Jewish youth movement, I had opportunities to speak with these refugees, and I learned directly from them their sad and terrifying experiences. Their accounts of persecution in Germany, France, Czechoslovakia, Austria, and Hungary were utterly foreign to our experience. While it was common knowledge that Jews were cruelly treated in Nazi-occupied countries, it was inconceivable to most Jews in Yugoslavia that the same tragedies could occur in our country, where a large population of Jews had for centuries lived in peace among the Slavs. Everyone was fearful, but most Jews simply could not accept the danger now on our doorstep for the brutal and mortal danger that it was.

Even so, by the autumn of 1940, many Yugoslav Jews, especially among the wealthy, had begun to obtain passports and visas for South America, Spain, or Portugal. Some Jews changed their names or even converted to the Christian religion. I felt that this was shameful and I fought back, speaking out publicly to affirm a Jewish consciousness among our people. I condemned Jews who so readily abandoned their tradition and their people. The members of my Jewish group were strong and proud in our solidarity and in our affirmations of our Jewish identities. During that late autumn and fateful winter of 1940–41, we were closely monitored by the police and by the Volksdeutsche organizations as well. And then, in those heady, disturbing days at the end of March 1941, we scattered into a thousand directions. The universities were closed. The students were on strike. War was at hand.

In the late 1930s, all of my friends in the Jewish youth movement planned to immigrate to Palestine. Palestine was a British mandate and immigration was restricted. The only way to enter Palestine was illegally, but this did not discourage us. We would not be permitted to leave Yugoslavia, however, until we had met our obligations of military service, so six of us petitioned to serve in the military. Our petitions were accepted, and we were sent to a reserve officer training camp in Sarajevo. There we spent nine long months. This was one of the most difficult periods of my life. Our superiors had no respect for us. As young scholars and idealistic citizens, this was a brutal shock to us. Obedience to orders was our first lesson. As our instructors taught us our duties as commanding officers, they suppressed our individual human dignity. I was assigned to the artillery. I studied military strategy, ballistics, calculus, and the use of guns and cannons, subjects to which I had never before given any thought. Throughout the troubled year of 1939, the Yugoslav army stood on alert while the government resisted intense pressure to enter into an alliance with the Axis powers. But our lives as soldiers remained uneventful, as we prepared for the officer exams that would mark our passage to the rank of sergeant. The day of our examinations finally came, on June 19, 1939. We celebrated our promotions when we learned that we had passed.

I was in military service when the Germans attacked Poland on September 1, 1939. By September 17, when the Russians struck Poland from the east, the Germans had shattered Polish resistance into isolated pockets of troops and had surrounded Warsaw. On September 28, Warsaw fell to the Germans. Although guerilla resistance persisted into the winter, the Germans had crushed the last fragments of the Polish army by early October. It was said that the Russian attackers stood aside while the Germans destroyed the Polish army, because the Russians were reluctant to stain their hands with the blood of fellow Slavs. The Russian butchery of Polish officers at a place called Katyn was not discovered until many years later.

If our lives in the Yugoslav army remained strangely peaceful during that autumn of 1939, the realities throughout Europe and within Yugoslavia were anything but calm. France and Britain had declared war on Germany after it invaded their Polish ally, but they didn't act militarily, and Germany, whose armed forces were greatly outnumbered by the French in the west, was left free to consolidate its conquest of Poland. We were saddened, but no longer surprised, when Soviet troops occupied Estonia, Latvia, and Lithuania in October. At the end of November, the Soviet army attacked Finland. We heard about naval battles between the Germans and the British, and we heard about the U-boat attacks against British shipping, but there was no real war in the west. France and Britain were at war with Germany, but they were still officially at peace with Germany's Axis allies, Italy and Japan.

Real war again broke out in Western Europe in March and April of the following spring. Hitler seized Norway and repulsed a British effort to prevent it. The Germans also occupied Denmark. In May, they attacked Belgium, the Netherlands, and France. The main thrust of the German attack had penetrated French defenses in the Ardennes, and German armored formations raced to the sea, cutting off the bulk of France's army in Belgium and northern France, thereby inflicting a complete defeat and disgrace upon that noble nation. During World War I, the French had fought at the side of the people of Serbia against the Austrian Empire and the Germans. The fall of France in those few weeks of late spring in 1940 had darkened many hearts among the people of Serbia, and we immediately had come to hate Italy when it attacked France, like a jackal, from the rear.

So, although all was quiet in our corner of Europe, the atmosphere was troubled with tension and intrigue. We had completed our reserve officer training, but we had to remain with the army to perform exercises and maneuvers, instead of returning to our studies at the university in Belgrade. The fall of France had saddened the entire world. We were fearful for the Jewish intellectuals who were concentrated there, and the signs of rising anti-Semitism within Yugoslavia had alarmed us. It was during this period that anti-Semitic laws were proclaimed in Yugoslavia for the first time. A *numerus clausus* imposed on the university limited the number of Jews who could be admitted.

———

Although the Second World War erupted in Europe in the summer of 1939, Yugoslavia managed to remain neutral until the spring of 1941. Geographically at the crossroads of east and west, Yugoslavia was almost completely surrounded by hostile nations. Austria, Hungary, Romania, Bulgaria, and Italy were all Axis nations allied with Germany. The international waterway of the Danube River flowed through most of these countries and played an important role in the geopolitical situation. Italy had occupied Albania. Yugoslavia's only friendly neighbor was Greece, with whom it shared a border on the south.

In 1941, I was completing my studies in architecture. As a member of the Jewish youth movement, I was planning to go to Palestine to live and work on a collective farm. I wanted to participate in recreating a new land and the realization of the ideals of Zionism as these had been taught to me in my youth group. I wanted to dedicate myself to the fulfillment of the Jewish longing to reclaim our ancient Jewish homeland. I fully understood the threat that the Nazis posed. I watched developments in neighboring countries during this period with mounting alarm. By the spring of 1941, the Nazis had been victorious everywhere, and hostile forces had all but surrounded Yugoslavia.

Belgrade, the capital of Yugoslavia, was a beautiful city situated at the confluence of the Danube and Sava rivers. Tensions had mounted in Belgrade in the first months of 1941, as the Yugoslav government struggled to balance internal and external pressures and tried to avoid being drawn into the European war. There were pro-Nazi groups and interests within Yugoslavia, but most people feared war and wanted to remain independent and at peace. Yugoslavia's closest allies—France and Czechoslovakia—had been defeated and were under Nazi occupation. Jews were fleeing all the conquered nations of Europe, many desperately trying to reach Palestine, in spite of a British blockade. The British controlled Palestine under a League of Nations mandate. In the late 1930s, the British had begun attempting to restrict Jewish immigration into Palestine, because of increasingly bitter strife between Jews and Arabs there.

Throughout the history of the Serbian nation, Belgrade had been the focus of Serbian life, the home of Serbia's Karađorđević dynasty, the seat of its government, and the headquarters of its military services. Prior to the First World War, it was the imperial capital of Serbia, under the Austro–Hungarian Empire. As the capital of the heterogeneous country cobbled together at Versailles from the wreckage of the Austro-Hungarian and Ottoman empires, Belgrade had grown into a cosmopolitan center, a magnet for many of the diverse peoples of Yugoslavia, and emigrées and refugees from throughout Europe. One million White Russians had fled to Yugoslavia after the Russian Revolution and the fall of the czar. Many of these had made their homes in Belgrade, within the city's mosaic of peoples.

Among the diverse peoples who made up the population of Yugoslavia there were also one million Germans. Called Volksdeutsche, these Germans mostly held menial jobs, working in such occupations as janitors, mechanics, and domestic maids. Almost all of them had been born in Yugoslavia. For the most part, they had always lived peacefully as full citizens of the country. But, by late 1940, the atmosphere within Belgrade had become increasingly infected with Nazi intrigue. During this period, some indigenous Volksdeutsche had become directly implicated in the cancerous growth of the city's panoply of Nazi organizations, German businesses, tourist agencies, and cultural bureaus. The German government sponsored these businesses and organizations, which often served as covers for subversive activity.

For the year and a half after the German invasion of Poland, while we followed the news of Hitler's conquests and domination of Western and Central Europe, life in Belgrade had continued more or less normally, at least at the surface. Schools were open. Businesses were functioning. But the atmosphere was becoming more and more tense with each passing week. People tried to remain calm, although everyone was frantically preparing for the worst. Everyone was hoarding food and other necessities. We stocked our home with supplies of all kinds, from sardines to sugar, from crates of soap to toilet paper, and any necessity that we could accumulate in the face of our fears of breakdowns in communications and transport, interruptions of electricity, in short, the disruption of normal civic order. With each passing day, the future became darker and more uncertain as the prospect of war and siege mounted.

People in the streets and cafés and other gathering places openly shared their anxieties and exchanged rumors of impending catastrophe. Nervous policemen were already breaking up public gatherings of more than three people. Friends met in private homes to discuss contingency plans for every imaginable emergency or disaster. The atmosphere in Belgrade grew daily more oppressive as intense pressures from Germany became threatening. We knew that we had great reason to be anxious about the fate of Yugoslavia. Britain's weakness at Munich was still fresh in our minds. We knew what had already happened to Czechoslovakia and Poland. The collapse of France had devastated us. We had grimly witnessed the coming to power of fascist regimes in neighboring Bulgaria, Romania, and Hungary.

Within the Zionist organization, we were all on the alert to do everything in our power to aid Jewish refugees to find safe passage to Palestine. Because the British held Egypt and the entire Middle East,

and the Royal Navy patrolled the Mediterranean, very tightly controlling the shores of Palestine, an overland passage offered the most
promising escape route for these refugees. Throughout 1940 and the
winter months of 1941, the movement of refugees through Bulgaria
and Greece, to Turkey and then Syria, toward Palestine, was still possible, though arduous, long, and expensive. Devotion, courage, and
cunning were all required to overcome the dangers and difficulties.

I was called to the south of Serbia, to Kumanovo, a completely Macedonian town, where I exercised with my battery and worked in the
quartermaster corps to accumulate foodstuffs of all kinds in the army
supply depots. When I returned to Belgrade from military exercises in
the south, I immediately applied myself to setting the affairs of my
family in order. I wanted to move my family's money, that of my parents and of my uncles as well, to a neutral country, to Switzerland. A
friend from Palestine, who was a representative of our Zionist organization, had the means to transfer the money safely, but my entire family was unmoved by my sense of urgency. They persisted in hoping
that Yugoslavia would not be drawn into the war. They remembered
the horrors of the First World War, but they refused to believe that
such dreadful horrors could ever again be repeated.

But the sorrows of the war that they remembered were nothing beside the horrors that I feared were coming. During the First World
War, the Austrians had imposed a regime that was harsh, but not brutal and savagely cruel. King Peter and the Serbian government had
escaped to the side of our ally, France, and, in the end, my parents,
who had been transferred to Paris with my father's bank, had emerged
from the war unscathed. My family did not understand that the coming
war would be far different. It would be a blitzkrieg war of lightning
armored attacks and unrestricted bombing, a war of destruction in
which the civilian population would be exposed to as much or more
harm and suffering as the soldiers. My family did not believe, could
not believe that, after a Nazi conquest, many citizens, and Jews in
particular, would be herded into concentration camps. All my efforts
to point to the grave dangers went unheeded. We remained in Belgrade, waiting for the drama to unfold.

The atmosphere in Belgrade approached panic in the winter of
1940. Fears of embargo, war, siege, and occupation intensified, and

prices soared as the population nervously continued to hoard goods of every kind. Yugoslavs wanted to remain at peace. Almost everyone insisted that Yugoslavia was unimportant, arguing that the Balkan country was isolated from the theaters of European conflict and could remain neutral. The government struggled for months to block or at least to delay any adhesion to an accord with the Axis powers. Throughout the winter, the issue of a treaty was hotly discussed, and the fears of the Yugoslav people were amply displayed in the pages of the country's newspapers. Although evaluations of the situation varied among the different politicians and commentators and the groups they represented, everyone felt a mounting danger. Prince Paul's sympathies inclined him toward Great Britain, but by spring, the German pressure on Yugoslavia to sign the Axis Anti-Comintern Pact had become overwhelming. Yugoslavia's prime minister, Cvetković, and foreign minister, Aleksandar Cincar-Marković, finally signed the Axis treaty in Vienna on March 25, 1941.

News came from all sides, and it was very difficult to discern what was true and what was false. At home, we had a powerful transoceanic shortwave radio, so we could listen to the BBC. This helped us to evaluate the barrage of news reports that we received. We finally learned that Prince Paul had instructed the prime minister and the foreign minister to go to Vienna to sign the pact. The news sent shock waves through the entire country. The reaction in Belgrade was immediate and outraged. Among the Serbs of the city, the reaction was almost violent. But it could not be said that the news was entirely unexpected, and it pleased certain sectors of the population, notably the Volksdeutsche and the White Russians of Yugoslavia, and an assortment of Slovenes, Croats, and Macedonians. Almost everyone else believed that Prince Paul had betrayed the country in agreeing to the terms that Hitler's Germany and its allies had imposed on his regime. And they believed that Prince Paul had betrayed the monarchy and the young prince Peter, in whose place Paul was serving as regent until Peter came of age to assume the throne. Many Yugoslav citizens, especially among the dominant Serbian population, jumped to their feet and demanded the overthrow of the government.

Three hundred young students went on strike in Belgrade on March 26, 1941, the day after the Yugoslav government signed the Anti-

Comintern Pact. As the students marched through the city, they shouted: "Let's defend our country!" They echoed the feelings of many of their Serbian elders, for in Serbia national pride and the imperatives of national liberty were from earliest youth deeply ingrained in the souls of the people and had assumed a spiritual, mythological dimension that was and remains even today fundamental to Serbian identity. The Serbs are a very proud people. The history and culture and the patriotic songs of the Serbian people are deeply infused with the desire for freedom and independence. The Ottoman Turks had occupied Serbia for five hundred years. The Ottomans had tried to convert the Serbs to Islam, but the Serbs took refuge in the high mountains of Kosovo, where they built monasteries and preserved their Christian culture. Out of their experience of resistance to the Ottoman occupation, the Serbian people had woven a uniquely rich and deeply ingrained folklore of heroism, resistance to slavery, and liberty. The first Karađorđe had led the successful rebellion against the Turks in 1804, and had founded the Karađorđević dynasty. Prince Peter was heir to the dynastic throne. In the minds and hearts of many Serbs, the young prince embodied the freedom and independence of the nation and the freedom of its people.

The Serbs of Yugoslavia could not tolerate being subservient to a foreign regime. In a united voice, the entire nation protested Prince Paul's submission to the Axis powers and the signing of the Axis pact, and proclaimed Yugoslavia's loyalty to the Allied camp. Our old friend France had fallen, and Britain had shown itself to be weak, but it was time to stand up for our independence at the side of neighboring Greece and at the side of Britain. Serbs believed it was time to depose Paul and to elevate Peter to the throne of an independent Yugoslavia.

Turmoil and confusion intensified in Belgrade the day after the pact was signed. Positions and opinions wavered, shifted, and hardened, some in favor of accommodating the regime, others insistent on overthrowing it. It was often difficult to determine who was for the pact, who was against it, and who was remaining neutral. The powerful Serbian Orthodox Church became very alarmed. People began to organize themselves in camps, and their debates grew increasingly shrill as many voices and conflicting interests struggled to be heard.

The Komitajis, an association of Serbian war veterans, began to mobilize its members, who were growing angrier by the hour. Many Serbs—especially our elders—were simply stricken with fear and grief, not knowing where to turn or what action to take. Most of the people felt that Prince Paul and his government had betrayed them. They were furious at this, but they felt trapped and powerless. Characteristically, many Serbs reacted quickly and violently. Much cursing and profanity could be heard in the streets. Some bewildered citizens took refuge in the coffeehouses, where they dulled their rage and anxiety with slivovitz, the plum brandy that was the Serbian national drink. There were no more jokes and smiling faces. The political wits that one had heard only a few days before had fallen silent, and people on the street read the paper over and over again, incredulous at what they found there, as if incapable of understanding or accepting what they were reading. Yet, at the same time, I noticed that many citizens began wearing the Union Jack and the crossed British and Greek flags on their lapels, plainly declaring where their sympathies lay.

The exploding unrest alarmed the government. Helmeted policemen rushed from one trouble spot in Belgrade to another, while the secret police began to round up and attack dissenters—patriots, communists, opposition politicians, and student leaders. The government forbade the public singing of patriotic songs. There was discussion of calling the army in to control civil unrest. The sentiments of the general staff were unknown, but the younger officers declared that they would never fire on the Yugoslav people.

The students of Belgrade University were especially active in their opposition to the government. Belgrade University was widely known as one of the most progressive universities in Europe. Government agents and police authorities were forbidden by law to enter the university grounds. As a privileged institution, whose integrity and autonomy were constitutionally guaranteed, the university immediately became a bastion of protest where all kinds of opposition activities were organized, and from which pamphlets were published and demonstrations were launched.

Amid the tumult of late March 1941, the new government struggled behind the scenes to avoid war. The overthrow of Prince Paul's government had been the result of a coup successfully launched by the Serbian opposition parties and officers of the air force. Under General Dušan Simović, it was this government that had ended the regency of Prince Paul and elevated the young crown prince Peter to the throne. Slovene and Croat ministers of the former government had remained in place. While the publicly declared sympathies of the new government were clearly with Great Britain and Greece, its representatives tried to hold Nazi aggression at bay by assuring Hitler and the Axis powers that the new regime would respect the terms of the Anti-Comintern Pact signed by the former regime. But Hitler had worked hard to render Prince Paul's government pliant, and the German dictator had not forgotten his bitter disappointment when Prime Minister Stojadinović, whose policies had been friendly to Germany, was dismissed in February 1939. So, the German armies deployed in Hungary, Bulgaria, and Romania were ordered to invade Yugoslavia.

The situation remained confused in Belgrade in those last days of March, as the government labored to forestall the invasion. Mobilization of Yugoslavia's large army of thirty-two divisions was not immediately ordered. In fact, full mobilization of Yugoslav forces was never completed, and the bulk of the nation's army was arrayed in defense of Croatia, exposing the rest of the country to German armored penetration from the east, and defeat, when the German attack came on Sunday, April 6, 1941.

Hitler had originally planned to invade Russia in 1943, but he had advanced the date of this attack to May 1941. Because of continued British resistance in Europe and the increasing hostility of the United States, Hitler wanted to accelerate the achievement of complete German domination of Europe so as to forestall American entry into the war. Yugoslavia was of no importance to the invasion of the Soviet Union, but before attacking the Soviet giant, Hitler had to eliminate any possible threat from the rear. He had already decided to attack Greece, which had turned back Italian attacks through Albania in the late fall of 1940 and the first months of 1941. Now, due to the change of government in Belgrade, and the uncertainties arising from it, he decided to strike at Yugoslavia before attacking the Soviets. This decision may have proved fatal to Hitler's Russian campaign, which, delayed because of the German campaign in Yugoslavia, was launched a month later than had been planned and was halted just short of Moscow, in the snows of a cruel winter.

While the new government frantically struggled to find some accommodation with Hitler, war fever was building within the country. The Serbian people were now enthusiastic for war. They wanted to fight to preserve their liberty. They would not surrender to the Nazis as the Hungarians, Romanians, and Bulgarians had done. The Serbs declared that Yugoslavia would not suffer the betrayal and defeat that had befallen Czechoslovakia. The nation would not crumble before the Nazi onslaught as had Poland, Norway, Denmark, the Netherlands, Belgium, and France. No!

The Serbian mind is very simple and values liberty above everything else. The Serbs are a heroic people. Serb history and folklore are crowded with epic heroes and brave warriors who fought for the freedom of their nation. The Serbian peasant is very proud. Disdainful of townspeople, the peasant is always ready to fight for his honor. Enthusiasm was high, but the nation, virtually surrounded by hostile forces, was in mortal peril. The Germans and Italians were poised to strike from Italy, Germany, and Hungary to the north, and German troops were ready to be unleashed from Romania and Bulgaria to the east. Treacherous enemies lurking inside the country would emerge on April 6, the day the Axis invasion began. These were the Volksdeutsche, the White Russians, and many Slovenes, Macedonians, and Croats, who together formed a powerful fifth column that committed sabotage and sowed chaos within the country, as it struggled to defend itself against the Fascist juggernaut.

3

The Debacle

On April 2, I finally received notice to join my unit, which was stationed in southern Serbia—more precisely, in Macedonia. I pulled my mobilization notification from the mailbox in the lobby of our building and was nervously reading it as I entered the elevator. The elevator gate slammed shut on my finger, and nearly broke it. A neighbor quickly came to my rescue and pried the gate open to free my gravely bruised finger. War had not yet broken out and I was already wounded! Although I was assigned to a mounted artillery unit, my training had instilled in me the expectation that my command would remain for weeks or even for months in the same position, so I anticipated a static campaign life, much like that recounted in Erich Maria Remarque's classic book, *All Quiet on the Western Front*. I left the next day.

The train stations were crowded with families and friends bidding farewell to the mobilized soldiers as they crammed into troop trains to depart to defend the country. The atmosphere was charged with enthusiasm, not so much now because we wanted war, but more due to the release of tension after many, many months of mounting anxiety. I encountered many friends on my southbound train, which was filled with laughter and commotion. Everybody was in high spirits. Exchanging jokes about the Germans, and especially about the Italians, was a popular pastime. When I arrived in Skoplje, the capital of Macedonia, where my division was headquartered, I was told to look for my unit in Štip. But Štip was almost one hundred kilometers to the southeast, and the directions were less than precise, so I only reached my battery two days later. Before setting out in search of my unit, I encountered my uncle Aron in Skoplje. He was also trying to locate his command.

I also hoped to see my uncles Isak and David, who were also serving as officers in the area. I kept my eyes open for them, but in vain.

On Saturday, April 5, I finally found my battery, which was bivouacked at some distance from the city of Štip. The Croatian commandant, the Macedonian first lieutenant, two sergeants, and all the troops—about one hundred illiterate Macedonians and a score of Serbs—were already in camp when I arrived. We had six horses and some forty mules to pull our four howitzers and field wagons. I learned on the spot that I had been promoted to second lieutenant. I was assigned a horse, an attendant, and a tent, and I was given a revolver, a sack of grenades, a gas mask, and all the other paraphernalia supplied to officers. I immediately settled into the life of the camp. Everybody was surprised that I was already bandaged, and the commandant made a few jokes about that.

Very early the following morning, on April 6, 1941, a trumpet sounded an alarm. It was already daylight, and a very beautiful day at that, with clear skies and a promising sun. Immediately after the call of the trumpet had died, we heard a rumbling in the sky, and suddenly the eastern horizon was crowded with heavy airplanes flying directly toward us. At this very moment, we received a telephone call from headquarters announcing that war had broken out and that Belgrade had been heavily bombarded. Our unit was ordered to move immediately toward the Bulgarian border.

When I received this order from my commandant, I had my first feelings of doubt. It was absurd to expose a battery—a long column of soldiers, equipment, and munitions—on the road in full daylight where any airplane could easily spot and attack it. It had been stressed in my training that mounted artillery should only change position under the cover of darkness. I pointed this out to my commandant, who told me sharply that orders had to be obeyed without question. We were to carry out—immediately—a forced march with full wartime equipment under the bright, hot sun, exposed along our entire route to air attack. A long, dangerous journey lay ahead of us.

We had been well trained to form up quickly. Our battery struck camp and was in line and on the march within an hour. My attendant packed my tent and luggage with the commissary and other support supplies that followed us at the end of the column. I was mounted on my horse, with my attendant marching along beside me. Airplanes threatened us as we advanced. We all had only one thought—to arrive rapidly at our destination and take up camouflaged positions. As if we were unaware of the danger, a motorcycle courier soon arrived with a dispatch ordering us to be ready to take cover off the road, because enemy planes were expected to attack at any moment. In fact, a few moments later, two small aircraft swooped down on our position and strafed the highway with machine-gun fire. We all dove off the road into the field. When we reassembled our column to continue our march, we were amazed that none of us had been hurt, and still more amazed were those of us who had seen Yugoslav air force markings on the two attacking planes. How could they have mistaken us for the enemy? I was rapidly becoming very suspicious that something very strange was going on.

The commandant remained calm and our troops kept good order. It seemed very strange to me that no one questioned anything. When we finally arrived at our destination, we encountered a chaotic situation. Columns were marching in every direction. When we reported to the commanding general, he cursed and screamed at us that he had not requested a battery, that he did not need one, that our orders were false, that a fifth column was operating in the army, and that the situation was spinning out of control. He ordered us to return to Štip, immediately. I was concerned about the battery's morale. Our troops had marched all day with hardly any rest, and we had to order them back without delay over the same route. It was already dusk, and it would soon be easier and safer to move, but the soldiers were exhausted, so we allowed an hour for mess and at least some rest before starting our return march.

Štip was in flames when it came into view at about two in the morning. Our route led us straight into the inferno of the completely abandoned and burning town. We tied cloths around the eyes of our skittish horses and mules and pulled them down the main street, where most of the two- and three-story wooden houses had already collapsed into piles of burning timbers. Except for the hissing of the fires and the occasional crashing of collapsing walls and second- and third-floor galleries, the town was deathly silent. The flickering flames trembled on the soot-stained faces of our silent, exhausted company. We were completely alone, as we toiled like automatons through the ghostly landscape of burning ruins. Only the soldiers attending the ammunition wagons betrayed a nervous energy, as they frenetically batted cinders away from their explosive freight. Less than a half hour later, we emerged from the flames of the destroyed town, which only one day before had been the center of intense, purposeful activity. We began to search for a place to entrench our battery and ready it for action.

My commandant indicated a position on the map to me, and pointed vaguely to high ground nearby, which he ordered me to inspect. I galloped off immediately to evaluate the site. Just as I arrived at the crest of the hill and was pulling back on the reins to curb my horse, a soldier came screaming out of the bushes, shouting that I should take cover immediately. He had just placed a charge of dynamite in an ammunition dump. It was going to detonate at any second. Terrified, I turned my horse around and raced down the road. Only a few seconds later, a violent explosion shook the entire landscape. I don't know how I managed to keep seated on my rearing mount, but I somehow steadied my horse with the grip of my legs and grasped at a telegraph pole for support. I was trembling like a willow. When I returned, the report I gave to my commandant was discouraging, so we decided to position our guns behind a small dip in the terrain just off the road about three hundred meters outside Štip. We would have some cover there, and a good field of fire over the town and its approaches.

It was deep night. We worked under the protection of darkness, the ghostly silhouettes of our exhausted troops eerily illumined in the glow of the burning town. It was a scene out of Dante's *Inferno*, but our men toiled on and kept up good discipline. My thoughts turned to my growing skepticism of our unit's Croatian commandant. I resolved to observe him very circumspectly, and to weigh his orders with equal care. While these thoughts were churning in my mind, the commandant suddenly called out to me and ordered me to lead a detail into the burning town to recover what we could from the army commissary stores, which he insisted were still intact there. Our soldiers were absolutely done in by their incredible fatigue and hunger, and I saw the sense in feeding them because I knew that the next morning would bring a very hard day, and a soldier with an empty stomach does not fight well. It was said that a Serbian soldier could go for days with a piece of bread and an onion, which is the typical food of Serbian peasants, but we did not have even that on hand. At the time, I didn't even think to ask what had happened to our field commissary wagon.

I hardly needed a map to find a way to the town, which was still illumined by the now abating flames that had all but consumed it, but I quickly realized that my party would have to move in front of our own firing line to reach it. Here was yet another instance of what had caused me to doubt the soundness of my commandant's judgment, if not yet his loyalty. I pointed out to him that the movement he had ordered us to make in front of our firing lines was forbidden by our own military regulations. Just as the commandant was stiffening to answer me, we heard the first bursts of heavy machine-gun fire, and I felt a rumble on the ground that signaled the approach of a large detachment of armor.

The black of night was fading to gray when I heard the thump of a rocket being fired and I saw in the sky a sudden burst of light that grew larger and larger until, within seconds, it had exploded and illumined the landscape in an eerie, phosphorescent glare. Seconds later, a heavy barrage of machine-gun and cannon fire raked our position. Everyone scattered, diving for whatever shelter they could find. For several minutes, we took heavy incoming fire, until the flare died, leaving the landscape shrouded in the mists and faint light of a day not yet dawned. The commandant was nowhere in sight, and our unit's first lieutenant had also disappeared. Most of the soldiers had turned their caps inside out to show the white cloth of the linings. They were surrendering. It was a terrible moment. I feared a horrible fate if the Germans captured me. The twenty Serb soldiers in the unit must have felt the same terror and not wanted to surrender.

With their hands raised high over their heads, frantically waving their campaign caps, scores of our men abandoned our position and walked toward the advancing Germans. I commanded the soldiers who remained—mostly Serbs—to take cover and fight it out. The Germans were still quite distant. Their tanks had only begun to lunge into sight behind the advancing infantry. I had never expected to use my knowledge of ballistics, but here I was, carefully gauging my instruments, making calculations, and shouting "Fire!" at precisely the right moment. Our howitzers knocked out four panzer fighter trucks before two Stukas shrieked down on us, spitting metal at our guns and their thin crews, pinning us flat to the ground while the German infantry marched quickly to reach us.

As soon as the Stukas pulled away, I ordered my soldiers to spike our fine howitzers and to follow me. The work was quickly done, and just in time, because we could already hear the voices of the fast-approaching Germans. We raced up the muddy slope, taking whatever cover we could among the rocks and bushes, small arms fire sputtering all around us. For almost two hours, we ran uphill across the stony terrain. When the German pursuit finally flagged, and we were out of danger, at least for the moment, we collapsed to the ground, more dead than alive.

We decided to take shelter among rock outcroppings in a forest of scrub pine until nightfall, when we would be able to move more safely. I studied my map. I knew that our only chance to rejoin our forces would be to ford the Bregalnica River, and then to head northeast across the highway toward Skoplje. I also knew that we were as good as lost, with only my battered field map and my field compass to point the way. At this point, one of our lookouts led six Serb soldiers to me. Like us, they were exhausted, battered refugees from the field of battle. Like us, they were lost, with no idea where to go or what to do. They did tell us that the fifth column had created tremendous havoc in the army, and had been responsible for many acts of sabotage in Štip and throughout the country. They also reported that the Croats had surrendered, and that a puppet government had been formed under Ante Pavelić in Croatia, that the Macedonians had surrendered as well, and that Macedonia would be annexed by Bulgaria.

We rested until dusk, and then moved on. We had not eaten for twenty-four hours, and we were still exhausted. After a full day of marching and our night countermarch of the day before, the firefight that morning, and our flight, we were almost completely spent. I don't know where we found the strength to go on. And, indeed, some of our men fell by the wayside as we made our way through the woods on the second night of the war.

We soon reached the Bregalnica. Many of the men refused to cross. I did not insist that they do so, but bade them well, leaving them under the nominal command of a Serbian corporal. Holding our weapons and ammunition packs high in the air to keep them dry, the chill water up to our chins, a good dozen of us braved the current, reached the northern bank, and then continued our journey through the woods. Drenched and shivering, we had to keep moving. Hardly two hours later, we reached the main highway. An endless column of German tanks was churning down the road at a steady speed of about twenty kilometers an hour. It was a surreal sight, that parade of steel monsters. The dim amber glow of their headlamps stretched out along the road like the luminescent scales of a huge serpent. There was no infantry with the tanks, no outriders, no trucks, no human presence visible anywhere. It was truly a strange spectacle.

Five of us ducked and slipped between two tanks, crossed the road, and silently glided through a hedge of trees into a cleared field. The sight of tilled land immediately brightened our spirits, for we knew that it meant there was a possibility of a friendly hearth and some food and shelter nearby. I had no doubt that we would quickly find some comfort. My four remaining companions were all solid Serb peasants. Returning to a landscape that was deeply familiar to them, they could now lead the way.

We were exhausted, ravenously hungry, and fearful. The pitch darkness of the night was mysterious and menacing. Like puppets on a confused and darkened stage, our forms, blotted out in the night, advanced heavily through a world of shifting shadows. My thinking was still clear—or was it? I wondered. I wondered if our situation was the rule throughout Yugoslavia on this night. Had the Yugoslav army—the soldiers, commissioned officers, the generals—all descended into this bizarre, lost world of shadows through which I was moving dumbly? And I was moving more and more with the force of an automaton, less and less with the conscious purpose of a man, as the shadows shivered and artillery growled in the distance. But, despite my exhaustion and the darkness, hope gave me the strength to continue.

We were greatly relieved when the door of a comfortable farm dwelling swung open and our request for food and lodging was granted. I remember little more than that I slept on a table and that I could not remove my boots, because they were new and had shrunk after being drenched when we forded the river. I don't remember even bothering to eat. As hungry as I was, I was all the more exhausted, and I slept the sleep of the dead. We breakfasted quite heartily the next morning. I do remember that. And we discussed plans to continue our journey.

We should have concluded that the divisional strength of the tank column we had crossed the night before meant that there was little doubt the entire region was firmly under German control, but this oddly did not even occur to us. We insisted on a rather indiscrete mode of transportation when we told the farmer that we planned to requisition two of his horses and his carriage. This did not please our host, who was as unpleasant as he was adamant in refusing it. I had always hated firearms, and had never thought to make use of them in negotiations, but war had already left its mark on even my own reasonable and peaceful disposition. Now I felt little inhibition in responding by pointing the muzzle of my revolver at his temple and coolly asking him to reconsider. Happily—and I do thank God for this, as I'm certain I wouldn't have known what to do next—he instantly became cooperative and suggested that he drive us. This was a fine compromise in our view, and we readily accepted it.

It was as bright and fine a spring morning as we could have wished for as we set out on the next leg of our journey to Skoplje, where we optimistically expected to rendezvous with a major concentration of the Yugoslav army. It was a perfectly peaceful morning, the landscape green with new life and the gentle air filled with birdsong. On the macadamized highway there was no sign of the ghostly tank column that had passed in the night, no sign indeed of anything amiss apart from the fact that the road was entirely deserted. We had traveled almost twenty kilometers before we encountered the rude awakening of a German roadblock and were obliged to surrender. One of the German guards immediately confiscated the camera that I had taken such care to preserve. Another guard took my knife. Yet another covetously examined my boots.

4

Prisoner of War

A SERGEANT ORDERED US INTO A TRUCK THAT HAD PULLED OFF ON THE shoulder of the road. We were driven to Kumanovo—the very city where I had not long ago performed military exercises—where we were herded with other prisoners of war into a public school building. There I was reunited with my attendant, who went to work immediately to ensure that I would be as comfortable as possible under the circumstances. Because my boots had shrunk and were stiff as bone and I hadn't taken them off for five days, my feet and legs were aching from poor circulation. My attendant found some lard—only God knew where and how—and spent an entire day rubbing it into my boots to soften them until finally—to my grateful relief—he was able to remove them from my suffering feet.

Until this time, I had not had a moment to think about my family. I had been entirely caught up in the fighting and in the flight to save my own life and the lives of my men. Now I was a prisoner of war, and time strangely opened to me, permitting me to reflect on matters beyond my own situation—not that my situation did not immediately demand some concentrated thought. Our makeshift prison was filled with spies and informers. There were Croats among us, and there were some Volksdeutsche planted among the prisoners. Agents of the Gestapo were present, and I was told that an SS regiment was bivouacked nearby. But I did think a great deal about my family, although my thoughts could produce nothing but memories of peaceful times and their faces as I had left them at home less than a week earlier, faces filled with pride, and love, and sorrow. Those faces had never left me. I could still see them now, perhaps better now than I had for many, many years.

Just before I left our home for war, my father had handed me a leather pouch containing fifty gold napoleons. It was a huge amount of money. Father cautioned me to use it only in special emergencies. In wartime, he told me, paper money quickly becomes worthless, but gold always increases in value. I was still carrying this gold, all of it, the pouch hanging from my neck, hidden beneath my shirt. I was also carrying a valuable watch that my uncle Aron had given to me as a graduation present when I finished *gymnasium*. My boots were my own, of the finest soft leather. Despite the beating they had taken in the past days, these boots had attracted the attention of many soldiers, both Yugoslav and German.

Conditions in the makeshift schoolhouse prison were deplorable. Almost one hundred prisoners were jammed into each of the classrooms, which were generally no more than sixty square meters in size. We slept without bedding on the floors, always grasping our meager belongings close to ourselves, sometimes forced to sleep piled on top of each other. The filth and stench and the infestations of lice and other pests were all part of the game, but we took this lightheartedly, because we had a feeling that it could have been much worse. The Germans, after all, did not enjoy a high reputation for their abuse and treatment of prisoners. The most brutal of our guards were the Bulgarians. They stood guard over us at night, while the Germans slept, and they could be arbitrary and cruel. They absolutely forbade nighttime use of the lavatory, which was a terrible hardship for all of us. We were enraged, almost to the point of attacking and killing the abusive guards, but it didn't come to that. We protested to the German command. We were all uniformed soldiers—there were some generals, colonels, and older reservists among us—and we were all entitled to at least some basic respect. The Germans finally saw our point. They even granted our request that they dismiss the Bulgarian guards, replacing them with young Volksdeutsche volunteers, who showed more humanity, at least in this instance.

We adapted to the monotony of prison life, as well as we were able. We organized our units and named senior officers as commandants. We gradually developed a rhythm of activity. We had sessions of calisthenics in the morning. We spent a great deal of time picking lice out of our clothing and our hair. We established friendships. We tried to communicate with the outside world. An iron fence surrounded the school but, in those first days of imprisonment, we did have some contact with people on the other side of the barrier. They tossed food and newspapers to us, and it was possible to have limited verbal exchanges with them. Many of these outsiders were searching for relatives. We all wrote cards to reassure our families that we were alive. Almost all of us had loved ones who were worried about us, just as we were worried about them.

The war had been a debacle for Yugoslavia. In less than two weeks, its armed forces had been completely destroyed. The capitulation was signed in Belgrade on Thursday, April 17. I still remember the sight of an old general in our prison. He wrapped himself in the national flag and sat weeping at the fate of the army. Many stories circulated about fifth column sabotage. Ammunition crates had been filled with stones. Gasoline had been adulterated with sugar to block oil filters and destroy automobile engines. False orders had been disseminated—especially by Croatian officers, it was said—sowing horrible disorder and confusion on all the battlefronts. There had been a big battle at Stražin, not far from where my battery resisted the advance of the German panzers. But, in general, our forces had simply collapsed and, in place of the bright pride and enthusiasm we had displayed as we went off to war to defend our liberty, we now wore the rags of misery and shame. Our countrymen on the other side of the prison barrier pitied us, but even then, in such a tragic time of war and common external enemies, most Yugoslavs despised the former state police authorities imprisoned with us. When our friends from outside the prison threw food to us, they usually told us not to share any of it with these police officials.

I had hoped to find my three uncles, who had also served on the southern front, and who were without doubt imprisoned somewhere nearby, but I did not find them at Kumanovo, and I heard no news of them. Nor were any of my Belgrade friends in our group. I did, however, become friendly with the ranking officer in our group of prisoners. He was from Belgrade, and had worked in my uncle's bank. I also knew a Greek family in Kumanovo. I had rented a room from them when I was there on military exercises before the war, and we had become great friends. One day, a young son of this family showed up in front of the gate. I asked him to get me a pad of paper and pencil.

I had observed so many fantastic poses of disheveled soldiers engaged in all kinds of activities, and I wanted to sketch scenes of prison life.

About two weeks after I had arrived at the prison, two German soldiers approached me and told me to take my boots off. Prisoners of war, they told me, were not entitled to have such fine boots. They jeered at me and tossed an oversized pair of infantryman's shoes in my direction. They were completely worn out and were far too large for me. I very angrily swore to all the saints I could think of, and started to think about where I could hide my valuables.

At that very moment, two Gestapo men called out to me and ordered me to report to the German command post. I feared that something terrible was about to happen. Subconsciously, I was already prepared for the worst. I knew that prisoners of war, and especially officers, were protected under international law, but I also knew that the Germans played by their own rules and that for them no law protected any Jews. Had I been denounced? Who had denounced me? I knew of only a few Jews in our prison. Could it have been one of them? I moved slowly toward the command post, fearful, my heart pounding. My friend, the ranking officer of our prison company, hurried over to ask me what had happened. Why I was going to the office? I told him that the two Gestapo men had ordered me to report there. Spontaneously, I tore the pouch of gold from around my neck and pressed it into my friend's hand. I told him that I didn't have any idea what would happen to me. I wanted him to have the gold. I certainly didn't want it to fall into the hands of the Germans.

When I entered the command post, I saw several German officers talking with two Yugoslav army colonels. Heavy machine guns and other weapons and tools were laid out across the floor. A German officer looked at me coldly and told me to remove everything from my pockets and to raise my arms above my head. I twisted slightly to the side as I emptied my pockets and managed to quickly remove my wristwatch without being observed. I clasped the watch in my palm and raised my arms high, fixing my eyes on the officer, who then immediately began to frisk me. When he had finished and turned toward his fellow officers, I slowly slipped the watch into my side pocket, wondering and knowing at the same time why I had taken such a mortal risk. Almost immediately, two of the German officers turned on me and began to scream *"Schwein!"* pounding at me with their fists until I fell backward over some metal machinery. They then struck me repeatedly with rifle butts, taking special aim at my kidneys. It happened so suddenly. I could not fight back. That would have meant instant death. I had no idea what they wanted from me. I remained prostrate at their feet while they beat me to a bleeding pulp.

The two senior Yugoslav officers impassively witnessed the horrible beating and my terrible pain, raising not a single word of protest. To the great astonishment of the officers present, Yugoslav and German alike, I did not utter one word during the beating. I twisted my body and raised my arms and hands to fend off the blows that were raining down upon me, but I spoke not a single word, made not a single cry, and did not once strike back.

When the beating stopped, the Germans ordered me to raise my shirtsleeves and show them my bare arms. I silently complied, not knowing what they could possibly be looking for. They seemed to be looking for tattoos or markings of some sort. I had only the freshly bruised skin of my arms to display to them. The bizarre examination puzzled me. Disoriented, I asked myself if it could possibly have anything to do with the empty leather sheath that still hung from my belt. I had kept my hunting knife in this sheath. But a German guard had seized the knife within minutes of my capture. I had owned it since my adolescent years. It was a very fine, strong knife, quite large, and very useful for many things. I was highly skilled in throwing it accurately from a distance. In times of war, it was a very useful item. I missed it.

An SS officer approached me and roughly pressed his cocked revolver against my left temple. Speaking emotionlessly, he threatened to shoot me on the spot if I didn't tell the truth. He wanted to know how many other Jews were in the prison. There were hundreds of prisoners being held in the school building, including officers, common soldiers, and police officials. And then there were our keepers, the German soldiers, the Gestapo, the SS, the Volksdeutsche, and the Bulgarians, all mingling inside the school and outside in the yard. I immediately understood that there was no way he could know or prove that there were any other Jews in the prison, or among our guards for that matter. There was certainly no way that he could know or prove that I knew of any others. The prison was too crowded. I had arrived only two weeks before. I knew nothing. I knew no one. That was my position.

I felt within myself a deep and scornful hatred for those monsters. Every fiber and cell of my being resisted cooperating with them in any way, on any level. My entire body tensed as I pulled myself straight. They could beat or torture me as they wished. I would not yield to any fear. I would not let them destroy my dignity. They would not make a traitor or informant of me. They could kill me on the spot without any ceremony. I was still in the uniform of a Yugoslav army officer and two of my superior officers were present. I pulled myself up straight and again I said, "No!"

Two soldiers finally removed me from the office and led me to a cellar door, which opened to pitch darkness. The soldiers shoved me down the stairs. When I came to, I was sprawled in chill darkness on a damp dirt floor. I lay there semiconscious for what seemed to be an eternity and then, gradually, fighting pain with each inch of movement, I forced myself upright and slowly began to orient myself in the darkness. I could not see my fingers in front of me. I moved very cautiously, fearfully and in sharp pain, step by step, my arm stretched out before me.

I reached an area where a thin gray light penetrated the darkness from some distant and yet unseen window, some unperceived crack in the wall, and I heard the murmur of voices, voices that seemed to be speaking in the Macedonian dialect. I called out, and three dim figures, suddenly silent, emerged from the shadows. I felt their presence with some sense other than sight, and we began to talk. As we talked, I began to see them. They all had beards, floating like dark patches in the gray light. They were all convicted murderers, they told me. They had been sentenced to life, but had escaped from prison at the outbreak of the war. The Nazis had recaptured them, and were holding them in the cellar while they decided what to do with them or where to transfer them. Murderers they might have been, but I was happy to have found other sufferers to share with me the darkness into which I had been thrown.

My meeting with these men, these criminals, was bizarre, and it was stranger still that they were cheerful, but I gratefully accepted their complicity and their friendship, their jokes and their laughter, in the darkness into which I had been thrown. They comforted me, assuring me that nothing would happen to me while I was with them. But I remained apprehensive. I knew more than they did.

This meeting in the cellar with these Macedonians was the first happy moment I had experienced since the beginning of my battery's forced march to the Bulgarian border. I wondered how they could be cheerful and unconcerned about their personal danger in the circumstances in which they found themselves. I ended by attributing this to their innate simplemindedness. They were living entirely in the present moment, living like animals, in degraded circumstances, but they were alive, and life itself seemed to be sufficient to them. They had no thought, no consciousness, of the war and of the destruction of the country. They knew nothing of the fears that I felt as a Jew, for myself, and for my people. I wondered why so many individuals, so many fortunate individuals, were unhappy creatures, especially those individuals called "intellectuals," for whom anxiety and alienation are fixtures of daily life, and whose actions are marked by discontent and irresolution at every step. I later reflected a great deal upon this subject, and concluded that the more one knows, the more of which one is aware, the deeper the chasms of ambiguity and compromise, the more varied the fauna of danger past, present, and future in human life. My Macedonian friends were exemplary of the simple men, the primal men, who can adapt thoughtlessly to the present, however horrible, with no expectation beyond the reality of the moment, no thought for the future, with a consciousness as dim as the penumbra in which we found ourselves imprisoned.

After I had been imprisoned for several hours in the dark cellar, a blast of light flashed from the stairwell, and I heard the clump of boots descending the rude wooden steps. A powerful beam of light jumped around the cellar and focused its blinding rays on me. Two silhouettes, almost entirely swallowed in the darkness behind the light, approached me. They were SS guards, one of them brandishing a heavy whip. Disembodied German voices harshly screamed at me, while the intense beam of light focused directly in my eyes, and the thick leather coil lashed out at me. My eyes remained wide open in horror. I wanted to close my eyes, to shield them, but I could not. Although both the intense, focused light and the surrounding darkness almost entirely blinded me, my instincts compelled me to fix my gaze on the shadowy tormentors who were violently kicking me and striking me with the whip and with their fists. This sheer torture continued unabated for five minutes, ten minutes, an eternity, and stopped as suddenly as it had begun, as if my torturers had satisfactorily completed a physical exercise prescribed for their own conditioning. They simply stopped, and then brought us our ration of bread and water. It was just a routine, and it was repeated twice a day, each and every day I remained confined in the cellar. This strange procedure terrified and confused the Macedonian convicts, but they were never touched. Their existence was only acknowledged by the rations of brackish water and rancid bread that they received.

I did not understand why the SS guards were directing the light into my eyes. My eyes were my most precious gifts. I was an aspiring architect and painter. Everything that I had dreamed of becoming depended upon what could come to me through my eyes. I asked myself how they knew I was an artist. Were their attacks on my eyes some methodical, scientific sadism calculated gradually to destroy my vision? Such thoughts proliferated as my mental stamina flagged. I even thought of asking the guards for an explanation of their treatment of me, but I realized that this would be as futile as attempting to discuss philosophy with rabid dogs. With each passing day I grew weaker on the regime of bread and water in the fetid dark of my humid, airless prison grave, filthy and sickened in its sewer of excrement and urine. The weight of suffering had progressively silenced the animal cheer of my Macedonian companions, and my life had become a nightmare of half sleep, punctuated by the beatings and feedings that were gradually becoming my only light. The light within me was flickering out.

After a hellish eternity of ten days, I was removed from the cellar and thrown into the excruciating noon brightness of the prison yard, where I collapsed like a limp sack. The guards dumped buckets of water on my filthy face to bring me back to consciousness, and told me that I could rejoin my unit. My commanding officer was extremely kind, and obviously relieved and happy to see me return alive. He brought me food and some fresh clothing. My attendant gently bathed me, washed my uniform, and did everything in his power to return me to strength. My commander returned my pouch of gold to me, telling me that he had borrowed two coins to help assure his own security and that after the war he would repay me. He had shown himself to be a fine human being. As a matter of record, he did repay the debt—to my uncle, since I never returned to Belgrade after the war—without any thought, apparently, of the debt I owed him of my own life.

Later that day of my release, when I had been properly fed and made as comfortable as possible, my commander sat down beside me where I was resting against the wall of the school building, shaded from the afternoon sun. He explained that he had done his best to help me. He told me that an officer named Avakumović had denounced me as a Jewish artist. He told me how he had protested my confinement to the prison authorities. I told him that I appreciated the risk he had taken in doing this. He then said that, regardless of his efforts, I would probably still be rotting in the cellar were it not for an inspection of a commission of the International Red Cross that was to take place the next day. That was why I had been pulled out of the cellar, so he told me. So, it was true, I reflected in silence, that they knew I was an artist and had wanted to destroy my sight methodically. That was why they had used that light. I tightly shuttered my eyes as a ray of the sinking afternoon sun stabbed into them. The light was painful, but I hoped that I would soon be able to adjust to it, and that the emotional scars of my torture would soon heal.

The discipline among the German soldiers had become increasingly lax, and they were mingling more and more with the Yugoslav officers. I understood enough German to be able to gather from their comments what they were up to, although they were anyway brazen enough in filching whatever they could take from us. I was keeping my watch carefully hidden, but had decided to give it for safekeeping to my Greek friend from outside the camp. I finally managed to speak to him through the fence, and he agreed to keep my watch for me. We were forbidden to go up to the barrier, so I began to toss stones and pebbles over it, as if idly amusing myself. I had wadded my watch in a small paper bag and when the opportune moment came I tossed it over the fence, afterward continuing my ruse of throwing pebbles. My Greek friend discretely picked up the package, gave me a knowing sign, and headed away.

Within a few days of my release from the cellar, a group of five
Jewish officers had formed around me. Four of them were doctors. I
had been casually acquainted with one of the doctors in Belgrade, and
it turned out that two of the others were from the capital as well. They
were very alarmed when they learned what had happened to me, and
they wanted to know all that I could tell them about my horrible experience. The atmosphere in the prison had grown more and more
threatening. An SS company was now bivouacked just outside the
prison gates, and the Gestapo was increasingly active in Kumanovo
and the region, hunting down Jews, Communists, Freemasons, Gypsies, and others on their endless list of victims.

After the first weeks, prison life became much more regimented.
Prisoners were selected and organized into work details, which were
assigned each day to hard labor. Our group of six Jews was placed in
the same detachment, which was otherwise made up of common soldiers. We were selected for the work detail because we were Jewish.
All other officers were exempted. Each morning, we were loaded into
trucks and transported to work sites. The details were mostly put to
work on road repair and clearing ruins. To my great surprise, my
group was taken to a place that I knew like the back of my hand, the
army storage depot where, a year earlier, I had been attached to the
quartermaster corps and had worked, requisitioning supplies of grain
and flour and stocking them in the warehouse. It was now our job to
empty the place.

Although I had been weakened by my ordeal in the cellar, and had
lost almost thirty pounds since the start of the war, I had recovered
much of my strength. I could handle the work, as could one of my
newfound companions who, like me, had served in the artillery. I had
had a lot of experience in this line of work. My army service with the
quartermaster corps had been administrative and supervisory. But I
had worked for an extended period at an agricultural station, an exact
replica of a kibbutz, where, as part of our preparation for immigration
to Palestine, my Jewish youth group had trained to live on a collective
farm.

But the four doctors in our group were much older than we were,
and they had never lifted anything heavier than their briefcases. I was
deeply concerned for them. How would they manage to haul fifty-

kilogram sacks of flour all day? The Germans pushed us all hard, especially the Jewish officers, or so it seemed to me, and it was a very sad sight to see the doctors stumble and collapse under their burdens. I showed them how to cradle the sacks at half-length over their shoulders so that they didn't even have to hold on to them, and how to position one hand on the hip so as to support the back. This did help them get by, but the work, difficult enough for all of us, was especially cruel for them. They were highly trained Jewish intellectuals. They had no experience of hard labor, and no aptitude for it. The work exhausted them beyond their limits. They were terribly sad and anxious, utterly depressed, almost in tears. I did my best to maintain their morale, but when we returned that evening to the prison, they broke down in despair and sobbed bitterly. I knew very well the anguish that their tears expressed, and I well understood where such anguish could lead.

Finally, we met together to discuss what course of action would be best for us to take. It was quite clear that we could only rely on ourselves. We were Jewish reservists. We felt abandoned. Our fellow officers did not want to intervene on our behalf. My commanding officer had been a rare and brave exception to this rule. The Germans could deal with us or dispose of us as they wished. We suffered all kinds of humiliations. One day, a trio of German sentries ordered me to water a garden, insisting that I wear only one shoe as I performed the task. I did as they told me, and they bent over in hilarity at the absurd spectacle that they had concocted for their own amusement. I watered the garden, silently despising them and the poverty of their imaginations.

The six of us decided to strip all signs of rank from our uniforms. We would try to melt anonymously into the body of common soldiers and share their destiny—a more prudent course, it seemed to us, than standing out as Jewish officers. A few days later, we were assigned to a unit of one hundred men that was being sent to repair roads somewhere near the Bulgarian border. We climbed into the open trucks with great apprehension. I gave the doctors a hand, since the truck beds were mounted very high, and they didn't have the strength to pull themselves aboard. Thus we started our journey. My commanding officer, kindness to the end, came to say good-bye. He was very worried. He had no idea where we were really going and, to be sure, nor did we. With the Germans, there were no guarantees—especially about life.

_____

After traveling for many hours, we arrived at a real prisoner of war camp, with six lines of electrified barbed wire strung between turrets in which heavy machine guns were conspicuously mounted. The German soldiers all carried submachine guns slung over their shoulders. The sight shocked us. My friends were sick with anxiety, and could barely remain standing after we clambered down from the trucks. We knew about concentration camps. The Nazis had set them up as soon as they came to power in 1933. We knew that people were tortured and killed in the camps. All the tragic stories of the refugees, nine years of grim documentation, flooded into our minds, and I must admit that even I was on the edge of abandoning all hope.

We were finally all called into the central assembly area where we were lined up, and an elderly Wehrmacht general stood before us and began to address us in German, which was immediately translated into Serbian. Some of the soldiers were already talking among themselves about how to escape. The general commanded all noncommissioned officers—mostly corporals and sergeants—to step forward. These men duly moved several paces ahead of the line. One of the sergeants told the translator that there were six commissioned officers in the group. The general in command of the camp demanded to see these six officers, so we advanced and lined up in front of him. We all spoke at least some German. When the general asked us why we had been sent to the camp, we forthrightly explained that we had been assigned to the work details because we were Jewish.

We later learned that the general, a graying man in his sixties, had led a battalion in the Balkans during the First World War. He was surprised that we had been sent to the camp, and he told us, almost remorsefully, almost as if to refuse any association with it, that the German policy against the Jews was harsh. He then asked us what we had done in civilian life and in the army. He was pleased when he learned that four among us were doctors. He immediately sent these men to the camp hospital, authorizing an orderly and an office for each of them. Because the remaining two of us spoke German, the general appointed us as translators, and we were also each assigned a private room and an orderly.

Our good fortune astonished us, but we soon adjusted to the routine of life in the camp. The soldiers set out to work each day, while we remained inside the camp, occupied with a broad range of administrative tasks. The food of the officers' mess was very good, the mountain air was invigorating, and the Germans treated us quite courteously. The guards were older and much more reserved than the bullies at the staging camp at Kumanovo from which, we had heard, most prisoners were to be eventually shipped to Germany.

I quickly became quite friendly with a German sergeant. He wore a soldier's uniform, but he was no Nazi. In private life, he had been a poet. We discovered many common interests. We talked about poetry and art, the Weimar Republic, Expressionism, Hölderlin and Rilke, Stefan George and Wedekind, about German movies, everything. Our doctors were content in their work at the camp hospital, where they mostly took care of our soldiers. German doctors attended to the German soldiers. All the doctors wore Red Cross armbands on their left arms.

Soon after our arrival at the new camp, we learned that all the prisoners remaining at Kumanovo were to be transferred there. Although we were happy that these prisoners would not be sent to Germany immediately, we did worry that the new influx of officers would complicate our situation by meddling, which would make our lives more difficult. The general, who, we soon realized, understood some Serbian, immediately sensed that the transfer of prisoners from Kumanovo had alarmed us. He reassured us that our situation and our quarters would not be changed. He planned to house all of the newly arrived officers in small, low, hangarlike, freezing metal barracks. The transfers finally arrived, and our camp was filled with what I thought must have been the entire Yugoslav officer corps, including many generals, colonels, and other high-ranking officers. I once again met Stojanović, the ranking officer of my prison-of-war company at Kumanovo. He immediately inquired about the conditions in the camp. As it turned out, the new arrivals were indeed housed in the metal barracks, and we continued to live in real houses. I was quartered in a second-floor corner room with two windows.

Sometime later, Bulgarian soldiers arrived at our camp and took up positions around it, while German soldiers continued to stand guard inside. Life went on. Despite the tightened security, a few soldiers escaped from the camp each night. The commanding general finally assembled all the prisoners and announced that we were to be forwarded to Tjustendil in Bulgaria, from where we would be sent to camps in Germany. This transfer was to proceed methodically, with truck convoys departing the camp every two to three days. I immediately studied the map, and determined that the distance from our camp to the Tjustendil railroad station was about fifty miles. I advised my friends to try to go with the first truck convoys, which were to transfer the officers. The troops would probably be forced to march to the station. I was not prepared for that ordeal. Frightening images of the forced marches described in one of Dostoevsky's novels, with scenes of soldiers beating and shooting anyone who lagged behind, haunted me. For this reason, I urged my friends to prepare to leave as quickly as possible.

I saw my sergeant friend at this point and asked him to try to assign us to the first convoy. He told me that we had been scheduled to be among the last to depart, and that he could do nothing about it. I wondered why they wanted to hold us for the last convoy. I was puzzled and frightened, and did not know what to think. Sleepless nights followed, for me and for my friends. The sergeant avoided me. He either knew something that he did not want to tell me, or he simply did not want to be disturbed by incessant questions for which he had no answers.

The convoys finally started to leave. As I had foreseen, first the higher officers, and then the lower officers, were transported in trucks, and the troops followed on foot. At this point, the general called the doctors to his office. He told them that he had received instructions from Geneva to release all doctors in accord with international law. He gave each of them a pass authorizing them to leave the camp immediately, naturally wearing their Red Cross armbands to help them move through the front lines. The doctors were jubilant to learn of their release, and I understood why the sergeant had stalled our departure. The Geneva dispatch had arrived a week earlier. The sergeant had seen it, but it was only later that the general had considered it. As jubilant as we were for the doctors, we were also very sad at the prospect of our separation. As friends, we had shared anxieties and uncertainties, fears and hopes. We had born witness to each other in terrible situations of degradation and moral weakness. Now the four doctors among us were free to leave, and the two of us who had served in the artillery would be transferred to Germany, where we would rot in a concentration camp until the end of the war—if we were to be lucky enough to survive.

This was a very hard time for me. All my inner forces were simultaneously in revolt, inflaming all my intelligence, sensitivity, and humanity. I had a deep love of life. I had plans for the future. I had to find a way to freedom. For three full days, I lay on my bed, thinking intensely, staring at the white ceiling, whistling Rachmaninoff's Prelude. Logic never abandoned me. I had been trained to think dialectically since the age of sixteen, and I always considered the negative and positive poles of things. I had studied the prophets and the Bible, Marx and historical materialism, and, at this difficult time, I called upon all my intellectual strength to find a solution. Anything was better than being transferred to Germany.

I started at the beginning and methodically assessed the entire situation. I realized that whatever I attempted would have little chance of success, but that I had nothing to lose in the effort. On the other hand, any action on my part could dangerously disturb the delicate balance of my situation as a prisoner, where my future was already closer to death than to the promise of life. But the general seemed to be a decent man of long experience. He had lived under the Weimar Republic. He had known life before Hitler. I was convinced that he valued human dignity, and that ultimately he was a man of religion. Even if were acting as a Nazi now, all of his earlier experience still had to remain within him—deeply buried perhaps, but still there. Also, he had authorized the release of our other friends. He knew that we had arrived at the camp as a group, and he had always treated us equitably. Perhaps he would also release my friend and me, even if we were not doctors. I had eliminated all other possibilities, and had come to the conclusion that the only choice left to me was to go to the general to ask him directly to let me go home. My remaining companion did not dare to do this, but my desire for life was so strong that I decided to take the risk. I could do nothing else. I couldn't break out of the camp and escape. I considered how the camp commandant might respond when I asked him to release me. I thought how I could respond to his likely refusal of my request.

My request might infuriate the general. He could take his gun and shoot me on the spot. He could strike me with a whip, or throw me into isolation, or find some other punishment for my temerity in asking him to let me go free. But I excluded these possibilities. The general was a mature and kindly man. He would not answer me with impulsive cruelty. On the other hand, possibly, just possibly, he might find in my request an opportunity to redeem himself and to dissociate himself from the terrible crimes that the Nazis were committing against the Jews. Perhaps the cost of such a gesture would not be too high for him. I could not confidently predict how he would react, but I decided that if I did not at least approach him with my demand, I would owe only to myself whatever miserable fate might await me. If I failed to try, and somehow remained alive, I would feel remorse for the remainder of my days. Summoning some fragments of desperate courage, urged on by the sheer instinct to survive, encouraged by my esteem for the man, I asked to speak to the general.

It was late in the afternoon of a desolate day. The mountains were blanketed with fog and low clouds, and a torrential rain punctuated with blasts of thunder was transforming the camp into a swamp. Everyone was huddled inside. I made my way to the general's office. When he received me, I immediately began to speak, looking directly into his eyes, making my appeal directly to his soul. I told the general that I was a young artist and an architect, that I was planning to do a lot with my life, and that I had a family and a girlfriend. I spoke with passion, telling him that I wanted to learn so much more and that I wanted to contribute to my community. I told him that my ideals were very high, and that I had high ambitions for my art. I pleaded that no one had anything to gain in holding me prisoner and in shipping me to Germany to perish in a concentration camp. I asked him man to man, "What will Germany gain or lose by killing me?"

The general heard me out. As I spoke, the color drained from his face, and I could sense that in those few minutes he saw his entire past in retrospect. He was absolutely silent for an eternity, and finally he said to me, "All right, go home, but I don't know that this is the better solution." He offered me transportation the next morning by truck to the railhead at Skoplje, about seventy-five miles away. I thanked the general, but answered that I would rather leave immediately. I could find some means of transportation. I thought to myself that I still had my gold. I could buy a truck, if that was necessary. And I didn't want the general to reconsider his decision over the coming night. Night is a mysterious time, when the thoughts of men can shift in tides of remorse and regret and fear.

Within five minutes, I was ready to depart. The general's office issued me a Red Cross armband and a pass in the name of Dr. Albert Alcalay. I would be able to move through German lines with these. I also kept my officer's raincoat, a splendid garment that had protected me on many occasions. I was at the gates and was just about to leave the camp when the guard told me to wait for the general, who was coming to see me. My heart started to pound. The thought that he had changed his mind terrified me. Instead, when he arrived, he shook my hand. Looking straight into my eyes, he told me, "Do not think that I like Jews. I only admired your desire to live and your civil courage." I thanked him politely, and walked though the gates.

Rain was pouring down steadily, but this did not slow my pace. Every step I took moved me closer to freedom. In a nearby village, I was fortunate to discover an old Model-T Ford. The car had a motor that still ran, and the owner was willing to take me to Skoplje for one gold coin. Skoplje was the principal city of southern Serbia. I could find a train there to take me north to Belgrade. Naturally, even before I left the camp, I had already heard all kinds of stories about how the Germans were treating Jews. Jews had to wear yellow armbands on which "Jude" was written. Jews had to take the most degrading work. But I did not see any Jews when I arrived in Skoplje. I concentrated all of my attention on catching a train to the north.

The railroad station was packed with people—soldiers, escaped prisoners, refugees fleeing bombarded cities, women with infants and young children, and the elderly. It was a sad tableau of panic and disintegration, that multitude of people, everyone carrying a bundle, everyone's face melting into the crowd of frightened faces. After waiting for many hours, I finally boarded a northbound train, but this train came to an abrupt halt only a few hours later at the important rail junction at Niš. The conductor announced that Niš would be the last stop, and ordered everyone off the train.

I climbed down to the station platform, where I found myself lost amid hundreds of people burdened with whatever they had been able to salvage from their uprooted lives: luggage, bundles, and cherished family pets. Miraculously, I caught sight of my four doctor friends. They had been unable to find transportation by truck to Belgrade and had been stranded at Niš for a week, waiting there for a train. Throughout that week, people had collected at the station, waiting. There was only one German sentry on duty. My friends told me that many trains had passed through the station, but not one had stopped. They were all hospital trains full of German soldiers who had been wounded in Greece, where the Greek people had fought heroically against the Nazis.

I assessed the overall situation. After all, I was wearing a Red Cross armband, which officially declared me to be a doctor. Why not gather the nerve to act like one? So, I called out to the waiting crowd, and told the people to collect their luggage and bundles into a huge pile on the tracks to block the next train. The German sentry started shouting *"Los! Los!"* (Get going! Get going!), but he quickly understood that the mob could crush him, so he retreated into the shadows and quieted down. Sure enough, a long hospital train soon approached the station and was forced to stop. As the train screeched to a halt, many German doctors leaped onto the platform to protest that the train was a hospital train that had to continue without delay. My friends and I approached the German doctors immediately. After all, even if we wore different uniforms, members of the medical profession still spoke a common language. We explained to the German doctors that the crowd had been waiting at the station for more than a week, without any hope of transportation. We told them that we only wanted to attach a few freight cars to the end of the train so that some of us could reach Belgrade. The Germans quickly agreed to this, but insisted that we lose no time getting it done. I had already mobilized the enthusiastic crowd, and we found a way to attach the freight cars immediately. The crowd almost smothered me with their embraces, which quite alarmed me.

5

Return to Belgrade

WE ARRIVED IN BELGRADE FIVE HOURS LATER. THE RAILROAD STATION and the entire surrounding area were ruins of shattered masonry and water-filled craters. Right away, I saw a work detail of ten Jews wearing yellow armbands, carrying shovels across their shoulders, marching under the command of a German soldier. It was a sight that I would never forget, and immediately the words of the camp commandant came to me: "Go home, but I don't know that this is the better solution." At that moment, my internal preparation, my capacity to deal with the Nazis, was to be tested.

I had trained myself to anticipate anti-Semitic acts without surprise, to be ready to resist them, and to support those threatened by them, to keep my balance. All the resources of intellectual analysis and mental preparation were in reach within me, but the raw emotional reality shocked and profoundly saddened me. Within minutes of my return to Belgrade, I realized that my life was going to be uncertain and difficult, that my humanity and dignity would be assaulted, that my very life would be in danger. All my mental preparation, my awareness of crimes against Jews, which I had heard so much about in the accounts of so many refugees, and the notion that my intellectual awareness was a sword and a shield, all of this meant little in front of the naked, shocking reality. My hopes were threatened. My vision of the days ahead was darkened.

But, at the same time, I felt strengthened and more purposeful. I understood that I would have to draw on all of my intelligence and cunning to stay alive. I knew that I probably would have to flee the country. The surprise of my release from the prisoner-of-war camp had exhilarated me. Now, returning to destroyed and occupied Belgrade, an accelerating series of shocking events and revelations began pounding at me. I finally collected myself, embraced my comrades in farewell, and started on the last stage of my journey home. I walked toward the center of the city. I had no idea what had happened to my family, to my home, to my friends, to my studio.

When finally I arrived in the center of the city, I encountered my good friend Jesha Konforti. We had been schoolmates since childhood, we had studied architecture together, and we had shared the dream of becoming painters. But Jesha did not recognize me. I was wearing my shabby uniform. I was filthy and bearded, and I had lost more than fifty pounds. When I called out Jesha's name, he stared at me, frightened, and, without saying a word, turned his eyes away and quickened his step to distance himself from me. "Jesha, wait!" I called. "It's me, Albert—Albert Alcalay!" He hesitated, looked back at me, his face gradually breaking into stunned recognition, slowly turned and, wordlessly, almost warily, approached me, his hand extended. Jesha told me that he had gone to my family's apartment to look for me, but had found it occupied by Germans. He had no idea where my family was, but they were certainly no longer at home.

I asked Jesha to accompany me to my family's apartment. When I rang the bell at the door, my heart was pounding furiously. It was the custodian's son, a *Volksdeutscher* (German settler living outside of the Reich), who answered. We had known each other for many years, but I had to tell him who I was, and I had to ask him if I could enter my own home to wash and find a change of clothes. He gesticulated angrily at me, screamed something to me in incomprehensible German, and slammed the door. Jesha put his hand on my shoulder, his eyes cast downward, as I stood there stunned and frozen in place. A few minutes later, the door opened and the young Volksdeutscher shoved a document in my face. In bold Gothic letters, across the top, was written *Beschlagnahmt*. This clearly meant that our home and all its goods and furnishings had been confiscated. Everything had been granted to the janitor and his family. Controlling my anger, I explained to the young man standing scornfully in front of me that I understood and accepted the situation. I appealed to him and tried to reason with him, saying that since my clothes could not possibly fit him, might he not at least give me some of them, as a kindness that I would remember and gratefully credit to him as a favor. He spit a stream of anti-Semitic obscenities at me and again slammed the door in my face, this time forever.

So I sadly turned away from my home and parted with Jesha on the street. I went off to see if I could find my uncles and others among my friends. I found my uncle David's wife and young child. Their apartment had been spared confiscation, so I decided to stay with them for a few days while I pondered what to do. Three months had passed since I had left for war, and no one had had any news of me. Jesha spread word among our friends that I had returned, and that I had not perished in the war, as everyone had believed.

Although the Yugoslav government had declared Belgrade an "open city" at the beginning of the war, meaning that it would not be militarily defended in the hope that it would not be scarred in battle, Nazi bombing had heavily damaged the city. The severe bombing had been the Nazi retribution for the jubilation the city had experienced on March 27, when its population had celebrated the overthrow of the government that had signed the Nazi Anti-Comintern Pact. German property in the city had been attacked and looted, and its German residents had been expelled or had taken flight in fear. When the streets grew calm after the intoxicating excitement of that day, many had fearfully reflected that the people of Belgrade and their city would be made to pay heavily for their boldness in demonstrating against the interests of the powerful Third Reich. And the bombers had come— wave after wave—in the first hours of the war on April 6, 1941, while my artillery unit and I were on our ill-fated march through southern Serbia toward the Bulgarian Border.

The German Stukas had struck at Belgrade's Jewish Quarter with concentrated savagery. Among the large population of Volksdeutsche who lived in Belgrade, many were employed as custodians, many of them in Jewish homes, and Volksdeutsche working as German agents had pointed to the Jewish Quarter in the center of the city as a prime target for bombardment. The streets of the Quarter were now filled with the rubble of broken masonry, twisted fences, collapsed stairways, and window sashes torn from the faces of the five- and six-story buildings that had lined these now sad streets. Few of the buildings that remained standing had escaped serious damage. Bombs had torn gaping openings in almost all of them, exposing interiors where the remnants of the civilization of my childhood and youth—carpets and furnishings, clothes and books—were precariously balanced, or hung suspended in the twisted wreckage. Bombed out Jewish families had crowded into the homes of friends and relatives, often in buildings that had been partially damaged and that were in danger of collapsing.

The Jews of Belgrade were now all obliged to wear yellow armbands on their left sleeves. They were all subject to any arbitrary command of the German authorities, and were forced to do menial and dirty work. Many Jews had been organized into work gangs assigned to clearing the streets of rubble and similar other tasks. The Jewish Committee had no power to question the German orders. Their only choice was to comply fully. The Jewish crews were made up largely of professionals—lawyers, doctors, merchants, teachers, and so on— who had rarely, if ever, in their lives performed manual labor. They made a pathetic sight as they worked clearing the streets, repairing bomb-damaged buildings, and hauling heavy containers of rubble and garbage. Many of them did not even know how to handle a shovel.

I refused to wear the yellow armband. Had I worn one, I would have immediately been assigned to a work crew and would have lost all freedom of movement. In these early days of my return to Belgrade, I despised the situation that I had found there. I hated the entire world. It was extremely dangerous for a Jew who was not wearing the yellow armband to be caught, so I moved very cautiously through the streets. I finally met with a group of my friends for a very serious talk about what action we could take. Yugoslav youth had begun to organize Resistance units. Most of these units were under the control of the Communists, whose command structure was highly centralized. There was a general consensus that it would be best to organize all resistance under a central command before initiating actions against the German fascists and their allies, and that we should struggle to replace Fascist authority with a progressive government.

All of my friends were Zionists above all. We had long and heated discussions over whether we should, for a time, abandon our Zionist idealism and our dreams of building a Jewish homeland in Palestine, or whether we should immediately join the SKOJ, the Communist Youth of Yugoslavia. Many among us pointed out that there was no way we could go to Palestine, and that our first priority must be to do everything in our power to defeat our Nazi enemies, but many expressed doubts that merging with the Communists was the best way to do this. We intensely debated these issues that tragic summer. Germany had long since consolidated its control of the entire Balkan region. The Greek army had surrendered on April 22, only five days after the capitulation of Yugoslavia. On June 22, the Nazis launched their attack on the Soviet Union. By midsummer, many Soviet armies had been encircled and destroyed, and German columns had penetrated deep into Russia, across a huge front stretching from the Baltic to the Black Sea.

The Nazi invasion of the Soviet Union was a tremendous shock to all of us—almost as great as the shock we had felt two years before when we had learned of the signing of the Nazi-Soviet nonaggression pact. We had all greeted with sorrow and outrage the subsequent Soviet participation with Germany in the dismembering of Poland, the Soviet occupation of the Baltic States, and the Soviet attack on Finland. Despite all this, despite the purges of 1937, despite the Soviet Union's abandonment and betrayal of the republicans in the Spanish civil war, despite the distrust that many of us felt for Stalin, most of us still revered the Soviet Union. Even in 1941, it was for many of us the best and the most honest country in the world. Little did we know!

Despite repeated warnings from his own intelligence services and from the British, Stalin had rejected any suggestion that war with Germany was imminent. He had refused to take any measures to prepare for a German attack, and had left his huge army of one hundred and fifty divisions exposed in advanced positions along Russia's extended western border. In the west and in Africa, hard-pressed on land, sea, and in the air, Britain stood alone against the Nazis. The United States remained aloof, across the Atlantic. So the Soviet Union stood without help against the blitzkrieg onslaught of Hitler's armies and those of its Axis allies. Many of us believed that the countries of the West—Britain's Churchill was notorious as an archenemy of Soviet Communism—were hoping that Germany would destroy the Soviet Union and its Communist regime. So, apprehensive for the fate of the Soviet Union, alarmed at reports of the defeat and destruction of its armies in that summer of 1941, we all considered joining the progressive youth of Yugoslavia—the SKOJ—to take a stand for the Soviet Union and to defend our own country in any way we could.

In casting our lot with the progressive forces, we would have been choosing to join in rebellion not only against the Nazis, but also against Yugoslav Fascists, who for many years had designated Communism as their primary enemy. When King Alexander had moved to reorganize the country in 1929, he wanted to create in Yugoslavia a nation whose citizens would place a higher value on loyalty to the country as a whole than to the many nationalities of which it was composed. This was a worthy goal, but Alexander completely failed to achieve it. In abolishing all political parties of a regional or religious character, and in curtailing freedom of speech and the press, the king had, in effect, abolished all political expression, and his regime had become a dictatorship with all the country's nationalist and democratic forces arrayed against it. The agents of Alexander's government applied increasingly brutal police methods to control the country, from the beginning singling out the Communists for especially severe repression. Yugoslavia was among the few nations in the world that had not recognized the Soviet Union. The Soviet Union itself had been unwilling to accept diplomatic ties with Yugoslavia until its government released many of its political opponents from prison, notably Moshe Pijade, who was serving a long sentence.

The Germans occupying the Balkans maintained their power nervously, through a reign of terror. The peoples of the region, especially the Serbs and the Greeks, were extremely proud. They were not prepared to accept Nazi conquest without a fight. No German could feel completely secure anywhere in the region. In Serbia, the Germans imposed a law of retaliation, declaring that they would execute one hundred Serbs for any single German killed. After Mussolini was overthrown, the Germans imposed a similar law in Italy, but there the measures were less severe, calling for the death of ten Italians for each German killed. Despite the draconian regulations imposed in Serbia, incidents of sabotage and attacks on German personnel had become daily occurrences. On one occasion, Serbian Resistance forces killed twenty-six German soldiers patrolling in the isolated hill country near the railhead at Valjevo, about ninety miles southwest of Belgrade. In retaliation, German soldiers immediately surrounded the large railroad station at Valjevo, where they stopped four long passenger trains and ordered everyone to disembark. The Germans then selected twenty-six hundred people—men and women, grandparents, children, and infants—and executed them, on the spot. Yet, both in spite of these brutal measures, and because of them, Germans were attacked and killed each day in an escalating spiral of violence and retribution. The Serb concepts of pride, freedom, and manhood would not be cowed. For them, a servile life was worthless. Nor did the women of Serbia hold back. They fought alongside the men in the front lines of their struggle for liberty. The Serbs were tough, very tough, and even the threat of death hanging over defenseless loved ones would not prevent them from striking out at their oppressors. This was the state of mind in Yugoslavia in the bitter summer of 1941, while Soviet armies were being pulverized and driven back to the gates of Leningrad, Moscow, and Rostov.

In Belgrade, the situation of Jews worsened daily. New restrictions were regularly added to a growing list, but this was done at a deliberately gradual pace, and the Jews of the city, who were desperate merely to survive, accepted the slow tightening of the noose around their necks. First, in the middle of June, when the weather was so beautiful, a 6 PM curfew was imposed on Jews. Soon afterward, Jews were forbidden to shop in the markets before 11 AM, and after that time only rotten foods remained for them to pick among, or there was no food left at all. Very soon after this, the Jewish merchants of the city were forced to close their shops, and all Jewish residents had to register and submit to periodic checks, as if they were paroled criminals. Jews could not ride on streetcars or take taxis. The list grew longer, and longer still. Then the Germans imposed on Belgrade's Jewish community a charge of five hundred kilos of gold to be paid within a week, under the threat that hostages would be taken if they did not meet the imposition in full. Jews were harassed at every level. Jews had become nonpersons. They had no rights. No indignities were spared them. Germans could treat Jews as badly as they wished, could invade any Jewish home, and could take whatever they liked.

Finally, it simply became too dangerous to be caught not wearing the yellow band, and I had to wrap it around the sleeve of my left arm. The commissioner of Jewish Affairs in Belgrade was a young man named Egon. While a medical student in Belgrade, he had already worked for the Germans as a spy. His best friends were the Margolis brothers, the sons of a Jewish internist. Egon ruled over all the Jews in Belgrade. It was a pitiful sight to see him lecturing to the senior Jewish doctors he had brought in to the Jewish Center. Egon preached at these distinguished men, screeching about the virtues of gymnastics, compelling them to run in place and to perform countless sit-ups and push-ups, as he drove those poor souls through such paces while his Gestapo overseers leered at the spectacle. Life was getting harder and harder and more dangerous with each passing day, and I simply could not understand how my fellow Jews could accept—as if it were normal—the process of their own destruction.

I had three uncles in Belgrade, all of them bachelors. One of them, Bukus Alcalay, a prominent ear, nose, and throat specialist, was a reserve colonel in the Yugoslav army. He was still in uniform and was working at the army hospital that summer. He moved around freely. Even the Germans respected him. My father's oldest brother, Bukus was not merely a marvelous doctor and surgeon—he also knew ten languages, six or seven of them fluently, and was an accomplished student of philosophy. He had always been very active in civic life. My second uncle, Nisim Alcalay, was also a doctor, a specialist in venereal diseases, but he was sick and had undergone an operation for an ulcer at the Army Hospital. My third uncle, Rudi Alcalay, was in the diplomatic service at the Turkish embassy. He suffered terribly from asthma, which was probably at least in part a psychosomatic ailment. During these difficult days, he suffered very much. Before the war, these brothers had all lived together in a large apartment with a fourth uncle, Isaac, who had been captured and was being held as a prisoner of war. Two other uncles—David Alcalay and Aron Alcalay—were also serving as officers in the Yugoslav army at the outbreak of the war. They, too, had been captured and imprisoned. Altogether I had seven uncles: three in Belgrade, another three in German POW camps, and another uncle, Jacob Alcalay, who died soon after the war, in Switzerland. We knew nothing at all of the whereabouts of my father and mother and Buena.

I visited my two uncles at the hospital whenever I could. From time to time, I brought them some food that my aunt—married to the only one of my father's brothers who was not a bachelor—had prepared for them. The hospital was on the distant outskirts of the city. I usually took the streetcar to reach it, although this was *verboten*. One day, when I was returning from one such visit, a young German soldier spotted me in the streetcar and ordered me to climb down immediately, which I did. But as soon as he turned away from me, I climbed aboard again, using the rear entrance. A few stops later he spotted me and came after me, working his way through the crowded cabin. Shrilly barking, *"Los! Los! Jude!"* (Get going, get going! Jew!), he tried to pick me up by my collar and shove me into the street. The streetcar screeched to a stop and I jumped off, the young soldier at my heels, shoving me and continuing his shrill abuse, as if he wanted to start a fight with me, to beat me, or to punish me. I turned on him, with my hands closed into fists. He flailed at me, and raising my arms to defend myself, I actually struck him. He immediately stepped back, suddenly silenced, clearly astonished that a "lousy" Jew would show his fists. He was not prepared for such a display and decided to leave me in peace. Within his sight, I mounted the next streetcar and went home.

The Germans only felt confident and strong when they were grouped together. Individually, their soldiers were cowards. Although they carried machine guns, they were nervous and frightened when they were alone. They knew that the people of the Balkans despised them and were ready to strike out at them at any moment. I remember the story of a young woman friend's experience. She was taken to a hotel where she was assigned the job of laundering German uniforms. While she was sweating and struggling over the wash, a soldier hung around her, harassing, poking, and pinching her, stupidly and abusively trying to wheedle favors from her. Exasperated beyond prudence and restraint, the young woman pulled the sodden, soapy mass of a brass-buttoned uniform from the washtub and swung it around in the air, striking the surprised soldier with such force that he fell to the floor. Embarrassed, he withdrew, excusing himself. This incident illustrated a point. We needed to show our pride and to be willing to stand up and defend ourselves. When confronted with any resistance, the Germans were often frightened and ran like cowards. But, in truth, they were dangerous and often quite ready to use their guns.

We felt black despair at the catastrophic news from Russia. The protective friendship of our great ally, France, was only a distant memory of disappointed faith. It appeared that Rommel would drive the British clinging on in North Africa into the Red Sea. The powerful United States remained asleep across the ocean. We felt completely alone, with only bare hope to sustain us. Hitler was in control of the entire European continent. Horrifying reports sporadically reached us from Poland about the fate of its three million Jews. And from the Jews of the Ukraine, Belarus, and Russia, there was only a crushing silence. And yes, we were dreadfully fearful for our destiny as well.

I tried to find a job as deeply within the Jewish community as possible, a job in which I would have the least contact with the despised Germans. I was highly motivated to find a position that suited me, and I proved myself quite ingenious in creating a very useful post that had not before existed. The Jews who had been assigned to work details gathered each morning at a central assembly point from which the various branches of the German occupation forces drew labor parties each day. A doctor was assigned to this staging area to verify the complaints of workers who reported themselves sick and unable to work and requested authorization to be excused for the day. I had observed the long file of people that each day lined up to wait to speak with the doctor, and had seen bitter quarrels breaking out in the exhausted and anxious crowd. Often these quarrels would arise from shameful disputes over someone's place in the line, with people taking sides and jostling, leading to shoving and more shoving, and sometimes outbreaks of fisticuffs. It was here that I was inspired and found immediate and useful employment. I would appoint myself marshal of the sick line! The morning immediately after my brilliant revelation came to me, I set a small table and chair at the head of the line and proceeded to register everyone by their name, alongside which I recorded their ailment. Everyone found this the most natural and useful job in the entire assembly area, and somehow the line was calmed by my presence. Scrambling over places in line and other disputes became rare. I accommodated everyone "officially," and they all felt reassured. The harassed doctor was pleased and relieved to have me as a gatekeeper to his office.

And so, I worked for a time, unmolested, until one day the Jewish commissioner went into a rage about something and ordered everyone to work—everyone, healthy and sick, workers and staff. And I was caught up in it, too. Fortunately, I was placed in a group with all my old friends. We were taken to a school, which we were ordered to clean. There was only one German sentry, naturally well armed, to watch over our group of ten. We were herded into a large, oblong classroom. The room was completely empty, but was littered with millions of bits of confetti, which covered the filthy and greasy floor. The German sentry immediately growled at us to clean this floor, not with brooms, but—with our tongues. We were to pick up all the confetti with our tongues! At first, we could not believe what he was saying, and started laughing about it, but he was very serious and barked the orders out again and shoved one of our comrades to his knees, motioning to the rest of us to get down to work.

One of my closest friends, Pajki, was in our group that day. He was only about five feet tall, but he was stout and strong, built like a Doric column, with the neck and shoulders of a weight lifter. I glanced sharply over at him, and saw the veins in his neck swelling with blood as his face turned red in fury. In a single movement, he swooped down on the German soldier and grabbed him by his collar and his crotch. Pajki heaved the soldier high in the air like a rag doll, all the military paraphernalia hanging from his belt like the strange charms of a bracelet, and threw him down on the floor with a force that would have shattered a stone. It was a splendid act of rage. We watched, frozen in silence, as the German soldier, his face chalk white, gingerly scrambled to his feet and, looking grimly at Pajki, said, "*Langsam, Langsam, Kamerad!*" (Easy, easy, friend!), and then sent us home.

Although they were the exception to the rule of desperate and bewildered submission among the Jews of Yugoslavia, such incidents were not rare in Belgrade, and they always took the Germans completely by surprise. They had not elsewhere experienced any resistance from their Jewish victims. But we were Sephardic Jews, and we were different. Our ancestors had deep roots in the soil of the country. We had come into the Balkans with the Ottoman Turks. For hundreds of years, we had lived in peace. We Sephardim were distinct from the Hasidim of Poland, with their caftans and beards and rigorously separatist communities. We were different from the Ashkenazim of Central

Europe. We were all enlightened Jews, steeped in the European tradition. Our fathers and grandfathers had fought in all the wars for the independence of the country, and although we did not have all the same rights as Christians, we had never suffered anti-Semitic pogroms, and we were not inured to brutality against Jews.

Now, however, the barbarians from the north had brought their diseased culture of persecution to the Jews of Yugoslavia, and our situation continued to become grimmer and grimmer. Because I was under continual police surveillance, I was forced to change apartments several times. And it had been discovered that my job had been a fiction, that no one had named me to my position helping the doctor in the assembly yard for the Jewish work crews. Deprived of this job, isolated from any responsibility, and with no sense of belonging to any group, I looked for employment at the Jewish Hospital, where before the war I had kept a studio with my teacher, Bora Baruh.

Of course, I did not ask anyone for work. I knew that I would be refused a position. Just as I had done in "finding" my former job, I observed the lay of the land, looking for some opportunity to fit in, to contribute to the efficient operation of the hospital. I was fortunate. My observations were rewarded with a possible solution. The hospital was a labyrinth of corridors of small offices and labs where Jewish doctors worked in a wide variety of medical specialties. In addition to these corridors of offices and labs, there were many operating rooms, X-ray rooms, wards, pharmacies, and so on, but there were very few intelligible signs to help orient patients and visitors to the hospital. So I climbed up to the fifth floor where my studio had been. I found an acquaintance of mine there, an architect who was responsible for configuring and reconfiguring space in the hospital in order to accommodate the shifting needs of its various departments. There was room for me in his office, and, with his unofficial assent, I declared myself a sign painter, and set about making colorful signs with the names of doctors, assistants, nurses, and other staff, and with the names of departments, labs, care units—anything that could be helpful. I began to place these on all the doors where they belonged, and everybody was happy. Thus, I became a hospital employee, and I worked there in relative safety.

One day, as I was strolling down the street outside the hospital, a woman friend of mine suddenly appeared, breathless and frightened, at my side. She was a member of my Zionist organization. She held a satchel of banned books out to me, and begged me to hide them for her, explaining that the Gestapo was pursuing her. With hardly a word, I quickly took the satchel and sneaked into the hospital as she hurried away, almost at a run. I went all the way up to the hospital attic, and hid the books between two girders in a dark and dusty corner. I immediately went back down to the street to see what had become of my friend. I later learned that she had managed to enter the courtyard of a house and had escaped unnoticed through its cellar into another street.

The next morning, when I arrived at the hospital to begin work, I was told to report immediately to the office of the director, Dr. Bukić Pijade. When I entered his office, he rose to his feet, his face beet red with anger. He screamed at me, asking me how I could have dared to jeopardize the entire Jewish Hospital community in hiding such books in the attic. I explained what had occurred the day before, and that I had planned to remove the books from the hospital and hide them or bury them elsewhere, but in the few moments I was granted to make my explanation, I realized that I had made a very grave mistake. The good doctor again burst into shouts of rage, ending in forbidding me ever again to enter the hospital under any circumstances, and, finally, adding that the books had already been burned. They were very valuable books, I sadly reflected, as I left the hospital. It was a pity that they had been destroyed.

Agitation among the youth was growing stronger by the day, along with the pressures placed on us to act against the Nazi occupiers. Orders went out to the youth Resistance cells that had been organized throughout Belgrade. I was skeptical of many of the assignments. They were all extremely dangerous, and they exposed us to risk of harm far more than they promised to deliver any real harm to the Germans.

My studio was still intact, and the building custodian was keeping an eye on it. He was also a Volksdeutscher. Prior to the Nazi occupation, he had always worked for Jews. As a very young man, he had taken custodial charge of the large building that housed a Jewish school, a Jewish hall and library, and many residential apartments in which Jews lived permanently. My studio was on the top floor of the building. Two of my uncles had lived there, including my youngest uncle, who was a prisoner of war, and had been vice president of the Jewish community. When this uncle had been mobilized the preceding April, he had spoken with this janitor, asking him to take good care of the building, but especially, if he would be so kind, to watch over his wife and his young son. This janitor was a Volksdeutscher, but he was no Nazi. He took excellent care of the building and he was faithful to my uncle until the end. His name was Herr Schitz. His own son, who was born in that very building, later denounced him as a Jew-lover, and the Germans executed the poor soul. But this was to occur much later, one more tragedy among the many millions of tragedies that unfolded in the Europe of those years of war.

Herr Schitz called to tell me that a German officer, an amateur painter apparently, had inspected my studio and had decided to appropriate it with all my supplies, and that a German doctor had made a claim on the office and research equipment belonging to my uncle, the laryngologist. Herr Schitz warned me that both the studio and the office, and all their contents, would very soon be confiscated. He told me to save what I most valued while I still could. I knew that Herr Schitz was taking a great a risk in telling me about this. All I could offer him were my thanks.

I certainly had no use for my uncle's research equipment, and at this point I needed nothing from my studio, but I didn't want anything to fall into German hands. I gathered a group of my friends, and late the following night we used the building elevator for many hours to shift all of my belongings out of the studio to my uncle's apartment. We also removed all the microscopes and other valuable instruments from my uncle's offices to the safekeeping of a friend's apartment in the same building. The next day, a still more numerous band of friends helped me move all these valuables to my own apartment, many blocks away. When the Germans came to take possession of my studio and my uncle's office, our valuables would simply be gone. Real risks were involved, of course, but fortunately, everything went smoothly and without incident.

A few days later, friends called to tell me that the Germans were moving everything from my family's apartment, so I went to look. I stood in the shadows on the opposite side of the street, not directly opposite, but some twenty yards away. I watched the Germans spill all the contents of our home out onto the street, to be hauled away: all my books and paintings, my drafting table, all our furniture, our clothing, our marble statuary, my father's precious collection of antique Persian rugs. I most regretted the loss of my books. They had been my real companions, my most faithful friends, and I owed them so much of my education. But I felt that even my books would be a burden in this time of danger.

As I watched the Germans pillaging the home that my parents had created with such love, I realized the futility of having removed the contents of my studio and my uncle's office. I became angry with myself for having exposed the lives of my friends and Herr Schitz to such danger by doing so. Within myself, I turned against the very possessions that had defined so much of my life. I realized that I had completely lost interest in these things, that they were entirely unimportant to me. I wished intensely that other Jews could feel the same way.

I became furious that my people were so attached to their possessions. I was furious that they had been too drawn in by bourgeois values. I was helplessly furious that our world was being torn apart, that so many Jews even then could not detach themselves from their blind middle-class love for beautiful objects, for chandeliers and furniture in rare polished woods and all those beautiful rugs and all the books and paintings. But I understood why these things were so valuable to them, seemingly more valuable than their lives. They represented the lifetimes of hard work that had been used to acquire them. Many Jews remained attached to their homes. They believed, despite the facts of the situation, and hoped, despite the utter despair that they felt, that, in the end, they would succeed in saving their homes, but the cost of this belief and this hope turned out to be the lives of so many among them.

In late July of that terrible summer of 1941, I began to work with the central committee that exercised authority over all the Jewish communities of Yugoslavia. If we didn't have any real authority or command of any real resources beyond our own dedication, we at least assumed responsibility to do all that we could to help the Jews of the country. The central committee was where the real work was being done. We worked with Jewish refugees from throughout Yugoslavia, handling thousands of difficult problems of every kind. I worked closely with many friends, but I was closest to Šalom Hornik, who had the most brilliant mind in our organization.

I worked with Šalom in the passport division. It was there, under his supervision, that I began to master the complex arts of passport and visa manipulation, administrative legerdemain, tricks of substitution, the craft of forgery, anything and everything, all to serve one aim, to sustain the flow of refugees away from mortal danger. We did everything that we could to help guide all the refugees as far as possible from Europe's vortex of murderous destruction, as far as Palestine whenever that was at all possible.

Sadly, our best efforts often failed. Many refugees were captured or killed en route. Many almost reached safety, only to be turned back toward their inevitable deaths. Many ended up in concentration camps. Some found improbable harbors of safety in which to wait out the war. And some reached their destinations safely and began to build new lives. We did our best, grimly aware of the dangers. We knew all the possible routes to Palestine, and their cost, through Greece, through Bulgaria, through Turkey via the Taurus Express through Asia Minor to Damascus, then on to Beirut and Palestine. We knew a hundred secret points of embarkation all along the Aegean coastline of Macedonia and all the stations along the sea route through the Aegean. We knew all the desperate games that had to be played to evade our greatest impediment, the British navy, but many of our friends ended up in the British refugee camps on Cyprus or in Italian camps on the island of Rhodes.

Our job was all consuming, and required great diplomacy and care. We worked with many underground organizations with varied needs and aims. And there were too many refugees who needed our help, and their numbers were swelling, a wave of refugees pushed in the only direction open to it by the force of a horrendous explosion.

We finally had to accept that our organization could no longer function in Belgrade or any other urban center where the Germans could monitor and repress our activities. Conditions were rapidly worsening, and our very survival was in doubt. We had to make clear to all our members that new sacrifices would have to be called for. The summer of 1941 was our darkest time. The Russians were reeling in defeat. The British had no help to offer. Their situation was desperate. In fact, the British were blocking us in the Aegean. The Vichy French were actively collaborating with the Fascists. In London, the Free French under de Gaulle and the Polish government in exile could only lay plans and make speeches. The United States remained dormant across the ocean. And, in Yugoslavia, the decision had been made to cease all resistance of any kind in the cities. The Communist leader Moshe Pijade had gone into the forest and had sent a call out to all the youth of the country to leave the cities and join the partisan groups that had begun to organize themselves to offer the threat of guerrilla warfare.

We all felt intense pressure to make a decision. We knew that we had just a few days in Belgrade before joining the Resistance units or setting off on the dangerous journey for Palestine. My friends and I gathered at the Ashkenazi synagogue in Kosmajska Street. We endlessly and emotionally discussed, questioned, and affirmed our leftist beliefs, trying to reconcile the conflicts arising from our attachments to the national cause of Yugoslavia and to Zionism. We debated how to continue our activities, and which course of action to adopt. We discussed the new dangers to our lives. We all knew that the struggle in Belgrade was futile. Staying on to continue our work there would surely lead to imminent arrest and internment in a concentration camp or worse. The real split in our group was between those who wanted to pull out immediately and make their way to Palestine and those who insisted that it was our duty to remain and fight the Fascists. Either choice imposed mortal risks. Even more deadly was the choice of doing nothing at all. Many members of our group already had clandestine ties to the partisans, and they urged us to join the forces of Moshe Pijade that were being organized in the forests.

After hour upon hour of intense and passionate discussion, we understood that there was no way to resolve the painful divisions within ourselves as individuals or within our group. Any decision would be very difficult to accept and would involve a harsh compromise. Many of us felt passionately that we were needed in Palestine, and that our primary loyalties should remain with our real dream of establishing a new nation there. But this was countered with equal force that it was in Yugoslavia that we should practice the ideals we had formulated throughout our young lives, and that we should remain and fight as revolutionaries in the front lines of the war against Fascism.

This meeting at the Ashkenazi synagogue in Kosmajska Street was the last gathering of our group. We knew that many of us would never see each other again, that we would be scattered across the globe, that many of us would face new battles at the side of comrades yet unknown, and that death awaited many of us in the near future. But beyond the uncertainties of the moment, as we embraced each other in farewell, we took some comfort in the faith and the hope that perhaps someday we would be reunited in Palestine. Whatever our choices, whatever the imperatives that finally determined them, we were united by the dream and the ultimate loyalty to the cause of a new land that then burned so fervently in our hearts. Now, years later, that passion, that dream, that hope, and that loyalty still binds us together, even as death has begun to divide some of us.

Many of my friends chose to attempt the dangerous and uncertain journey to Palestine. I cast my lot with them. Some arrived at their destination quickly: for some, the journey was long; for some, the attempt was fatal, their deaths anonymous, their graves unknown. Among those of us who chose Palestine, life carried some, such as me, on a different path, to a different destiny, away from Palestine. For the others in our group, the well-organized partisan units offered their young recruits a more certain escape from the cities. This fact alone played a role in the decisions taken by many. But even this was dangerous and required extreme caution. Belgrade was thick with spies and Volksdeutche, and any even seemingly sure-footed steps to contact the partisans could lead one straight into the hands of the Gestapo.

Early in the morning of the day after our meeting, a terrible and decisive event occurred. A Jewish boy named Emil Almoslino, who was working for the Communists, threw a bomb under a truck. The bomb exploded, killing five German soldiers. The boy was never caught. Egon, the Jewish Commissioner, arrived, pale and extremely disturbed, at the Jewish Commission offices at around 11 AM. He could not tell us what had happened, but he ordered all the Jews of Belgrade to assemble at 2 PM the next day at Tašmajdan, a large open place where the municipal tennis courts were located. The employees of the Jewish Commission were instructed to go throughout Belgrade to tell the Jewish people that everyone, every Jew, was ordered, without exception, to report to the square. We had a very hard day as we fanned out through Belgrade to inform the Jewish community of the order to report to Tašmajdan. My two uncles were far away at the Army Hospital. I hoped to myself that they would hear nothing of this. I was not going to tell them anything.

The next day, at 2 PM, many thousands of fearful Jews had assembled, but the Germans corralled the men only in the fenced area enclosing the tennis courts. The women and children were told to remain outside. A large contingent of SS troops and officers was present, and the Gestapo was well represented. Finally, the German officers ordered the Jewish men to separate into groups according to their professions. There was considerable confusion at first, and sharp screams of abuse from the Germans, but quickly doctors, lawyers, merchants, and teachers, and so on, had all lined up in separate groups. Although I could have lined up with the students, I took my place with the teachers. Finally, the Germans started to count down the lines, taking every fifth man out. I was counted fourth. We were all then ordered to leave, except the designated fifth men. We all felt a foreboding of tragedy, but we dared not fear the form that it would take, so many of us removed our jackets and gave whatever other clothing we could to those who remained, as well as all the money we were able to collect on the spot. We moved spontaneously and quickly to do these things, and we were relieved that the Germans permitted us to make these gestures. As we left the enclosure, the women outside the gate strained to see their husbands, brothers, and sons, and greeted them with hugs and tearful kisses, but a pandemonium of grief soon broke out among the many women whose loved ones had not returned. It was a cruelly hard day, and we all left the scene filled with apprehension. I had many friends among the unfortunate men whom the Germans had retained, and I reflected with a strange combination of bitterness and gratitude on the luck that had stayed with me since the outbreak of the war.

The next morning, when I arrived at the Jewish Commission, the large front gate was tightly shut, so I went in through the back door, which was really the entrance for the employees. Everyone was in a somber mood. Some people were huddled in corners, weeping. Doctors in the basement were giving injections to girls and women. I immediately learned that all the personal effects of the men the Germans had selected the prior day had been returned. We immediately concluded that they had all been shot as punishment for the truck bombing. It was a terrible day. We were under siege at the Commission. Outside the gate, women were screaming, cursing, weeping, collapsing. Many pounded on the gate, desperately beseeching help where we had none to give. It was as if the entire Jewish people were sobbing and stricken with grief.

For the first time, the Jewish community of Belgrade had been struck with the full force of the reality of its situation. It was a great tragedy, a tremendous psychological shock that I hoped would awaken the Jews and incite them to flee the danger, but it did not. For my part, I resolved to leave Belgrade, to leave Yugoslavia, without any unnecessary delay. I called Šalom Hornik to tell him how I was planning to escape and to ask him if he wanted to join me. I planned to forge an Italian passport, not for Italy, but for "Free Dalmatia," which Italy had declared an autonomous territory. If Šalom wanted a similar passport, I could make one up for him as well. I had forgotten that Šalom was married—to Vinka Baruh.

I told Šalom that I was leaving as soon as I could forge my passport. I had no intention of traveling directly to the west, since that route would take me through Croatia. The Croats had behaved viciously toward the Jews, and toward the Serbs as well, even more so than the Nazis. I planned to travel south until I entered Italian territory. The Italians were not at all anti-Semitic, so I could at least hope for a better chance once I reached territory under their jurisdiction. Šalom liked the sound of my plan, and agreed to travel with me. We decided to take Vinka, too, to leave her in Niš, where she could stay with her sister until we crossed the border into Italian-controlled Kosovo. There, in Priština, which we knew was in Italian hands, we could obtain some kind of lasciapassare (laissez-passer) for Vinka so that Šalom could go back and pick her up.

I made quick but meticulous work of forging the passports, choosing Armando Moreno as my false name. I concocted a similar alias for Šalom. We decided not to carry any luggage, but we did ask two German Jews who were returning from Belgrade to Priština, where they had found refuge, to take a few things with them and keep them for us there. The next day we set out on our dangerous journey. I did not have time to say farewell to my uncles, but I sent them a letter in the care of a trusted friend. Šalom and I had decided that it would be wiser to depart as quietly as possible, so I did not attempt, nor did I have time for, a complete round of farewells to all my friends. Many among them had in any event already left the city, or had disappeared from view, and were doubtlessly preparing to leave. I exchanged warm embraces with the few friends I did see before leaving, always saying that we would be joyfully reunited in Palestine. I left my apartment and all my belongings to my friends Flora and Mladi.

Early the next morning, I slung my raincoat over my shoulder to hide my yellow armband, and made my way cautiously to the railroad station, where I was to meet Šalom and Vinka. We planned to board a train to the south. The day was overcast, so it was not out of place that I was carrying my raincoat, and if some Volksdeutsche recognized me and asked me why I was not wearing the armband, I could readily display it. The walk to my destination was nevertheless extremely tense, and I was perspiring more and more profusely as I approached the railroad station and as the number of German guards increased.

Šalom and Vinka were waiting for me when I finally entered the station. We purchased tickets for Niš and quickly entered the train. Šalom and I immediately went to the men's room, where we hid in the toilet stalls and stripped our armbands off. We then joined Vinka to take our seats and await the departure of the train. A steady stream of people mounted the train, until finally it was full and ready to depart. But before we departed, two German soldiers, their machine guns at the ready, passed slowly down the center aisle, carefully fixing their gaze on every passenger, one after another. My heart was pounding so furiously that I thought it was going to jump out of my body. Finally, they passed, and the train started rolling slowly southward.

I was leaving Belgrade. Even then, I expected never to return. I thought of the three uncles I was leaving behind. I had tried to persuade them to leave. And I was wondering where my family was now, where my mother, my father, and my sister were. I had not heard from them for many weeks.

6

My Father's Journal: Part I

MY FATHER KEPT A DIARY THROUGHOUT THE WAR. IN THE FOLLOWING extract from this diary, my father relates what happened to my family from the beginning of the war, when I was away with the army in the south, to the day I rejoined them, when the strands of our fate and destiny became re-entwined:

Sunday, April 6, 1941

There are sirens and alarms throughout Belgrade at 3 AM. We sit together with our landlord, Isak Tuvi, in his apartment, trying to find out what is happening. By 5 AM, the alarms have gone silent. We return to our apartment to go to bed, since it is Sunday and we can sleep the whole morning. I turn the radio on. I immediately hear the proclamation to the German nation that Hitler has declared war on Yugoslavia. I try to tell this news to my wife and daughter, but they are so tired that they have fallen asleep. I remain awake and wait. At 6:30 AM, another alert comes, and I wake my wife and daughter, since a bombardment has followed the alert and I hear the sound of antiaircraft guns. The German Luftwaffe is attacking Belgrade.

We hurry downstairs to the cellar, where many neighbors have also come, sleepy, unwashed, half-dressed, disheveled. We can hear heavy detonations, and deduce that fires are breaking out and buildings are collapsing. Some wounded people enter our cellar at this point. The first wave of bombers passes. Some of our acquaintances run into the streets. When they return, they tell us the names of the first casualties. The City Theater is in flames. The second wave comes very quickly afterward. It strikes much harder. Bombs hit all the buildings around us. We can feel the earth shake from the explosions. Women scream and pass out,

89

among them my daughter. The men are silent and pale. The doorman and the servant of our landlord, both Volksdeutsche, *comfort us, telling us that there will not be any more attacks from the air. They tell us that the bombing was only a punishment for Belgrade because of the demonstrations of March 27. Afterward they both go to the roof of our house—nobody knows why—and then they escape across the bridge to the bombarded city of Zemun on the opposite bank of the Danube. We spend the whole morning in the basement, waiting.*

For lunch, we have a little bread. There is no water. The toilets are already backed up, and the stench is horrible. Police are cruising the streets, trying to stop the looting of the bombed-out stores. At about 2 PM, I go to our bank, followed by our maid. All the streets are deserted. The Serbian King Hotel and some bombed-out shops, mostly Jewish-owned, in King Peter Street, are on fire. I stand, helpless, in front of the big safe at the bank. The second key is with the bank's cashier, and I cannot open it. We return home. We have to think about a shelter for the night, since everyone cannot possibly sleep in the cellar. Then a car arrives to pick up Mrs. Steiner, one of our neighbors. Everyone begs the chauffeur to take them, but my offer of one thousand dinars prevails. But we have to start at once, without any of our things or any luggage. I just want to pick up my prepared suitcase, which is in the cellar, but I cannot find it quickly in all the confusion—someone is sitting on it. Women are pulling at my sleeves and my coat and will not let me go. "Take me, take me! I want to go with you!" they cry. Finally, we pull away. I promise them that I will send the same car back to pick them up.

We leave our home in this manner, leave everything behind, and we depart without even an extra handkerchief in our pockets. While the car is driving through King Alexander Street toward Grocka, the air is filled with trembling sounds and the tremors of bombardments. When we arrive in Grocka, we see our friends Mirko Pollack and his family riding on a wood and coal wagon. They are all black with soot. Their house had collapsed on top of them, and they had barely saved themselves by crawling through a cellar window. It is hard to believe how Mirko's 300-pound wife could have passed through the cellar window. After a little talk, they agree to look for shelter with us that night in

Grocka, and we also agree to continue together toward the resort of Aranđelovac. One of the peasants offers us shelter for the night at his place. From his courtyard, we can see Belgrade burning in the night sky.

Monday, April 7, 1941

This morning, our peasant host comes to wake us and tell us that there was an alert. In the harbor on the Danube, a ship had been sunk. We depart over the mountain with many other refugees to get away from the Danube. We walk for the entire day, as fast as we can, over small goat trails, to avoid the highway. We can see German planes flying southwest to bomb Smederevo, Kragujevac, Mladenovac, and other towns. It starts to rain. Soaked to the skin, we arrive that evening at Duboka, where we pass the night in a peasant's house. He suspects that we all might belong to the fifth column and wants to take us the next day to the town hall. One of his grandsons—some kind of wunderkind—*improvises his own songs on a gusle, a one-stringed instrument, generally played as accompaniment to the recitation of Serbian epic poetry.*

Tuesday, April 8, 1941

When we wake this morning, the entire village is filled with refugees. We continue, walking through the mud, but we realize that we are circling the Kosmaj Mountain. We pass through Mladenovac. It is deserted, but very lightly damaged by bombardment. As we go toward Aranđelovac, we are caught by a very strong wind, followed by snow. Half frozen, under very difficult conditions, we arrive at a resort hotel and find an apartment.

Wednesday, April 9, 1941

We rest in Aranđelovac. We can see the full image of war there. There are no provisions. All the stores are closed. The coffeehouses are full of soldiers, the streets full of refugees.

Thursday, April 10, 1941

Today is the first day of Passover. Our lunch consists of a lump of sugar with a piece of bread that we received from a friend. Our friend Mariška and my wife are sorrowful about Passover, and they weep bitterly. We hear all kinds of news. The German radio "Dunav" declares that their "courageous" army has occupied Skoplje and Niš. At the same time, the town hall of Aranđelovac, through its town crier with a drum, tells us that the enemy has not even passed the border and that our army has destroyed 600 tanks at Kačanik. In the distance, we can hear heavy artillery. Somebody comes who says that the Germans had taken him prisoner but that they released him when he told them that he was a merchant. A great number of refugees are going toward Rudnik.

Friday, April 11, 1941

Soldiers had first been moving to the east. Now we see them moving to the west. Dead horses lie in the streets. The snow is as thick as in January. I see a Gypsy dressed in uniform, begging. I promise Mirko Polack that I will take care of his wife and two small sons, but only if they obey me when I signal them to move ahead.

Saturday, April 12, 1941

The situation in Aranđelovac is not good, and I don't like it at all. I would like to depart, but now I am bound by my promise. Word is spreading this evening that the Germans have arrived. There is a general scare. We pass the night, three families together, dressed and sleepless.

Sunday, April 13, 1941

Finally, our soldiers are ready to move. This is a good sign. I advise some friends that they and their families should move with us toward Bosnia, but they refuse. Finally, I ask Mrs. Polack to either free me from the promise I had made to her husband, or depart with me. She then decides to depart. I ask her to tell nobody about our intentions. At about 2 PM, when it is time to depart, I go to get her and her children. There is a whole crowd of women and children behind her. She says that she is sorry, that she had told only one person. With a lot of effort and fatigue, we succeed in getting ahold of the train that is transporting troops and is going to Lajkovac. Some soldiers, mostly from Belgrade, tell us that the Germans have entered Belgrade from the south. Both bridges on the Sava and Danube, great large bridges, have been destroyed.

Monday, April 14, 1941

In Čačak, the railroad station is full of people. I bump into my brother David. We have been waiting all night in the station. My brother and his colleagues are still searching for his command, which, they say, can be anywhere from Banja Luka to Mladenovac. His entire command has disappeared. He complains to me that his wife has not escaped with us but has remained to protect the furniture.

Tuesday, April 15, 1941

We travel toward Užice. Rain falls all day. We often hear alerts, as the German airplanes are almost always in the sky. I say good-bye to David, who continues with his friends toward Sarajevo and Banja Luka. We take another train. There are many people from Belgrade on the train. Some woman says to her companion: "Look, darling, how the Jews are the first to escape." I can't bear it, and react by telling her: "Yes, Miss, we are escaping because we fear Hitler, but why are you escaping?" We arrive in Pale late at night. There we hear that Sarajevo has been bombarded. Why do we decide to descend from the train? It takes such a long time to find a shelter for the night. While I am pounding at the door of a summer villa in which Mrs. Polack had lived last year, somebody calls out my name. Out of the darkness appears the head of a peasant who asks, "Who is it—Alcalay?" My wife answers him, and then he says, "I would like to do something for you, since Dr. Bukus Alcalay [my oldest brother] saved my life at the Army Hospital." My wife asks him to find us a shelter for the night. He does find us shelter.

Wednesday, April 16, 1941

With terrible difficulties, and at considerable expense, we find a little bit of food. In the coffeehouse, people are talking about some kind of concluded truce. A certain colonel, who has a room next to ours, advises us to go to Sarajevo. "Go and get lost among your people. I am advising you as a friend." We part from Mrs. Polack, who tells us that her husband has arrived by truck and that they are going toward Užice, and that only we, but not any of the other people that are increasing by the minute, can go with them. Because Mrs. Romano implores us not to leave her alone, we decide to go to Sarajevo, and leave immediately for the railroad station. At a distance, in front of another train, I spot a group of officers. I think that maybe David is among them, but instead I run into old Dr. Kujundić from Belgrade. I follow his advice and, instead of going to Sarajevo, we return toward Užice. In the train, I have a quarrel with a major.

"Look, they are evacuating the children. Haven't you heard what the premier said? Everyone should perish on the threshold of his house," the major shouts.

That is too emotional for me, so I yell at him, "Why, sir, are you escaping and saving your life instead of fighting on the front?"

"Who are you?" he asks.

"I am Alcalay from Belgrade."

He answers, "Ah, so now I understand why you are escaping."

We descend the train at Ustiprača. The major tells us to wait for the train and go to Užice.

It is completely dark and impossible to see anything. We are becoming desperate. Then an officer approaches me and asks me what I am doing in that darkness.

"We are waiting for the train from Užice," I tell him.

"Užice is in enemy hands," he answers.

"What are we going to do now?" I ask, full of apprehension.

When the officer then asks if we would like to come with them to Montenegro, I answer, "Certainly!"

The officer, Captain Bojović, orders some young men equipped with bayonets to push an empty freight car, which in a moment is full of people. Very soon, the train starts toward Plevlje, but it stops at Rudo.

We pass another night filled with apprehension, between enemy columns. At a distance, we can see the lights of cars. People are saying that the king and the whole government is leaving to go to Montenegro. Madame Romano and her husband and their children are sobbing and saying: "Why are we getting farther away from Belgrade?" As if the stove, the house, the maid, and card games were all waiting for them there!

Thursday, April 17, 1941

Very early this morning, the train starts backing toward Ustiprača. I tell the Romanos to return if they think they would be happier, and they did. They are very sad that we don't want to return with them. Captain Bojović immediately sends his armed students to the highway, and these students succeed in bringing back three empty trucks. A great many refugees fill them up in no time. The officers who are staying in the coffeehouse remain there, yelling and shouting, "Bojović! Wait for us!"

He answers them, "You are the fifth column! Stay there and die!"

I never thought that I would see such a moment. It was like some kind of German propaganda movie. A group of Montenegrins is waiting for us at Moljkovac. They think that we are "Croatian traitors." It takes a lot of effort on the part of Captain Bojović to convince them that we are not. Finally, we can continue. In an old highway tavern, one Montenegrin says to me, "Mister, have you ever seen such a debacle? There hasn't been such a disaster since Kosovo!"

Dead tired, in the complete darkness of late night, we reach Kolašin, where we find supper and a night shelter.

Friday, April 18, 1941

Today, I meet with a German Jew. He advises us to remain in Kolašin and wait for the Italians. Mr. Ergas, our travel companion, wants to go toward Peć, but Captain Bojović tells us that a big snow has fallen on Čakor Mountain and that it is impossible to travel there. We part from him. He gives us a truck and advises us to travel toward the Italian army. We embrace each other like brothers, exchanging our ad-

dresses, hoping that we will see each other again. Captain Bojovič is first going to Andrijevica with the young students, and then afterward he will join the partisans.

"You will hear about us," he says in farewell. We start moving toward Podgorica, where there is a camp of Italian troops. We do not dare to enter the town, but instead turn toward Nikšić.

The road to Nikšić will remain forever etched in our memories. We encounter our whole army there, destroyed and completely bewildered. We see our artillery and, in each car, a small Italian soldier. Our soldiers look like giants compared to the Italians, although these giants are now their prisoners of war. There is one of our majors sitting atop a cannon, sitting and crying, and we in the truck start to cry also when we see such a sight. The broken fuselage of an airplane is lying by the road. Sporadically, we can see groups of our infantrymen and dumps of ammunition and stacks of rifles. The rain is pouring down. A great number of our officers walk with bowed heads, staring down at the muddy road. My wife immediately recognizes the son and son-in-law of Mariška in a distant group. She calls out to them to come join us, but they do not hear, since the truck is going in the opposite direction. Entering the forest, we notice many soldiers hiding their rifles or banging them on stones in order to break them. But we do not pay too much attention to this. We distribute the rifles that are in the truck to the Montenegrins, and they are as happy as little children.

We arrive in Nikšić at sundown. The town is full of our army and refugees, but it is not occupied by anybody. We are advised to move ahead—otherwise our truck will be confiscated. We continue toward Trebinje, where our travel companion, young Armand Amodaj, has a relative, Dr. Levi. Night falls, and we are stuck on a muddy road, among idling Italian trucks. We pass the whole night on the truck, listening to cries and screams and sobs, but we can't tell where they are coming from, or why they continue all night long.

Saturday, April 19, 1941–c. May 15, 1941

We have been in Trebinje one full month. Our whole army arrives in the town as prisoners of war, and then is moved to camps in Albania and Italy. One day, I notice a great number of our higher officers in the restaurant. Our friend Ergas tells me that they have come from

Skoplje. I approach their table. One of the generals asks me, "Are you the writer who wrote about Moses?"

"No, that is my brother Aron," I answer.

"I just wanted to ask about him, since he was in Skoplje, serving as captain."

"Colleagues! Do you know anything of Aron Alcalay?" the general asked the other officers.

But nobody knows. I ask them for news about the Seventh Division, in which Albert is serving. The general tells me that our army has had heavy battles with Germans on the Bulgarian front. I cannot learn anything new. It is natural we should worry a lot about Albert. I write to Sarajevo and Zagreb, and I receive a telegram from Zagreb that says that Albert is alive and has been taken prisoner in Kumanovo. My wife and I cry tears of joy.

People are arriving from Belgrade. One postman tells me, "If you are Jewish, do not return to Belgrade, because it is terrible there for Jews. Others are not being molested."

Life in Trebinje has been monotonous. All our soldiers have been sent off as prisoners of war, all except the Croatians, who have been set free to return home. We are mostly with the Ergas family, who joined us in Aranđelovac. With them is a young Jewish boy who has decided to return to Belgrade to see what has happened to Mr. Ergas's store. He returns after a few days and brings us Albert's letter, written from the POW camp in Kumanovo. Albert had thrown the letter over the fence, asking that somebody bring it to me. This letter somehow came into the possession of Aron's wife, Fini. Albert is worried about us, and he has lost all his things. By the same boy, we send him money, clothing, and food.

I go to Dubrovnik, where I find a great number of people from Belgrade. There is great commotion, because of an agreement between "Independent Croatia" and Italy. Dubrovnik and Trebinje are going to belong to Croatia, so all Jewish refugees are intending to flee, but where?

c. May 17, 1941

. . . This morning, swastikas appear on all the front doors in Trebinje. With almost no hesitation, we decide to take the bus through Du-

brovnik and go to Herceg Novi. We find many of our friends there. We immediately find an apartment in a house close to the shore in Topla, on the highway outside the town. The room is very beautiful, and looks out onto a lovely garden. The landlady is a very kind, older woman, named Nasta Spirtović. She has one unmarried daughter and another daughter married to a Croat, but a good Yugoslav, by the name of Martin Sager. Life in Herceg Novi is not without commotion, but the Italian authorities here appear to be very tolerant.

. . . We have had a sketchy correspondence with Albert. He has returned to Belgrade and is working with the Union of Jewish Communities. We have advised him to come join us here, and have sent people to bring him, but he doesn't want to come. He wants to remain with his friends and my brothers, to share their destiny in Belgrade.

. . . We pass the time reading or talking with our hosts or promenading to "Boka," where all the people from Belgrade gather together. My brother Rafajlo suffers from bad asthma. My brothers Bukus and Nisim are serving as doctors in the army hospital. All three have remained in Belgrade. My other three brothers, Aron, Isak, and David, are prisoners of war in Germany. Our major preoccupation here is collecting provisions. Food is getting scarcer every day. I go to the market in Herceg Novi, but cannot find anything to buy.

. . . I have written several times to Albert to come join us here. I have sent some men to bring him, but he has rejected the idea of leaving his friends and his work in Belgrade. My brother Bukus, still wearing the uniform of a colonel of the Yugoslav army, is working at the army hospital. Nisim is also working as a doctor there. All the time, new refugees arrive with news that the Jews in Belgrade have to do compulsory work without pay. I learn that my cousin, Alfred Hason, Jr., was hanged. His brother is a physician in Herceg Novi. I have implored the people not to tell him anything. The attempt to form an independent state in Montenegro has not succeeded, and a revolt has broken out. Here among the inhabitants of Herceg Novi displeasure towards us Jews is more and more apparent, because food is getting more and more expensive, and we will pay any price demanded for it. One of the officers has told me that we are going to be interned, but nobody believes him.

June 1941

Suddenly we are being arrested. The Italians are confiscating all our money. They are saying that we "financed" the Montenegrin Revolution. They say they are going to send us to Italy. They take all the Jews to a school. We remain there a whole night. My wife becomes ill.

. . . The Italian authorities send us by truck to Kotor. A great number of Carabinieri accompany us. The authorities tell us that they will return our confiscated money when we arrive in Kotor. But instead of going there, we are hurried aboard the ship Alexander with a crowd of Montenegrin women and children, as well as some young people from Herceg Novi, who are all considered communists. We sleep on the floor of the ship's dining salon. The guards are constantly at our heels, even when we go to the toilets.

. . . We have been transferred from the Alexander to another ship, the Kumanovo, which is anchored in front of Tivat. The personnel of the Kumanovo are treating us much better. We have been assigned cabins. The Union of Serbian Sisters of the town of Kotor has sent us food. Many stories circulate about where we are to be sent—to Italy or to a concentration camp somewhere. Three men from our group from Herceg Novi are allowed to return there to collect our belongings. They bring us back a letter from Albert asking us to help him escape from Belgrade. Unfortunately, it is now too late. We are interned. But what is happening in Belgrade? My wife is torn with worry. We barely manage to keep her calm. We are all very worried about Albert.

. . . We are suffering terribly in this heat. It is impossible to sleep in the cabins. We sleep on tables in the various salons of the ship. Finally, the ship starts sailing. The sea is very rough outside the harbor of Kotor. We look out for the last time at Herceg Novi. We have had to leave a great deal of our money there, all consisting of gold coins. I say to myself, "It is better for it to be lost than for the enemy to take it and buy more weapons with it, against all our hope—an Allied victory."

. . . We land in Durrës, where we climb into a huge bus and set out for a camp at Kavaja. The bus discharges us at the gate. We are taken into the camp without any formality and are pushed into a large stable, into which are crowded three rows of rough wooden bunks, really little more than crude shelves. The hygienic conditions here are terrifying.

Filth and garbage are piled everywhere. The women and children start to scream and cry, especially those who believed that we would go to Italy. One of the Italian officers has told one of our people, Lela Mevorah, "Sarete delusi, andate in un brutto paese" *(You will be disappointed; you are going to a horrible land). We have all been given two blankets, a spoon, a fork, and a container for soup. There is no running water. They deliver water in two big barrels. There are no toilets. They plan to dig a crude latrine. The heavy atmosphere is black with mosquitoes and insects, so thick that it is impossible to stand still. It is even impossible to lie down. A squat Italian major lines us up in two columns, one male and one female, and in a very vigorous voice declares,* "Signori e signore, c'è che c'è, c'è" *(Ladies and gentlemen, what we've got is all we've got). But as soon as he hears the women crying, he runs to us men and, with tears in his eyes, declares,* "Prego, dite alle signore che la vita non è sempre di rose. Non devono disperare! Calmatele, prego!" *(Please, tell the women that life is not always a bed of roses. Don't despair! Quiet them down, please!)*

. . . What can we do? We must accept reality. We have to take care of ourselves first. We are going to have to take responsibility for a general cleaning of the camp, especially our shelter in the stable, which the Italians are calling a capanone *(a huge barracks). Yesterday, the Italian officers and soldiers were very sharp-tongued. Today, they are polite and ready to help. They complain themselves about being obliged to live in Albania under such conditions. We have filled a freight car with garbage. The camp is infested with rats and frogs. The clouds of insects are a constant torture. We are going to have to do our best to clean them all out. Somehow, we are going to improve conditions and become acclimatized to the situation. I don't know if we will be able to do anything to improve our crude sleeping quarters. That the men are isolated from the women and children is an additional hardship for many of us. What can we do?*

. . . The steady rainfall has transformed the camp into a muddy swamp. Many of the women and children are feverish and sick. Some of the men have also fallen ill. We have soup with macaroni, canned food, and some kind of coffee for breakfast. Everything tastes good enough. The Italians have granted our petition to permit one of our men to go to town every day to purchase fresh food. Some of the men

are very depressed. I am trying to comfort them. Who knows how badly off Jews are elsewhere in Europe? Some of the people, especially those who are well-to-do, have not lost hope that the Italians are going to send us all to Italy.

. . . Women and children from Montenegro are quartered in other stables—capanoni—in our camp. We don't know why they have been brought to Kavaja. We are forbidden to communicate with them. We are somehow getting used to this new life. The women are washing the laundry, starting to take care of themselves, and not crying anymore.

July 1941

It is Sunday today. I meet a lawyer recently arrived from Belgrade who tells me that Germany and Italy have declared war on Soviet Russia. This is hard to believe, but it confirms other reports we have heard, and many of us feel new hope because of it. The Axis have made a major mistake. The lawyer has told us that the Germans have advanced deep into Russia, and that the Germans are sinking many British ships. It is certain that the war is going to be very long, but we are going to win. The news from Belgrade is not good. The destiny of us Jews is growing darker.

August 1941

We have made great progress in improving conditions in the camp. We have cleaned up all the garbage dumps. Dry weather over the past weeks has helped us a lot, but we choke in the dust stirred up by passing truck convoys. The Italians have built covered latrines for the women. We can walk outside the wire in the afternoon, but only within the limits of the camp. Today, a great number of Montenegrins arrive. They are put into a separate compound, but we manage to speak with them. They tell us that the revolution in Montenegro has been crushed. Last night, a Montenegrin woman gave birth to a baby. Our Dr. Bauer was invited to help her. He told us that they live in great misery. Many among us, especially those who have money, still believe they will be sent to Italy. Some have lost hope, and believe they are going to perish here. Dr. Bauer, his brother, and I have decided to start studying the Italian language. Everyone else is studying English.

August 14, 1941

My daughter returned from a walk today and pulled at me to go with her.

"Don't you see that I am busy?"

"Come, Father, come now!"

She pulls me by my wrist with both of her strong, tiny hands. The moment we were alone, I ask:

"Where is he?"

"Who?"

"Albert."

"How do you know?"

"I feel it. Why would you otherwise call me away like that?"

"I saw him in front of the camp."

"Alone?"

"Yes."

7

The Quest for Freedom

As the train left Belgrade, my mind was spinning in thought. I had left Belgrade without hesitation. I knew in my heart that I would never return. Although I had wanted to rejoin my family and had had many opportunities to leave before, I felt that I should remain in the city with my friends and my uncles. There was important work to do in Belgrade. Many of my friends and I believed that we could do the most damage to the Germans if we remained in the capital and joined in the resistance to the Nazi occupation there. But the situation had changed by the time I left the city behind me on July 30, 1941. The Soviet Union was at war with Germany and was reeling in defeat across the Ukraine and western Russia. The British were suffering terrible losses at sea, and, in North Africa, Rommel's Africa Corps had driven them back to the Egyptian border. The Yugoslav Resistance had all but abandoned Belgrade to the Germans. And the repression there had intensified far beyond our breaking point. The situation of the Jews in the city was hopeless. It was a dark, grim time. All that remained to us was the struggle to save our own lives, if even that would be possible. When Moshe Pijade declared that there was nothing more that could be done in the cities, and called to us to join the partisans in the countryside, and when the Germans began their wholesale massacre of the Jewish population, departure was the only choice. And so we left Belgrade, those of us who could, either to join the partisans in the countryside, or to try to reach Palestine in any way possible, as many others and I had chosen to do.

We finally arrived at our destination, the important rail junction of Niš, and climbed down from the train. In better days, international trains, the famous Orient Express among them, had passed through the city. Vinka went to stay with her sister. Šalom and I set out to find my "godfather," Dr. Albert Beraha. I had been given his name when I was circumcised in Paris. Dr. Beraha was a very prominent Jew. The Nazis were watching him closely, and the doctor and his family lived in fear, so it was far too dangerous to stay with them for even that single first night of our arrival. The doctor even refused to let us enter his home. We could not go far. A curfew was in effect, so we decided to seek shelter among Gypsies whose caravan was camped on the outskirts of the city. The Gypsies greeted us with warm hospitality, sympathizing with our plight, because they were no strangers to Nazi persecution.

The next morning Šalom and I managed to hire a taxi. We had to cross the border into Italian-controlled territory at the village of Uroševac, a dangerous Shqiptar (ethnic Albanian) settlement. It was no longer the border between Yugoslavia and Albania, but now the border between German-occupied Serbia and Italian-occupied Albania. I told Šalom that I would do the talking when we arrived, that he should just get out of the taxi and remain standing beside it. These Macedonians of Albanian extraction were a very simple and poverty-stricken people who lived in small groups in small shelters scratched into the ground. I had seen many such Shqiptars in Belgrade. Woodstoves were the principal source of heat in wintertime Belgrade, and migrant Albanians found work in the city as woodcutters before the war. Though they were paid very poorly, these migrant workers managed to save enough to be able to return to their villages and marry. In their home region, Shqiptar men were considered thieves and cutthroats by the local Slavs. These fierce men were allies to the Nazis. With the war, they had obtained real power. Dressed in Nazi regalia, they were heavily armed and could murder a stranger for a few coins. But if our luck held, we might yet be able to cross the border at Uroševac without incident.

When Šalom and I arrived at Uroševac, I emerged from the taxi to deal with the Shqiptar border guards. They were all heavily armed, some carrying two or more pistols, most with bandoliers of grenades slung over their shoulders and knives hanging from their belts. Some carried submachine guns. Most of them had adorned their hats and boots with skulls and crossbones. They were all quick to jerk their arms into a rigid Fascist salute. On my lapel, I wore the sign of the three lions, the emblem of Free Dalmatia. Our passports indicated that we were returning to Split.

I instantly understood that I had to take the initiative. Any hesitation on my part would invite dangerous mischief on theirs. So I crisply returned their salute, and immediately began to stare intensely at the youngest among them. When this youngster realized that I was staring at him, he uneasily asked me why. Assuming a self-assured stance, I declared that I had seen him working at Pelivan's, in Belgrade. Pelivan's, a shop and café in Belgrade, was famous for all kinds of Turkish pastry. It was a landmark and a great meeting place in central Belgrade, which was a largely Jewish section of the city. I had often passed by this shop and would visit it at least once a day. I knew Pelivan, the owner, very well. He was a good friend to the Jews, and his daughter and my sister attended the same school and were friends. Pelivan had traveled frequently to the Shqiptar region and often returned to Belgrade with a few young ethnic Albanians in tow to work in his pastry shop and learn the trade. Now, I knew there were only two possibilities. The young man had either worked for Pelivan, or he had not. Even if he hadn't, he would know about the shop, and I would have established at least some common ground with him and the other border guards. Fortunately, I guessed right and immediately found myself in an animated discussion with the fellow about Turkish pastries, while his colleagues looked on with friendly interest. I told them that the Pelivan shop in Belgrade had been destroyed in the bombing. Minutes later, we shook the hands of those murderers, bidding them farewell, and left in peace. They didn't even examine the passports that I had worked so hard to forge.

Šalom and I finally arrived in Priština. Before the war, this town, the largest in the province of Kosovo, was within the southern border of Serbia. The Italians now administered the town and province as part of a greater Albania. There were no Germans in the region at all, so it was at Priština that we could finally catch our breath, relax, and enjoy some food. Many Jews from Germany had halted in Priština before war broke out between Yugoslavia and the Axis nations. Many of these Jews had remained here, because they felt relatively safe in the forgotten and remote town.

The buildings in Priština were low. Many were built in the Turkish style, with their upper stories projecting out a little over the street so that the women could look down into the street without showing themselves. The town had a bazaar and many houses, and generally gave the impression of a town in Anatolia, but it also had a typically Balkan character. Otherwise, there was nothing of particular interest there.

Priština was crowded with refugees when Šalom and I arrived there around the twelfth of August. The Jews whose flight from Germany and Central Europe had come to a halt in the town had been augmented by recent arrivals from German-occupied Yugoslavia. There was great misery among many Jewish youths who had arrived in the town without their parents. They slept in school buildings or out in the open. By day, they wandered around the marketplace, scavenging for food and desperately looking for work of any kind. I felt that I had to do something to help them.

I had always made a great effort to collect money for the Jewish cause. I had collected for the Jewish National Fund, for the Hadassah summer camps, for the World International Zionist Organization, and for a variety of other organizations and institutions. Among the Jewish population of Belgrade, I had had a reputation as a public fund-raiser, and often members of our community there had greeted me with the question, "Hi, Albert! How much?" So, on my second day in Priština, I started a collection for the Jewish children and youths who had been orphaned or had been separated from their parents. I called on the Jews of the town and refugee community and tried to persuade them to offer gifts of money to help provide for the young people. I succeeded in collecting some funds, which I then distributed among the destitute youths.

Soon after I had distributed the money, and just as Šalom and I were seeking out a man who could make up a passport for Šalom's wife, Vinka, we became aware of a great commotion among the Jewish refugees in Priština. What had happened? We soon learned that somebody had bombed the Hotel Park in Niš. Five Gestapo men had been killed in the bombing. A large group of Jews had fled from Niš, fearing retribution against the Jews there, as Jews had been killed in retribution for German deaths just two weeks earlier in Belgrade. Šalom and I searched for Vinka and her sister among the newly arrived refugees from Nis, but we found no sign of them.

Šalom was supposed to return to Niš with a passport for Vinka. That night, we could not sleep at all. Šalom was deeply torn and could not decide what to do. I could not be of any help to him. I did not know myself what I would have done in such a situation. I left him alone with his conscience to make the decision. After all, Vinka was his wife—although we had all promised each other that we would remain together and watch over each other as much as we could, and I did feel a certain responsibility. It was very difficult for Šalom, but as the horizon grayed with the light of a new day, he finally accepted that he could not go. Even if he could make it back to Niš, it was almost certain that once there he would be trapped and would not be able to return to Priština. The Germans were now on the alert. Besides, I wasn't sure of the depth of his attachment to Vinka; it had been a great surprise to all of us when he decided to marry her. She was rather simple, whereas he was one of the most intelligent and sophisticated people I had ever met, and we were all rather mystified about the attraction she held for him.

Once Šalom had reached his decision, he no longer seemed to be at all troubled. He dashed a letter off to Vinka, sending her the address of the Jewish Community in Vienna, through which he hoped they could continue to communicate. We decided to leave Priština immediately. We had a long journey before us. We said our farewells and boarded a bus to Prizren, from where we hoped to find a way to the west, across northern Albania to Skadar. At Skadar, we planned to take a ferry across Lake Scutari to Montenegro. There, we would then descend the slope of Lovčen Mountain to the Bay of Kotor, where I hoped to find my family, get more money from them, and go on to Italy, Switzerland, Portugal, Mozambique, Egypt, and finally—to Palestine.

Our bus arrived in the central square of Prizren in the early evening, about 6 PM. The city was swarming with Italian troops, because it was the principal base of the Italian campaign to suppress the Communist insurgency in Montenegro. The soldiers were suspicious of everybody. Several black-shirted Fascists roughly ordered us to open our suitcases in the middle of the square, so they could inspect them.

I felt completely lost and scared. In a frantic, almost paranoid state, I told Šalom in Hebrew that the Fascists were going to cut our throats and no one would ever even know that we had been killed. I was in a frantic state, one of almost paranoia. My irresistible instinct was to push ahead. We had to get out of Prizren immediately. I was suddenly struck with a brilliant, insane, impossible idea, but an idea that—if it worked—would be our salvation. I took two gold napoleon coins in my hand and started to play with them, while I asked a taxi driver if he would drive us south to Tirana, the capital of Albania. The driver shook his head and said, "Tirana is in another country."

Looking directly into his eyes, I replied, "I know."

He looked at me as though I were a madman, telling me that his old vehicle could not possibly make it across the high mountain passes at night, on horrible roads, through country infested with murderous brigands and thieves. I accepted all his arguments, but I was determined to get out of Prizren at that very moment. I told the driver that we knew the risks, and would deal with the dangers as they arose. I was ready to pay him generously, in gold. In the end, those two gold napoleons, shining and clinking in my palm, were sufficiently convincing.

We climbed into the battered taxi and drove the entire night. Fortunately, we weren't waylaid and attacked. As to the roads and bridges, the Italians had greatly improved them. We paused for sleep in the high mountain village of Kukes, about forty kilometers southwest of Prizren. But sleep was almost impossible, the mosquitoes were so thick. Swollen from their bites, I tried to cover myself with my raincoat. Early the next morning, we continued southwest to Tirana. When we arrived in the Albanian capital, late in the day, we learned that the ferry service across Lake Scutari had been suspended because of the fighting in Montenegro. So, Šalom and I decided to go on to Durrës, a small Ionian port about sixty miles by road from Tirana. We hoped to find passage there on a ship that could take us north to the Montenegrin port of Bar.

Durrës is a beautiful city, nestled on the slope of a mountain called Tomori. The daily paper there was also called *Tomori*, but Šalom and I did not know a single word of Albanian or Italian, so we couldn't read it. We finally found a place to sleep at a caravanserai. This was a kind of inn or hostel for travelers and their horses. The caravanserai in Durrës was quite a large building with wide halls, in each of which some thirty rude iron beds were lined up in two rows, like in a hospital. No attention was paid to hygiene! The vermin-ridden sleeping pallets were stained and greasy. The poorly ventilated halls were thick with the nauseating odors of stale sweat and filth. The Turks and Shqiptars who sheltered there were a rough crew. They all snored loudly. Šalom and I were shocked, and almost decided to sleep outside, but we made the difficult adjustment to the grim accommodations.

Obtaining food was another big problem. Food was sold on the street, usually from tables laden with deep greasy pots swarming with flies. The most popular dish appeared to be a kind of thick, viscous, dark-brown stew. We could not touch that food at all, so we searched for some bread, plain bread, or some buns called *lepinje,* which look like Syrian pita. We finally did find some ordinary bread. To my surprise and delight, we also found some halvah, which was enough for me, since I had eaten halvah all my life. That was how I knew Pelivan so well—because he made the best halvah in Belgrade!

We finally found a ship that would be steaming to Trieste, but it was not scheduled to leave for another fifteen days. We had no choice but to accept this delay, glad at least that we had found a way to move north. There were no signs of danger in Durrës, so we took life easily and explored the town. One day, soon after our arrival, I noticed a tailor shop whose sign bore the name of "Samuel and Jakoel." I remarked to Šalom that it was surely a Jewish establishment, so we entered the store and found out that the owners were indeed Ladino-speaking Sephardic Jews. Neither Šalom nor I spoke any Italian or Albanian, but I knew enough Ladino to be able to communicate with the tailors. They told me that many refugees from Yugoslavia had been collected in a large refugee camp at Kavaja, only eighteen kilometers to the southeast. Now I can't say exactly why I was so interested in seeing this camp and was prepared to take the risk of approaching it. I did have confidence in my forged Italian passport, and I certainly had a lot of chutzpah, so I decided to take the bus and go there. Šalom did not want to go, so he stayed behind, and I set off on a bus with Samuel, one of the tailors who had offered to accompany me.

When I descended from the bus at Kavaja, I saw a large camp only a little more than one hundred meters away, but a large sign clearly barred me from approaching it. I stared intently at the barbed wire fence, and even at that distance I immediately recognized my sister and my friend Jaša Almuli behind the barrier. But the moment I caught a glimpse of my sister, she hurried away and out of sight. She had also seen me, and had run immediately to call my father, who was at that moment studying Italian with Dr. Bauer.

"My daughter is coming in from her walk and calling me to go with her," my father told Dr. Bauer. Turning to my sister, he said, "Don't you see that I am working?"

She replied urgently, "Come, Father, come now!"

My father later told me that he had immediately felt that perhaps I had arrived. He asked Dr. Bauer to excuse him. As soon as my father and sister were alone, my father asked, "Where is he?"

My sister looked up at him and asked, "Who?"

"Albert," replied my father.

"How do you know?" asked my sister.

My father answered, "I had a premonition. Besides, why else would you have called me as you did?" He was agitated now.

My sister said, "I saw him in front of the camp, and he was alone."

My father and sister hurried toward the camp gate, where an Italian officer was chatting with Rafa Konforti. The officer looked toward my father and asked him, "Are you Alcalay?" When my father affirmed this, the officer demanded, "Who is the youngster who is looking for you?"

"I don't know," my father replied. "Let me get out to see. Maybe he is the son of an Albanian friend." The officer agreed to allow my father to meet with me, but he ordered a soldier to accompany him and to remain with him during our conversation. Rafa also came with my father and the sentry.

The moment they approached me, I came out from behind a large tree outside the gate and quickly spoke to my father in a low voice, "Don't do or say anything that will tell them that you are my father." We shook hands, and Father asked me when I had left Belgrade and how I had found them. Very briefly, I told him that the Germans in Belgrade had shot 103 Jews, Mikica Bararon among them, and that I had escaped with my friend Šalom the next morning, intending to travel to Herceg Novi, where I had expected to find all of them. Our journey had been difficult. We had not planned to travel to Durrës, where only that morning I learned about the refugee camp. My father then told me that he had received a letter from Marcel Farhi in Belgrade, with the news that all the Jews there had been interned. He had also learned from this letter that my father's brother Bukus had given me several thousand dinars for the trip, and that Uncle Bukus was now stranded in Belgrade, without money.

My father asked me if I wanted to join them in the camp, but I answered no. I outlined my plan to enter Switzerland illegally, and to travel from there to Lisbon, Portugal. I explained that I could then take a ship around Africa, by way of Angola and the Cape of Good Hope, to Lorenzo Marques, Mozambique, and then travel by rail across Africa to Cairo. I planned ultimately to cross the Sinai into Palestine.

"How do you propose to travel so far without money?" Father asked me.

I answered that I had been counting on him to help me with that. My father then told me that the Italian authorities had confiscated the family's gold when they had arrested them in Herceg Novi, although he had managed to hide some there, which I could have, if I could reach the town and find it. He then gave me eight hundred lire, which was all that was left to him. Father told me that he would try to borrow money for me from friends inside the camp. He would arrange to go out of the camp the next day to buy the food in the market for those in the camp who had enough money to purchase food from outside, and he would then give me whatever money he managed to collect for me. I told him that I would try to meet him at the tailor shop on the main street in Kavaja. It was at this moment that Samuel Haim, the tailor from Durrës who had accompanied me, indicated the approach of the camp commandant and warned me to leave. I grasped my father's hand firmly, and looked into his eyes. I then turned and followed Samuel away from the camp.

8

My Father's Journal: Part II

MY FATHER RECORDED IN HIS JOURNAL WHAT THEN HAPPENED INSIDE the camp.

Wednesday, August 13th, 1941

I ask Rafa not to tell anybody about Albert's arrival. I also ask Mrs. Almuli and Jacqueline Russo, who has seen him, to keep quiet. I tell my daughter not to say a word. My wife is playing cards. I decide to leave her undisturbed. I will tell her after supper when we are alone. But my dear wife Lepa talks constantly with everyone around her, and, before I can speak with her, Avram Aladem, who has somehow learned of Albert's appearance, asks her, "Lepa, why haven't you told us that your son came to the camp gate today?"

"My son! When? How?" she cries. Lepa starts to sob, and faints. With great effort, we succeed in reviving her. Through her sobbing and tears, she reproaches me for concealing from her the news of our son's visit, and so on. Within minutes, the entire camp gathers around us and is assaulting us with questions. It takes quite an effort to quiet everyone down. I tell them that I am going to see Albert again the next day, if I can arrange to leave the camp with Ergas to go to the market. The conditions inside the camp remain terrible. We have arranged to send a delegate out into the town each day to buy food there. Mr. Haler has served as the designated buyer, but he is now stricken with malaria. I myself hope to replace him, so as to then be able to leave the camp. Rafa Konforti, who was educated in Italy, is the only refugee in the camp who can really speak Italian.

Thursday, August 14th, 1941

Thanks to Rafa, I am permitted to leave the camp this morning with Ergas, a local Greek who has befriended us. An Italian guard accompanies us. I need a pretext to free myself to look for Albert, so while Ergas is buying vegetables, I ask the soldier to let me go to the toilet. I hurry down the principal street of the town, looking desperately for some sign of my son, searching for the tailor shop where we have arranged to meet. I quickly find a tailor shop, but there is no sign of Albert there, and the young man at the counter seems to speak only Albanian, and I cannot make myself understood. Rushing back into the street, I encounter two Carabinieri, whom I ask for directions to a public toilet, thinking that this would give me a pretext to prolong my search for Albert. The Carabinieri point to a spot about one hundred meters down the street. I ask a passerby if he knew of any tailors in the town, but he knows nothing. I finally ask another passerby, but this time in Serbian, "Is there a tailor around here?" He knows a little Macedonian, but he does not understand the word for "tailor." With some effort, I explain it to him, but he too knows nothing, so I continue on my way.

Soon there are no more houses. The road opens into a landscape of fields sown in corn. In the distance, I can see a half-demolished mosque. I realize that our guard will by then be more than suspicious and will be looking for me, and that there will probably be unwelcome consequences to my prolonged disappearance. I hurry back to the market, where I excuse my absence as well as I can. On the way back to the camp, Ergas tells me that the guard has become very nervous and has continually been asking why I was taking so long. Ergas adds that he has managed to calm the soldier down, and that I will probably be able to leave the camp tomorrow to try again to contact Albert.

Friday, August 15th, 1941

I am able to leave the camp again today with Ergas. Rafa Konforti, who acts semiofficially as our liaison with the Italian authorities, asks the guard to take me to Samuel Haim's tailor shop to pick up a pair of trousers that he has ordered there. When we arrive at the shop, Ergas learns that the tailor behind the counter is originally from the island of Corfu. Ergas starts a long conversation with him in Greek, to gain time, in the hope that my son will appear. Ergas finally turns his conversation to the guard and somehow manages to draw him off with him to the vegetable stands outside, leaving me alone to speak with the tailor. He tells me that Albert has returned to Durrës, but that he would certainly be back soon. He explains that Albert has to travel between the towns on the bus, and the bus isn't expected back until later.

The tailor tells me that he has helped interned Greek Jews reach freedom, and that he will help our entire family if he can. He also says that the Italians have been speaking bitterly about the war in Russia, so that it seems the Germans and their allies are struggling there more than many people suppose. Time passes very quickly as we talk, but there is no sign of my son. At about 11 AM, Ergas returns with the guard. He delays, conversing for yet another half hour, but then we finally have to return to the camp. I am very worried about Albert. We have decided to try again for a third time tomorrow, but I don't know how long we can continue like this.

Saturday, August 16th, 1941

Disaster! The camp officials seal off the camp this morning. They forbid anyone from going into town. The faces of the Italian officers are very dark and stern. We are all ordered to assemble. The commanding major arrives and gives a speech, declaring that he has proof that we have tried to contact people on the outside. He tells us that he is determined to put a halt to this sort of activity, and that any break in discipline will be punished. His words hit me like a hammer. I am intensely concerned about Albert, who knows nothing about this turn of events. Rafa is going to try to get word to the tailor about this tomorrow.

Everyone in the camp is now asking me, "Isn't Albert going to Herceg Novi to get your gold?" They think that I am Croesus, and that my fabled riches will save us all. They want Albert to fly by plane to Split to inform their families and friends about our situation. They are so desperate to find a way out that they have lost their senses. But I don't argue with them that it is not at all likely that Albert could fly anywhere, and I certainly do not ask them if they really believe that their families and friends, whether they are still in Split or anywhere else, are in any position to help us. I have been given a large packet of letters to give to Albert, and have been promised money to help Albert reach his destination and deliver them. I have been told that it is necessary to make such a sacrifice to save the whole group.

How can I even inform Albert about any of this? I am being closely watched. I am terribly anxious. Rafa is certainly being watched, too, but he has such a cool head, and the Italians like him so much that they would normally be more likely to laugh than to harm him if they catch him at anything. But this is far more serious. Anyway, Rafa tells me not to worry, that he will take care of things. Everyone contributes what little they can. They have even collected almost six hundred lire for Albert's friend, Šalom. My camp roommate, Pepo Sasson from Sarajevo, has offered to lend me one thousand lire. I am deeply touched, and take it with gratitude. Lepa gives me another thousand lire. I had no idea that she had anything left at all. So, we can give 2,000 lire to Albert in addition to the eight hundred I gave to him on Monday morning.

With all this going on, we still hold our regular Thursday night entertainment. It is difficult to tell jokes at such times, but laughter is so important, and I manage to cheer our friends up a little with humor, though this evening it takes quite an effort.

Friday, August 22nd, 1941

Rafa has managed to get the money and the letters to Albert. When he returns, he tells us everything he has heard from Albert. There are more details about the massacre in Belgrade. The Germans there shot 103 Jewish men in retaliation for a truck bombing, committed by a youngster, which killed five German soldiers. Rafa mentions the names of several of our friends who were killed in the massacre. Word about this instantly spreads through the camp, and, within minutes, many of the women burst into tears and lamentations. It was very hard to quiet them down. I pray that Albert can move forward safely.

Saturday, August 23rd, 1941

If I did not feel great joy for his mother, who has longed to see him, I would feel even greater anger toward Albert for his irresponsibility.

He has taken an enormous risk in showing up at the camp today, "cleverly" posing as a nephew who is traveling in the area, who has heard that we were in the camp, and who wants to pay us all a call. I wonder if the Italians tolerate the charade because they find its absurdity so appealingly amusing. They are capable of guiding their actions by such feelings. The commandant, the expression on his face hidden in the shade cast by the visor of his cap, simply looks at us the entire time that Albert was inside the camp.

All our friends gather around Albert with a cacophony of greetings and questions. We have no chance to speak with him about our own family and a thousand other things, but Lepa clings to his arm the entire time and slips her diamond ring to him when he departs, indiscreetly embracing him with an affection that surely betrays Albert's comically transparent alias. I hurry the boy away, before the tastes of our Italian audience shift from comedy to tragedy. After Albert's departure, we all become very quiet, plunging into our memories of the past and the uncertainty of the future.

I am deeply concerned about my son. Rafa assures me that Albert has good false documents. He is traveling under the name of Armando Moreno, a student from Split. Everyone has been continuously talking about the shocking news of the shooting of the hundred Jews in Belgrade. Avramče Mošić cannot believe it. "Germans can beat people, but they will not kill. They are cultured people!" he says.

Later this very day we are moved to another barracks closer to the entrance of the camp, and also very close to the office. We receive permission to write letters to our families in Belgrade and other cities. Rafa Konforti and Miša Alađem are the only ones among us who speak Italian well. They work in the office the entire afternoon.

9

A Voyage to Italy

SEVERAL DAYS LATER, ON WEDNESDAY, AUGUST 27, THE FREIGHTER THAT
Šalom and I had been waiting for was ready to steam north along the
Adriatic coast to Trieste. We were happy to board the ship and be on
our way. We planned to get off at Split, where I was now charged to
deliver the letters that had been entrusted to me in the camp. Šalom
and I had a cabin to ourselves, and we were really able to somehow
detach ourselves from the horrors we had witnessed on land since the
eruption of war in early April. The weather was beautiful. Our trip was
almost like a vacation. We felt a release of tension as soon as we were
out to sea. The burdens of our responsibilities and worldly cares
ceased to be oppressive. We were certainly conscious of matters that
we would eventually have to deal with, but, for the moment, the weight
of their gravity had been lifted from our shoulders.

The ship first called at Herceg Novi, and then sailed into the Bay
of Kotor, to Kotor, before returning to Herceg Novi, where it stopped
again. I felt the strongest temptation to get off the ship there to look
for my father's gold, which he had hidden in the hotel room when the
Carabinieri came to arrest my family. But I resisted this temptation,
because the risk was too great. Herceg Novi was by then under Croatian control, and the Croatians could be very nasty. We stopped in
many small harbors along the Adriatic shore—Dubrovnik, Šibenik,
and then Split, where we disembarked and passed through the customs and passport controls. As it happened, we were extremely lucky
to arrive when we did. Our documents were valid until exactly that
day, August 31, 1941. They would have been expired had we arrived
only one day later, which would have led to dangerous complications
with the authorities. An angel was surely watching over us.

We found lodging and soon discovered that many of our friends and acquaintances from Belgrade were in Split. What we had heard was soon confirmed. There were indeed many wealthy Jewish refugees in the city. I dutifully made the rounds with the letters that I had promised the inmates of the camp at Kavaja I would deliver. Somewhat to my surprise, I found almost everyone to whom a letter was addressed, often at addresses other than those that were indicated, but almost always settled in relatively comfortable circumstances. These letters were appeals for help from relatives whom fate had treated less kindly than the family members I was carrying them to. Many of the letters also requested that help be extended to Šalom and me as well.

I met with many of these wealthy Jews in various cafés, but no one expressed any concern or made any gesture of assistance to me or to anyone else as far as I could see. I wasn't even offered a cold drink, not to speak of money. It seemed that these fortunate people were not even aware of the many young refugees in Split who had no shelter, no food, no proper clothing. These fortunate people were all hungry for news. They all wanted to know what had happened in Belgrade. But their only real concern, it was clear to me, was to live as comfortably as possible. They spent money as if there were no tomorrow, as if it were pointless to help anyone else. Admitting that there was some truth in both of these points, I still hadn't expected to see the kind of behavior that they displayed, and it demoralized me quite a lot.

As disappointingly indifferent as they were to the needs of others, these wealthy Jews also seemed unaware of their own peril. The Fascist authorities were watching closely, as more and more of them crowded into the city alongside the influx of orphaned children and the poor. I tried to understand the lack of concern these wealthy Jews showed for themselves and for others. They were simply trying to maintain normal lives. But prices for the most basic necessities were soaring, as demand pressed upon limited supplies of housing and food. Even if their resources were not seized beforehand, these well-to-do people would be progressively reduced to poverty, and they, too, sadly, would probably be sent to camps.

But even if I could understand the sad psychology of the situation, I was outraged at the complete disregard by the fortunate of the needs of others. Instinctively—I could not do otherwise—I began a campaign to collect money on behalf of the starving children and young people. For me, there was nothing new or difficult in knocking on doors to collect money to help those in need. I went about this conscientiously, and was utterly undeterred by the resistance and cold-blooded irresponsibility I encountered almost everywhere. I will never forget the shock and dismay I felt at the reaction I received from one of the richest ladies of Belgrade, who, in better times before the war, had herself been active as a philanthropist. She answered me, "How do you expect me to give to you, Mr. Alcalay, when I escaped with only one million dinars." And I was asking her for a mere ten or twenty dinars! Despite such resistance, I did manage to collect a handsome sum, which I gave in its entirety to a trusted friend, who distributed it carefully among the youth in greatest need.

I was extremely anxious about the dangerous and resentful social climate that the extravagance of the wealthy was creating in Split. I knew that the authorities could react at any moment with an order for the deportation or internment of masses of people, so I urgently tried to obtain new documents that would allow us to escape from the town before the trap sprung closed on everyone there. Fortunately, Šalom and I were able to establish contact in Split with several important Zionist organizers who trusted us. They had known us in Belgrade through our years of active work in Jewish youth groups. British visas authorizing their entry into Palestine were being held for them in Switzerland, but they could not leave Split. Even if they could have left, they would have had almost no hope of reaching Switzerland. So they provided Šalom and me with a letter authorizing the transfer of the British visas to us, leaving us with the problem of obtaining documents to cover our passage into Italy, where we would have to find a way to continue on illegally into Switzerland. The way was half opened for Šalom and me to resume our journey—and we had managed to keep most of our funds intact.

———

At the end of September, a month after our arrival in Split, Šalom and I were ready to set out once again. I had accumulated a few belongings during our stay there, but I gave most of these away and sold a few items, reducing my baggage to what could be carried in a satchel. I wanted to travel very lightly. We had no definite plan, other than to cross the Adriatic to Italy, and then somehow find a way to enter Switzerland. We said good-bye to all our friends, with the promise that we would all someday meet in Palestine. I had discarded my outdated false documents and was now traveling under the name of Alberto Alcalla, posing as a citizen of newly "Independent Dalmatia," the coastal region of Yugoslavia then occupied by the Italians. As my cover, I assumed the role of a student. I was to be traveling to Italy to study Italian language and culture. Our voyage across the Adriatic took only one full day. Šalom and I disembarked at Ancona on Wednesday, October 1, 1941.

Our plans at this point were still vague, and neither of us knew more than a few words of Italian. We did have some contacts in Milan, where we hoped to find a guide to take us into Switzerland. We should have pressed on immediately. But we were young men with a renewed sense of freedom, and we were caught up in a sense of adventure, after having left behind a brutalized country where we both had witnessed so much Nazi killing. The first thing we noticed when we arrived on shore was a large sign promoting the artistic exhibition, Biennale di Venezia. This was enough to distract us from our immediate goal. Instead of traveling immediately to Milan, we bought train tickets to Venice to see the Biennale, rationalizing that we could move on to Milan afterward. After all, in traveling north to Venice, we would be that much closer to our ultimate destination.

The Biennale is a competitive international exhibition of painting and sculpture. The exhibition in the autumn of 1941 was the last one to be held until the end of the war. Futurist works of art dominated the show. Many of them displayed a fascist inspiration. Nevertheless, the sight of so many paintings was intensely exciting to me. I entirely forgot the hated Nazis and the war, which since April of that year had shattered my life and completely turned me away from my passion for art. Now I felt all of this passion flooding back into my spirit. Inwardly, I needed to separate myself from the bitter tragedy of the time, the anxiety of flight under an assumed identity, the uncertainty of the future. I had always longed to see the work of Giotto at firsthand. Realizing that the great Giotto frescoes of the Capella degli Scrovegni could be seen in Padua, which was nearby, I urged Šalom to visit there. Šalom was quick to agree. Having arrived in Italy without any problems, we were both feeling liberated and free, and ready, for a time at least, to set our cares aside.

We traveled by train to Padua, where we found the chapel in the main park in the center of the old city. The beauty of the Giotto frescoes was overwhelming. We studied them undisturbed for several hours. Emerging from the chapel, Šalom and I walked slowly through the old quarter of Padua, admiring the beautiful old buildings and observing the people of the city. As we were discussing what our next move would be, we were absolutely astonished to hear a voice calling out to us by our real names, when even between ourselves we were using the false names on our passports. The voice belonged to Geri Weiss, our longtime friend from Zagreb. He was as astonished to see us as we had been to hear our names being called out. He asked us what we were doing in Padua. With an unthinking lapse of indiscretion, I explained that we were traveling with false documents and were planning to cross the Alps into Switzerland. I then asked Geri what he was doing in Padua. He explained that the Italian authorities had confined him in Padua along with three other friends of ours. They were living together, quite comfortably, in a pensione whose address he then gave to us.

At that moment, two plainclothed detectives approached us and asked Geri if he was Geri Weiss. When he confirmed his name, they asked him to come with them. I suppose that Šalom and I looked innocent enough. The detectives did not even bother to ask to see our papers. The incident perplexed and troubled us. Geri accompanied the detectives without protest, and without once looking back at us. Šalom and I silently walked away from the scene. It was evening. We could not leave the city until the next day. And we had no intention of leaving until we saw our close friends Bibi, Hedva, and Miriam, and told them about Geri's encounter with the police.

Just as Geri and we had been when we met, our friends were utterly astonished to see us. They were concerned about Geri, but they reassured us that such police checks had become an accepted part of their lives. Even more of our friends were living in the pensione, and everyone gathered together. The night passed in warm embraces and subdued, intense conversation. A room was available—the landlady was becoming accustomed to the arrival of foreign refugees—so we decided to stay there for a few days while we decided on our next move.

Padua had been Dante's home during several years of his exile from Florence. The site of one of the world's oldest universities, the city remains to this day extraordinarily beautiful, filled with history, and endowed with rich art treasures and splendid architecture. As pleased as we were to have found old friends, and as charming as Padua was, Šalom and I realized within a few days that we had to reapply ourselves to the task that we had agreed to accomplish. Although we had agreed from the very beginning in Belgrade never to separate, we now could see that it would be easier and much safer if only one of us went on to Milan, especially because we didn't have confidence in our false Italian travel documents. Šalom wanted to go. We planned to maintain contact by telephone. In Milan, Šalom would try to find a way to purchase Latin American passports, or to find a guide who would agree to guide us through the Alps, and on to Zurich.

Šalom departed for Milan by train. I remained at the pensione with our friends. I did not think much about it at that time, but I was certainly unwise to stay there, because my papers would not have borne close scrutiny, and the police surely watched the pensione, which was well known as a place where refugees gathered. All the residents here, apart from Geri, were registered with the police. My concern heightened when Geri failed to return, and we finally discovered that the police had arrested him for presenting false identity documents and had sent him to a prison camp on Lipari, a desolate island to the south, just north of Sicily.

Nevertheless, I remained at the pensione and settled into life in Padua. I wrote to my father to let him know where I was. He arranged to have Swiss friends send money to me, so that I could buy winter clothing and painting materials. I began to study the history of art and to paint—mostly portraits at this time. Time passed for me in a most agreeable atmosphere of friendship and art. I found an understanding companion in Miriam, Bibi's sister. There were also the two brothers Baum from Zagreb, whom I had known in the past, very intelligent men, whose company I enjoyed. We all had a good time together. I explored Padua. I was particularly interested in the city's medieval history, especially the period of Dante's exile. Food, clothing, and other necessities were all rationed, but we had enough of everything we needed. I waited to hear some news from Šalom—he would remain in Milan for several months. Fall was almost over.

10

My Father's Journal: Part III

W EEKS AFTER MY ARRIVAL IN PADUA, THE INMATES OF THE CAMP AT KA-vaja were moved to a larger camp—to the Ferramonti di Tarsia refu-gee camp—in Calabria, in southern Italy. My father wrote me letters to reassure me that the family was all right, and that the Italian au-thorities were doing everything possible to help them. They had a dif-ficult ordeal in Kavaja. My father recorded it in his journal.

Monday, September 29, 1941

We have been suffering terribly from the heat. The filth and foul air of the latrines has added to our discomfort at Kavaja. We have spread a tarpaulin between our barracks and the one next to it, to make an outdoor dining area where we have at least some air and some relief from the heat. The camp authorities are also providing us with more drinking water. We continue our Thursday night programs of entertain-ment. Everyone enjoys these events, and they help boost our morale. I perform little skits, in which I parody various camp personalities and poke fun at everyone's expectations of better treatment. I perform these skits in rhyme, for which a certain talent remains from my youthful days of writing poetry. I am always on the lookout for new material. Italian newspapers printed in Tirana are made available to us. They bring us news of Axis victories in Russia and North Africa. Everyday we collect bread for the poor Montenegrins who are interned nearby. The Italians treat the Montenegrins harshly, because of continuing armed resistance in the province to Italian occupation. It reminds me of the way the English treated the Irish.

. . . Uncertainty about the future aggravates the anxiety we are all feeling. Everyone is on edge. Petty quarrels are common. The smallest

arguments quickly burst into bitter disputes. I busy myself with my study of Italian, and with rehearsing comic skits for our Thursday night entertainment. We have to do all that we can to keep our spirits from sinking too low. The commandant has urged us to organize a petition to be relocated to a camp in Italy. Conditions have been so difficult here, and people will support almost anything that promises hope for some improvement, so almost everyone has now signed the petition. Many have written letters of petition as well. I resist the idea at first, and I still believe that we Jews are better off here in Kavaja, at least for the moment, as bad as things are. But I agree to sign. Who am I to resist the general will? Many of our people advance their petitions with claims of having had many commercial contracts with Italians. What can I cite to support our petition? That I have read Matilde Serao, Marco Praga, or DeAmicis?

. . . The young people are adjusting well to life here. They enthusiastically participate in the classes that are organized for them. They have their endless discussions. Like some among their elders, they play cards, that old Jewish malady. The commandant takes some of the ladies and girls to the beach in Durrës, but they return disappointed, because the beach was deserted. The commandant is also allowing small groups to go into town to see movies at the theater there. Ergas tells me that Albert has arrived safely in Split. A Jewish firm in Kavaja has received a card from Nissim Russo to that effect. I feel much better, but I am impatient to hear directly from Albert.

Friday, October 3, 1941

September has passed, and there has been no change in our situation. Ergas tells us that the tailor Samuel Haim can safely guide the family to freedom. He is not asking too much for this—only a few thousand leks, Albanian money. Though Haim seems to be well-meaning, I am skeptical. But I would go ahead and somehow find the money for this had I not heard from so many others of their bitter disappointment with him. I drop the plan.

. . . Heavy rainfall has made the situation inside the camp even more desperate. We are crammed into the barracks. There isn't room for everyone, and the damp air inside is incredibly foul. Some of the sick

have been sent to the hospital in Tirana, and some are being held in a temporary emergency clinic here. Poor Šlesinger suffers terribly from a worsening leg infection he contracted when he refused to remove his prosthesis during our sea voyage here. He is also in great pain from the injury he suffered when he slipped and twisted his spine. His constant moaning is terrible. Despite all this suffering and degradation, which worsens daily, life goes on here in a cacophony of hundreds of simultaneous conversations, punctuated by quarreling and songs. The endless card games continue. Fantasy has become part of the fabric of our daily lives. So many among us bury our anxieties in dreams about the future. So many argue over where they plan to live in Italy, as if the choice will be theirs to make. People are drawing lots to determine who will be with whom. And no one really has any idea what is going on in the world, what our fates will truly be. The tailor tells us that everything is all right.

Wednesday, October 15, 1941

The camp commandant received a telegram today. He has it read to us, with the express instruction that we listen calmly, without expressing our feelings about it. No applause. No criticism. "Il Duce ha accolto le preghiere degli Ebrei d'essere transferiti in Italia, in luoghi da designarsi." (Mussolini has heard the prayers of the Jews to be transferred to a new home in Italy.). The crowd doesn't dare applaud, but the joy that almost everyone feels on hearing this news is clear. As for me, I am not sure what is best, or what will happen next.

Monday, October 19, 1941

Six days pass, and there is only silence from the commandant. There is no further word about our transfer to Italy. The blackest despair has by now replaced the joy and relief that so many had felt earlier. The Italians have made many promises that they have been able to keep. Why should this be any different?

Wednesday, October 21, 1941

I have finally received a letter from Albert. He is living in Padua, apparently quite happily. He writes that he has received no help from our community in Split. He did succeed in extracting some funds for the poor refugees and orphans there, but he doubts that any help will be sent to us here, despite all the letters that he delivered. I feared this, but it is nevertheless a great disappointment, one that I shall keep to myself. Why should I extinguish the hopes of others? The days pass in uncertainty. The commandant has assured us that our departure has only been delayed by a lack of transport, ships, convoys, whatever. We can only wait. We give money to Samuel Haim, and give a nice present to the major. We can only wait. I shall try to have money sent to Albert through friends in Switzerland. The poor boy doesn't even have a winter coat.

Sunday, October 26, 1941

Everything has happened so suddenly. The entire camp was emptied last Friday. We were transported in relays by truck from Kavaja to Dur-rës, where we were hurried onto a large old freighter. We crossed the Adriatic due west to Bari. The passage lasts twenty hours. I am told that the distance is about 120 miles. After we debark at Bari, we are transported by truck to a newly built camp in Calabria. It is called Camp Ferramonti di Tarsia. The director of the camp, accompanied by a number of Yugoslavs, welcomes us. Families are assigned separate apartments. Single men and women are housed in barrack dormitories, which accommodate twenty-five to thirty persons.

The camp has been built on reclaimed marshland. It is already enormous, and new barracks are still being built. There is plenty of water, even electric lighting. A barbed wire fence surrounds the camp. Police and security agents circulate inside the fence to maintain order. Appel (roll call) is held for families only in the morning, but Appel is held for single men and women both in the morning and at noontime. Apparently, single people escape more readily, because they are not attached to their families. In the evening, we are forbidden from going beyond the unfenced courtyards of our barracks.

Thursday, November 6, 1941

What little money that was left to us is gone. We can't do anything in this camp without money. Everything, even the smallest service, has to be paid for immediately. In the smaller camp at Kavaja, where there were fewer than three hundred people, we were able to maintain some communal life. Here, there is no sense of community. This is understandable, since there are more than a thousand people from all over Europe. Our group from Kavaja has been dispersed throughout the camp, and has already lost its identity. Only the young people sheltered in Barracks Number Nine still somehow maintain a communal life.

Even so, Ferramonti is loosely organized into a small Jewish republic. There are two synagogues, one for orthodox Jews and one for conservative and other Jews. Friday and Saturday, synagogue services are very pompous, and they remind everyone of home. There are also schools for the children, but lessons are given only in German, because most of the refugees in the camp are from Germany and Austria.

Those people who have certain skills can make good money here. A black market is booming in the camp. Our arrival has caused a rise in prices for many items, and the other internees bitterly reproach us for this. Arguments and quarrels often erupt, but these disputes have been smoothed over so far. A kind of tribunal has been organized in the camp to hear cases. We want to avoid involving the Italians in our internal squabbling as much as possible. In addition to our group from Kavaja, there are many other Yugoslavs here, but Jews of German origin make up the majority of the camp's population. Few families have managed to remain together. I meet a lawyer from Zagreb, who tells me that he has been with my brother Aron on the Bulgarian border.

Tuesday, November 18th, 1941

Today, I receive a reassuring letter from Albert. He writes that he has sold his mother's diamond ring on the black market in Milan, and that he now has enough money and is living comfortably among friends in Padua. He has bought a good winter coat in Milan. He says nothing of the dangers he must be facing, to avoid giving me cause to worry about him, I am sure.

We pay almost five lire each day for the food that we receive from the camp kitchen. We are not being given enough food, and the weather is beginning to turn cold. The Italian authorities have granted us a subsidy for our food, but this does not cover the cost of bread. I give lessons in Italian and French for three lire per hour, teaching students in groups of three. In this way I make twelve lire daily. A friend from Herceg Novi has telegraphed us a bank draft for 2,000 lire, but I have not been able to cash it. I ask my cousin Dr. Sima Adanja for a loan of two hundred lire, but he excuses himself, saying that he does not have enough, and gives me only one hundred. Everybody knows that he received 29,000 lire last week. He spends at least five hundred lire every day. But this does not matter. When times are difficult, we learn who our friends are!

11

Interlude in Northern Italy

I COULD NOT FORGET THE WAR AND MY WORRIES ABOUT MY FAMILY AND so many friends, but I enjoyed my life tremendously during this period in Padua. I moved about the city freely, and I also made excursions to Vicenza, Spa, and other towns in the region, even to Venice. Padua enchanted me. It is an almost completely medieval city of the trecento—there is relatively little Renaissance architecture of the quattrocento—with long, colonnaded streets and beautiful old buildings with mysterious gates that open into central courtyards adorned with handsome gardens and statuary. There is a large outdoor market and also an impressive indoor market, a vast, completely open space beneath a soaring, vaulted roof. I spent much of my time studying Italian and the fascinating history of the city and the region. I also purchased a good stock of art materials and sketched and painted outdoor scenes.

Miriam Smetterling was my constant companion throughout my stay in Padua, and I enjoyed sharing the magic of the city with her. One memorable Friday evening, a very old Jewish family of Padua invited us to their stately home for dinner. The house was filled with many reminders of their ancient ancestry, and we felt that the Jews had been here since the beginning of the world. I learned that evening that many Italian Jews—neither Sephardi nor Ashkenazi in origin—were descended from Hebrew slaves who had been brought to Rome after the emperor Titus destroyed the Second Temple of Jerusalem in 73 AD. Most of these devoted Jews and their descendants had remained in Italy, and they could trace their ancestry to the very distant past. During the Inquisition, many outwardly agreed to accept Christianity, but they secretly maintained their Jewish faith in their hearts. There was a synagogue in Padua with a large congregation.

A few days after this dinner, Šalom telephoned me from Milan. He told me to quickly find a bride and get married, because he had found a way to obtain a family passport for me. I thought about this, and even discussed it with Miriam, but Šalom called back a few days later and told me that the passport was no longer available. So many people were desperately seeking passports, and it had sold for much more money than I would have been able to pay. So I continued my idyllic life of exile, painting and studying in Padua, and trying to master whist. I discovered that I have no talent at all for cards!

November had almost arrived, and the weather was turning cold. It became more difficult to find decent food. Even the bread at the market was becoming inedible, with more and more sand mixed into the flour. I remember one day noticing some graffiti scrawled in front of the large statue of Julius Caesar: *"Questo pane nero, mangia tu, Julio Cesare, con stomaco di ferro!"* (Eat this black bread, Julius Caesar, with your iron stomach!)

One day, I heard the landlady calling me. A police agent had stopped at the pensione to tell my friend Bibi that his mother was coming from Ljubljana, in Slovenia, to visit him. The policeman had checked the pensione's register of tenants and had noticed my name. Because I was unknown to him—he did know all the other residents of the pensione—he wanted to check my documents. When I showed the detective my *lasciapassare*, he noted that my two-month visa had already expired, and asked me why I had not returned to Dalmatia. I explained that I had stayed to study Italian. With better skills in Italian, I said, I would later be able to help my people back at home. The policeman smiled at this with an air of friendly suspicion. Many false documents were in circulation, he said, and in any case, my documents were no longer valid. He retained them, and also demanded that I surrender to him any ration coupons that I might have. He then ordered me to report to the police station the following morning, to clear up my situation.

I realized that I had been stupid to remain living in the pensione with my friends, especially after my papers had expired. I did report the next morning to the police and persisted with my explanation that

I had overstayed the term of my visa in order to study Italian language and culture. I said that I needed more time in Italy to advance my studies. The officials were polite and understanding, and assured me that everything would be all right. They could extend my visa, they said, but first they had to confirm its validity and its original date of issue with the authorities in Split. They would telegraph the authorities in Split to check. Until they received a response authorizing the extension of my visa, I was to report at the police station every morning at eleven o'clock.

While I had found the courage to report to the Italian authorities that first morning, I knew that I could not return to the police station. The officials would soon learn from their office in Split that there was no record of any visa in my name, and they would arrest me, and perhaps send me to the prison camp on the island of Lipari where Geri had been sent. So, that same day, I packed up all my belongings, which by this time had become quite cumbersome, and took a train to Milan. I did not have a single identity document and—far worse—I no longer had any ration coupons for food.

I arrived in Milan without incident, and checked my bulky parcels at the station, stuffing only the most essential items into a satchel. I then set off in search of Šalom whom, to my great relief, I finally found. Šalom had managed to avoid the police, but his papers, which were identical to mine, had also expired. Of course, we were both extremely anxious. Without identity papers, it was almost impossible to find lodging. Šalom and I searched throughout the city, but had no success in finding a place for me to sleep. I couldn't stay with Šalom. The concierge of his pensione watched everything like a hawk and was the type to report anything suspicious.

So I began to live the life of a homeless vagrant, spending night after night in the waiting room of the railroad station. With no place to hide, I was always on the alert for the police, and was afraid even to sleep. It was already well into November when I arrived in Milan, and the nights in the northern Italian city were bitterly cold. I felt worse than a dog. Kindhearted Polish refugees who Šalom knew would take me for one or two nights from time to time, but this was only infrequently, and we found nothing else. Šalom and I met at the Brera Library every afternoon at four, where at least there was some heat.

Šalom brought me what food he could find. In the evenings, I found some refuge and warmth in the theaters of the city, but I spent most of my nights at the railroad station.

The situation in Milan, and in Italy in general, was becoming more alarming with each passing day. The atmosphere was very heavily charged. The Germans—dissatisfied with the lack of enthusiasm that the Italians were showing for the suppression of the Jews—were descending into Italy in increasing numbers to deal with the situation themselves. Milan was full of German spies and Gestapo agents. They sometimes raided the movie houses and other places of public assembly in search of Jews and Communists. War was raging on all fronts, and Germany and its allies appeared to be everywhere triumphant. News of the London blitz, as well as news about the German advances in Africa, had a tremendous impact on me. I prayed that the Nazis could be stopped before reaching Cairo, and I was terrified that they might even reach Palestine. I was an illegal trapped in a hostile city. I had no idea what to do, but I was determined not to surrender. So I tried to survive and avoid trouble.

My nerves were taking a severe beating. Tortured by the uncertainty of my situation, constantly alert to danger from all directions, unwashed and exposed to the elements, with very little sleep and poorly nourished, I managed to keep going, strengthened by the hope within me that I would find a solution. One day, Šalom failed to keep our usual late afternoon rendezvous at the library. I was filled with apprehension and foreboding. I didn't know what to think. I was completely alone in a hostile city. I somehow survived the night, and returned to the library the next day at the same hour.

Šalom was there, badly shaken. The previous day, as he was sitting in his room, the police had knocked on the door. Šalom told me that his first thought was that I had been arrested and had confessed to everything. He immediately shredded his identity documents and flushed them down the toilet, knowing that it would be better to be caught without documents than with falsified ones. He then opened the door and was taken by the two agents to police headquarters. When they arrived there, Šalom was ushered into the office of the chief of police, who took one look at Šalom and said, "I regret our error. You are not the man we are looking for." Šalom was released immediately. The police didn't even ask to see his papers. Perhaps they were embarrassed!

Šalom and I were crossing the Piazza del Duomo as he related his story. Despite all my troubles, I burst into roars of laughter in the midst of the crowd. And I could not stop laughing. It was mostly laughter of relief that Šalom had escaped real danger. It was laughter at the absurdity that he had been taken before a high police official and that the police had not even asked to see his papers. The whole affair was tragicomic, and now Šalom himself had no identity papers, although his papers had expired many weeks ago, like those that had been taken from me in Padua.

It was now almost the end of November. Šalom and I still met at the library each day, but I was exhausted, and my nerves were worn razor thin. We were intensely aware of the Nazi presence in the heart of Milan and had heard news of their atrocities in the city and throughout Italy. We also knew that the Italian authorities in Padua were searching for me. I was reaching my breaking point. Life was becoming more and more unbearable for me with each passing day, and the nights were even worse. I thought of borrowing or stealing a passport and taking a sleeping car berth in the overnight train to Trieste. On this train, the conductors collected passports before the border was reached. The passports were monitored at the border, but they were not checked against the passengers, who presumably were asleep. That would be one way to leave Italy without directly confronting passport controls at the border, and in Trieste I could hope to find some ship that would carry me to a safer place. I also considered going to Genoa.

Travel and identity documents, forged or authentic, were not available anywhere—not for love or for any amount of money. Trains were now being rigorously monitored, so it was very difficult to travel. I went by bus to the Swiss border near Lake Como, only twenty-five miles from the heart of Milan, hoping to find a guide there to help me find a way into Switzerland. But the entire area was crawling with security agents, and even if I had found a guide, any attempt to cross the border there, if not absolutely impossible, would have been extremely dangerous. I was trapped. My physical and mental resources were severely depleted. The circle of danger around me was tightening. I was terrified that the Germans might capture me.

Although Šalom and I had started out on our journey pledging to each other never to separate, I knew that this was now inevitable. Šalom probably could continue in Milan for a while longer, but he no longer had any papers and would have to lie low. He had a place to stay. He had some ration coupons for food. Even so, he was at great risk, because raids were becoming more frequent every day. The circle was tightening around Šalom as well. He would have to make a move soon. After I returned from Lake Como, I realized that I had to leave the city immediately, but that I no longer had the strength to dream of breaking out of the prison of Europe to reach Palestine, which itself was already threatened by the Nazi war machine in the desert. Šalom still harbored some hope of reaching our goal. So, he and I decided to set out on different paths. I assessed what scenario could work the best for me.

Ferramonti di Tarsia in Calabria

While I was in Padua, I had learned that my parents and sister had been transferred from the camp in Albania to a refugee camp in southern Italy. It was a large camp. My father had written to me that the Italians were treating them with some kindness, that they showed a special consideration to family groups, and that he and my mother and my sister were managing rather well there. I blamed myself for having wasted time in Padua, for having too willingly settled into a comfortable life there while I relied on Šalom alone in Milan to arrange a means to continue on our journey to Palestine. The ordeal of the past month had utterly exhausted me and shattered my nerves, leaving me an anxious and angry shell.

I was reluctant to leave Šalom, and I hated abandoning our dream of traveling to Palestine, but I could see no way to sustain any effort to advance toward that goal. How could I travel without identity papers, without ration coupons, and with relatively little money? The Italian police were already looking for me, and they had my photo. After carefully taking everything into consideration, I understood that surrendering myself to the Italian authorities was my best and most rational option. At this point, an Italian prison would be the safest place for me, where the police in Padua would not search for me, and where the Nazis did not yet have the authority to interfere.

These thoughts emerged naturally as I assessed all the other possibilities, and it became clear to me that I had no viable choice other than turning myself in to the Italian authorities. It would be terrible to be confined in a prison, but at least there was some hope that I could rest there undisturbed, and perhaps gather my strength and recompose my nerves. I would declare my true identity and ask to join my family in the refugee camp. If only somehow I could find my way back to my family. I realized now, and perhaps too late, what I should have understood long before—that my place as the only son of the family was at the side of my parents and my sister. Had I behaved selfishly without a thought for my duties to my family? Was I now exchanging the rags of my failure for the bright garments of filial piety? Perhaps the only viable option for my own survival was to join my family. But truly regardless of these considerations—and they did weigh on me—I had finally understood that I must join my family and share the fate of my parents and my sister, and do all that I could to help them to continue on the hard road to survival.

So I decided to go to Vicenza, a beautiful small town about twenty miles northwest of Padua. There, I would present myself to the police. Vicenza was the last stop on the train before Padua, and it was unlikely that the authorities would monitor the train before it reached the city. I also thought that it would be clever to turn myself over to the police in a town near Padua, where no one would have thought of searching for me, surely assuming that I had fled further away. Besides, my good friend Hanan Praeger—also a member of the Zionist movement—was living in Vicenza. He was free to move around the town, but was confined there with a small community of Jewish exiles from Belgrade, who were in the same situation.

I said good-bye to Šalom. I fervently wished him well in continuing the quest to reach Palestine. I gave him some money and the addresses of friends and family in Switzerland who would help him on his way. I told him to pause for some time and gather his strength once he reached safety in Switzerland, and I warned him above all to avoid traveling through France. I adamantly and urgently insisted that it was simply too dangerous, even with the best documents. He should fly directly to Lisbon. We embraced each other and exchanged promises that we would meet again in Palestine. It was a painful moment, two friends saying farewell at the diverging roads of their destinies. As strong as our friendship was, the real pressures on us to separate were even stronger. We had to take our lives in our own hands, and could no longer support each other's progress down a shared path.

I don't know if I was led to my conviction by the concentrated force of circumstances or by some inner urging, but I felt that in these heavy hours, I had to share the destiny of my family. After reaching this decision, I was completely at peace with myself, and felt an inner serenity that I had not known since the beginning of the war. And so, I left Milan, an exhausted scarecrow, my nerves stretched to the limit, aware and fearful of the dangers still threatening me, especially from the Germans, but ready to turn myself over to the Italians, with some hope that everything could yet work out for the best. An inner peace and resolution had been restored to me, but I craved solitude and some way to heal the wounds of my recent hardships and disappointments.

I arrived in Vicenza very early on the frigid Thursday morning of December 11, 1941. I sought out the relative warmth and shelter of a church and heard the morning mass, and then went to a bar for something warm to drink. I could have gone directly to the police station, of course, but I relished these last moments of freedom, and I was certain that whatever office handled illegal aliens would not be open before 9 AM. As I was sipping my cappuccino and listening to the crackling of the radio over the bar, I was shocked to hear Mussolini's voice declaring war on the United States. I was stunned that a small country like Italy would declare war on such a great power.

Naturally, this was an emotionally charged moment, for myself and for all the Italians around me. The Italians are a highly emotional people, with deep ties to the United States. The announcement was extremely unwelcome news to them. An exchange of fierce opinions erupted in the bar. Some of the Italians started cursing. Some openly wept. I remained silent at my small table, transfixed by the sad spectacle. At nine o'clock, I slipped away and crossed the street to the police station.

I had not spoken my real name for a long time, and it sounded strange to my ears when I announced myself. I was ushered into the office of the Ufficio Stranieri (Aliens Office), where an older policeman was sitting at a desk reading a newspaper. The balding officer was dressed in a black shirt adorned with a Fascist insignia, but his kind face and pleasant features revealed a good nature. He asked me what I wanted from him. I said that my name was Albert Alcalay and that I was in search of my family. Friends in Slovenia had told me that they had gone to Italy, so I had crossed the border illegally at night at Postumia and continued to Trieste, where I had heard that my family might be in Vicenza, since there were some Yugoslav Jews living in that town. When I had finally reached Vicenza that morning, I had learned that my family was now in a refugee camp at Ferramonti, in Calabria, far to the south. Because I had entered Italy illegally, and didn't have any documents, I could not travel any farther in search of my family, so I had decided to surrender to the Italian authorities, in the hope that they would make it possible for me to join my family.

The officer listened carefully to my story, although I could see that he was distracted, probably by the news of Mussolini's declaration of war against the United States. He asked me how long I had been in Italy, and where I had traveled. I told him that I had been in the country for three days: the day of my arrival in Trieste, the following day in Venice, and now the third day in Vicenza. He looked at me with absent eyes and said, *"Va bene, figlio mio, vieni domani!"* (Very good, my boy, come back tomorrow!) His unexpected response shocked me. I had come from a country that had been at war with Italy; I had entered Italy illegally without documents; and he was telling me to return tomorrow! I could not believe my ears, but I left the station and found a room at the nearby hotel.

I visited my friend Hanan Praeger that afternoon. I entrusted my remaining gold to him. I kept a large sum in Italian currency, which I had raised on the black market in Milan by selling my mother's diamond ring and exchanging two gold coins. Hanan thought that my decision to turn myself in to the Italians was wise, and he promised to do all that he could to help me.

The next morning, I reported to the station at 9 AM, feeling hopeful that I might not be confined in a jail. The officer had treated my situation so casually, and he had seemed to be a kind man. I thought that I might be able to convince him to allow me to remain at the hotel, while arrangements were made for me to join my family. With this in mind, I entered his office and repeated my story, hoping that I would be able to reason with him. This time, the officer was much more alert. When I finished speaking, he looked down at his hands, clasped together on the desk before him. He then looked into my eyes, with an expression of weary kindness on his face, and said: "All right, we shall immediately look into the matter with the Ministry of Internal Affairs and see what can be done. In the meanwhile, we shall have to detain you here, but this should be for only a short time."

Encouraged by the officer's apparent kindness, I told him that there really was no need to detain me. I had turned myself in, and it was clearly in my own interest to wait for a reply from the Ministry. Of course, I wouldn't leave. I could wait at the nearby hotel and report to his office whenever this was required. The officer listened patiently, but replied that he had to follow regulations strictly. Otherwise, he could lose his job and his pension. He explained that he was only months away from retirement, and that he had a large family to support. Even so, I persisted, insisting that I could pay for the hotel. Confronted with my resistance to the idea of being locked up, the officer patiently explained that he understood my position, but that he was obliged to detain me!

Finally, in an attempt to find some way to accommodate me, he called two officials to his office and asked them, in my presence, if some way could be found to circumvent the regulations. The men shook their heads, and said that there was no way to do so during wartime. The regulations were designed to protect the state against spies and foreign agents. They agreed that I didn't seem to pose any threat, but they insisted that there was no way around the regulations. After all, I had no documents, and they had no way to confirm my identity. They would have to hold me until they could clear up the situation. They all tried to comfort me. Conditions in the jail were not bad, they told me, and I would probably be confined for only a few days. Finally, seeing that I had exhausted all possible arguments, I accepted that I would have to go to jail. I realized that I had pressed the limits of official kindness, and thanked everyone for having been so patient, and for having shown so much consideration to me.

Everyone was very courteous. The officials asked me for all my valuables, and sent for my belongings at the hotel. I had left my gold with Hanan Praeger the prior afternoon, but I was carrying a considerable sum in Italian currency. When the officials saw this, they told me that they could put the entire amount into an account against which I could charge any extra food that I wanted to order from outside the jail. I agreed to this arrangement, and thanked them. I was then led to my cell, where I was left alone.

The cell was quite Spartan in its simplicity. It was small, about ten feet long and seven feet wide, although the ceiling was quite high. The large slabs of granite that formed the walls, ceiling, and floor gave it the aspect of a medieval monk's cell. Opposite the door, a tall, narrow, barred window looked out onto the prison courtyard and a patch of sky. From the left corner beside the window stretched a double bunk, rudely fashioned in wood, each bunk furnished with a straw mattress, one pillow, and two blankets. At the end of the bunk beds, a small shelf was built into the wall. A wooden table projected from the wall opposite the bunks. In front of this table, a simple chair was fastened to the stone floor. A pail, which served as a toilet, was set in the corner beside the door. A bare electric lightbulb was suspended from the ceiling. Its aggressive, bright light shone night and day.

When the heavy door closed behind me, I sat down on the bed. I was overcome by a strange feeling of peace and security. I was completely alone. I had found a quiet corner. I looked at the gray stone walls of my cell and focused on the muffled sounds that penetrated the door and window. The gray walls exuded damp cold and stillness, a sense of timelessness and history. I shuddered at the cold, and realized that it would grow colder still at night as the December days fell away into winter. I wondered how long I would remain in the cell. I was exhausted. After so many sleepless nights, I was sure that I would sleep soundly, but even with the blankets pulled over my head, the strong electric light irritated me, and it was several nights before I adjusted to it.

I was awakened abruptly several times that first night when the guard outside made a great commotion, singing and banging on the bars of the windows. The guards, I learned, did this regularly, to be sure that none of the prisoners had begun to cut through the bars in order to escape. Apparently, the bars rang somewhat differently when they were cut. Being Italians, and hence innately civilized and playful, the guards were not content merely to strike the bars, but felt compelled to make concerts out of their inspections. Eventually, I became accustomed to their percussive serenades, and they ceased to awaken me at night—ample proof of the fantastic adaptive powers of the human animal!

It took me only a few days to develop a new routine—washing, cleaning my cell, meals, emptying and rinsing out the pail, exercise, and sleep. The prison regulations were not harsh. I adjusted to the damp chill of the cell, and the solitude of my first days in prison was a blessing to me. The prison food proved to be neither ample nor good. When the heavy door of my cell opened on the second day of my stay and the guard handed me the menu of the nearby trattoria, I eagerly ordered a sumptuous lunch. I was ravenously hungry, and I reasoned that an ample meal now and then would help me to withstand the cold. Miraculously—at least it seemed a miracle to me—this small prison at Vicenza was equipped with a library from which I was permitted to borrow books. I started a program of reading with several heavy tomes—*The Count of Monte Cristo, Les Misérables,* and several others. I read these books slowly at first, since I did not know much Italian, but I quickly began to master the language. I was alone all the time, and barely spoke to the guards. I purposely ordered extra food and left it for them when I was done with my meals, because they all appeared to be famished.

Several days passed with no news from the Ministry. I was beginning to feel lonely and restless, when a young American was assigned to my cell. He was an American citizen, but he had been born in Italy and he spoke hardly a word of English. I was pleased to have some company, but this unfortunately lasted for only a few days. One day, as we were getting ready to go out for our daily exercise, this fellow somehow managed to dislocate his shoulder as he was pulling his coat on. He was instantly in excruciating pain. He began to scream, he was suffering so terribly, and soon the entire prison was in turmoil. It seemed that the entire prison staff came rushing into our small cell and the features of the director's face were so drawn in anxiety that I was certain he feared that Roosevelt would declare a separate war on the prison for war crimes! My roommate was taken to the hospital. I never heard any word of what became of him. No one else was ever assigned to my cell. I remained completely isolated, even when I went for my daily walk, for the term of my stay in the prison, which eventually lasted almost three months.

As the December days grew shorter, the cold became sharper and sharper. There was little I could do to stay warm, other than to remain huddled in my bunk fully dressed under my blankets. I did spend a great deal of my time standing on the sturdy wooden table across from the bunk, stamping my feet, and beating my hands across my chest, while I whistled my way through my extensive repertoire of music. I have always had a terrific musical memory. I would often start with the symphonies of Beethoven and then move to his quartets, but I could also choose from a broad selection of works by other classical composers. I also knew an enormous number of Israeli and Serbian songs. Sometimes I could hear the voice of a fellow prisoner shouting into the courtyard: *"Alcalay, basta fischiare!"* (Alcalay, stop whistling!). But this whistling was my way of combatting loneliness, and I restrained myself only at night, when I withdrew in favor of the opera of our Italian guards. My reading kept me quiet a great deal of the time. I would have been quieter still if we had been permitted paper and pencils for drawing, but these supplies were granted to me only occasionally, for the sole purpose of writing letters. This restriction had something to do with my status as a "political" prisoner, although I couldn't see that there was anything particularly political in having entered the country illegally.

As cold and lonely as I was, I made the best of things and settled into prison existence. My belongings were finally delivered more or less intact to my cell. I arranged these across the upper bunk, from which I had removed the pillow and blankets for use below. I accumulated various cans of food, whatever delicacies I could obtain—

chestnut marmalade especially—and artfully displayed this bounty on the small shelf set into the wall at the end of the bunk. I did everything possible to fight the cold. Despite all my efforts, my feet were twice frostbitten, and I was taken to the prison infirmary, where my feet were cured by soaking them in hot water. I decided to let my beard grow, after I learned that the prison barber shaved prisoners with cold water and used the same razor on the entire prison population. I can still feel that blade on my face! Once was enough!

After a few weeks, I was permitted some visitors, thanks to the efforts of Hanan Praeger, who was on friendly terms with the director of the prison. Hanan and his wife were the first to visit me. Hanan's wife brought me some fresh clothing, which was very welcome, and she insisted on laundering my soiled garments, which were so filthy from constant wear since leaving Padua that I was ashamed to surrender them to her. Hanan and his wife came to see me as often as they could arrange to do so. They were in contact with our mutual friends in Padua—Bibi, Hedva, and Miriam—who all came to visit me as soon as the Praegers told them that I was in prison in Vicenza. I was especially joyful to see Miriam again.

It was during one of their visits that Bibi informed me that Šalom had managed to cross the border into France, but had not been able, for some reason, to get a flight to Lisbon. I never understood why Šalom hadn't been able to stay with his original plan, as he had promised me he would. What had compelled Šalom to risk taking a train through France? Bibi told me that Šalom had promised to send a cable as soon as he reached the safety of Spain. Nothing had been heard from him, and we all feared that he had been captured in France and sent to a concentration camp in Germany. We never received any news of him. I searched for him in Israel for many years after the war. We had promised each other that we would meet there, but we never did. It was a great loss for all of us, for me especially, because Šalom and I had sworn an oath that we would never separate, and yet we were forced to do so.

December gave way to the frigid days of January. The Ministry had not yet responded to my petition. In itself, the Ministry's delay did not really bother me. Despite the bitter cold, I was regaining my strength—mentally as well as physically. But it was extremely cold, usually more than twenty degrees below zero, and often even colder at night.

A guard always accompanied me when I went into the prison court-yard to take my daily exercise. I had no contact with the other prisoners. I tried to talk to the guards, but was always met with silence. I was a stranger to them, and they wanted to keep their distance. The natural friendliness of the Italians was one casualty of that bitter winter of war. One day, I noticed something white lodged in the bristles of the broom that the guard gave me to sweep out my cell. Inspecting this, I saw that it was a scroll of paper wrapped around a small pencil. A note in Serbian was scrawled on the paper, asking for news of the progress of the war. I knew nothing. Hanan, his wife, and our friends had all refused to speak of the war, as if what news they could share was too bad to tell. I also sensed a trap in the situation, so I pushed the paper and the pencil back into the broom and returned it to the guard. But I wondered if perhaps some captured Montenegrins or other Yugoslav Resistance fighters had been transferred to Vicenza from Kavaja or elsewhere. I never learned anything more and no further efforts were made to contact me.

Time went by very slowly, as I awaited clarification of my situation. January had almost passed, and the Ministry still had not responded to my petitions. I continued to read voraciously, and was beginning to achieve a real command of Italian. I was eating quite well, and was living an almost entirely sedentary life. Despite the cold, I had already gained back almost twenty pounds, although I was still well under my normal weight.

From the beginning of my imprisonment, I had been able to correspond with my father. At the end of January, I received a letter from him, in which he wrote that he had met with an important inspector at the camp. My father had appealed to him to help resolve my situation, explaining that I had not been able to cut through the slow bureaucracy and red tape at the Ministry of Internal Affairs, and that I was freezing in the prison at Vicenza. The inspector had assured my father that he would expedite the resolution of my case. Father optimistically expected that I would soon be released from prison and sent to join the family in the camp at Ferramonti. He told me not to bring money into the camp, because it would be useless there. He advised me to spend whatever I had left on any necessities I could obtain before leaving Vicenza.

In the middle of February, I was, in fact, called to the office of the prison director, who told me that I was to leave for Ferramonti the following day, accompanied by a police agent. I overheard the agent who had been chosen to accompany me boasting to his colleagues that he would extract money from me and use it to buy olive oil in Calabria in the south. He planned to return north with this oil and sell it on the black market. The agent did not know that I already understood Italian quite well. Although he spoke quite fast, I understood what he was saying, but I remained quiet and indifferent to his little speech, as if it did not concern me in the least.

I wasn't going to be traveling light. I had accumulated an ample array of belongings. In addition to the valise I had carried with me from Milan, I would need at least two more large suitcases in which to pack everything. I also had a large box of painting supplies. I had hardly touched it since Bibi and Miriam had brought it to me in December, but I had no intention of leaving it behind. Since I was to leave the next day, I requested permission to go into town to buy luggage and a few things that I needed. My request was granted, and I went into town, naturally accompanied by a guard.

I found two suitcases at the first store we visited. They were old and battered, but quite ample and sturdy, inexpensive and perfectly suitable. We then went to Vicenza's principal grocery store, where I purchased a variety of things, including such luxuries as toothpaste and shoe polish. I noticed a large stock of marked-down tinned sardines piled on a high top shelf in the store. I asked why they were on sale. Were they too old? The storekeeper explained that he could not sell the sardines because they were packed in vinegar instead of oil, and no one wanted sardines packed in vinegar. I had never heard of sardines being packed in vinegar, so my curiosity was piqued. I examined several of the tins and noticed that they had been imported from Spain. The label indicated that the sardines were packed in *aceite* (oil). I almost laughed out loud when I understood that it was a subtle linguistic nuance. Vinegar in Italian is *acceto*, so the grocer's customers had interpreted *aceite* on the Spanish label as meaning vinegar when, in fact, as I happened to know, *aceite* means oil in Spanish. I told the shopkeeper that I happened to like sardines in vinegar, very much, that my whole family liked them. For next to nothing, the shopkeeper was thrilled to be rid of his entire stock of Spanish sardines, and I was quite pleased with myself for having found such a bargain in wartime for excellent Spanish and Portuguese sardines. This transaction puzzled the guard, who looked at me in amazement, not knowing what to think. And so we returned to the prison, where I organized my baggage and ordered a superb supper from the trattoria, supplemented, of course, by an ample serving of sardines. I was ready to set out on the long journey to the south, along the entire length of the Italian peninsula.

The officer assigned to accompany me tried to cultivate my goodwill from the moment of our departure. He began by telling me that regulations dictated that I should be handcuffed throughout the journey, but that he did not think this would really be necessary. He esteemed me, he explained, as a civilized individual who surely wouldn't take advantage of his liberality by attempting to escape. I told him that he could do whatever he judged to be necessary. If regulations required that I should wear handcuffs, then so be it. I reflected to myself that if I were restrained in handcuffs, at least I wouldn't have to carry the luggage that I had accumulated. Naturally, I did not thank the officer for his pretended consideration. Having overheard him saying that he planned to extort money from me, I was well aware of his real attitude. A black-shirted Fascist official, I despised him.

The trip on the train to Rome was rather comfortable. The official reserved our compartment for public security purposes, placing a sign on the door to that effect, so we traveled alone and had plenty of room. The officer tried several times to engage me in conversation, but I was unresponsive. Although my Italian was rather good by this time, I had no desire to practice it with this man. The trip passed without incident, but as soon as our train had screeched to a halt in the station at Rome, something extraordinary occurred.

Sirens suddenly began to scream an alert of an enemy air attack. Everyone naturally feared that the railroad station would be a prime target. The scene in the station instantly became chaotic, as people scattered in all directions, looking for shelter. My guardian and I fled from our train, leaving all the baggage behind. I ran into the station café, where I stopped and waited, having lost sight of my guardian and not knowing where else to go. We could hear the staccato thud of bombs exploding on the outskirts of the city, but Rome itself was not attacked, and no bombs struck the railroad station. Apparently, the Allies were respecting Rome's declared status as an open city. When the sirens wailed the all-clear, I walked back and boarded the train, which very shortly afterward jerked into motion to continue the journey to the south.

Because of the confusion caused by the attack, and the sudden departure of the train from the station, the corridors of the train were jammed with passengers struggling to return to their compartments. Many new travelers had boarded the train in Rome, adding to the general disorder. There was no sign of my guard, and I was alone in my compartment with neither tickets nor identification. When the conductor came to collect our tickets, I had a hard time explaining to him that during the alert I had been separated from the official accompanying me, and that he was probably somewhere on the train. The harassed conductor looked me over dubiously, and told me to stay put. He said that he would search for the officer, but would have to turn me over to the authorities in Naples if he did not find him.

I was extremely fearful that I might be thrown into another prison for only God knew how long. I restlessly paced in the swaying compartment, continually opening the door and straining my head to the left and right to see some sign of my guardian over the heads of the crowd jammed into the corridor. Finally, just as the train was arriving in Naples, I saw a comical figure far down the corridor struggling to make his way through the crowd. It was my guard, quite disheveled, without his jacket and tie, and evidently quite anxious to reach me. When he had finally fought his way to the compartment, he embraced me like a long lost brother, thanking heaven, God, and Mussolini that he had found me, for otherwise, he confided to me, he would have been sent to the Russian front or to a forced labor camp.

I was also quite relieved for myself. I spoke more openly with the man, with a new sympathy for his situation. We discussed what had happened between our separation in the chaos at the station in Rome and our arrival in Naples. I explained that I had not really been frightened during the air alert, convinced that, because Rome had been declared open, the Allies would not target the railroad station in the center of the city. But I confessed how fearful I had been to find myself alone in the train without any papers. Our train left Naples without delay. Before many hours had passed, we had traveled more than 120 miles to Cosenza, a large town in northern Calabria, deep in the south of Italy.

We immediately boarded a local train to Mongrassano, a small medieval town in the hill country about twenty miles to the northwest. There, my guard hired a carriage drawn by two horses, which, after slow progress, finally delivered us in front of the gate of the camp at Ferramonti di Tarsia, where I was expected. The inmates of the camp had observed the approach of the carriage. My searching gaze quickly found my parents and my sister in the crowd gathered at the gate to greet me. And so I arrived at the camp, pale from almost three months of confinement in prison, but rested, and with a little more meat on my bones. The sun was shining. The day was warm. My father, my mother, my sister, and I joyfully embraced, and we were all pummeled in the affectionate embrace of the joyful friends gathered around us. The prodigal son had returned. From these moments of reunion with my parents and my sister until after the end of the war, I shared their destiny, not merely as a support to them, but also taking into my hands decisions about our next moves on the road to survival.

12

My Father's Journal: Part IV

My FATHER, MOTHER, AND SISTER HAD BEEN INTERNED AT THE FERRA-
monti refugee camp since late October. I had been imprisoned at Vicenza for almost a week, when my father recorded the first of these
entries in his diary:

Wednesday, December 17, 1941

*We are in the south of Italy, yet none of us has ever experienced such
bitter cold. The Ministry in Rome has authorized the distribution of
blankets here. In recent days, some members of our group have been
released from the camp to free confinement,* confino libero. *Dača Azriel
and his family are the first to be released, followed by both Bauer brothers, and then others. Rumors are circulating that bribery was involved.
This doesn't seem to be the case, although it is clear that all those who
have been freed have adequate resources to support themselves and their
families outside the camp.*

Friday, December 19, 1941

*We have just today received a letter from one of Albert's friends in
Padua. He writes that our dear Albert came to Italy to look for us, and
surrendered to the police in Vicenza when he learned that we are here
in Ferramonti. He has petitioned to join us here, but he has to remain
in prison until the Ministry of the Interior rules on his petition.*

Monday, December 22, 1941

*We at last receive a letter from Albert. He tells us that he has been
well treated in the prison at Vicenza, and that we should not worry*

about him. I can't sleep at night. Each time I hear a train pass in the distance, my heart leaps with hope that it is bringing our son back to us.

Sunday, December 31, 1941

While Albert was in Padua, he received a letter from my brother David. This has been the only sign of life we have had from my three brothers since we learned they had been sent to a prisoner-of-war camp in Germany. David says he is well, but it is clear that he has had to write this for the censors. He says nothing of his wife and child. We are sick with worry and sorrow for the miseries that they all must be enduring.

There is a Catholic priest who works as a missionary inside the camp. He is very diligent in his efforts to convert the Jews here to Christianity, and almost thirty have joined his church. We are all anxious to learn what has happened to the Jews who remained in Belgrade. No one knows anything. The Catholic missionary has told us that he is making every effort through Vatican channels to learn something about the situation.

Many of us who fled from Belgrade have left substantial assets behind. With the help of the camp authorities, who have encouraged us to be optimistic, we have taken the first steps to free assets that were frozen in the disruption of the German invasion last April. The camp authorities have repeatedly said that we will receive everything back. I simply cannot believe this, but am certainly hopeful that we might recover something . . .

. . . Life inside the camp is monotonous and gray. We live day to day. How can we think of the future? The barbed wire that surrounds us protects us from the evil in the outside world. My friend Solomon Mošić organizes a kitchen for Yugoslavs. Knowing that I cannot pay eighteen lire each day for my wife, my daughter, and myself, Solomon does not invite us to join. I don't even go to the café that was organized by Ilia Talvi, since I don't have any money to spend. Despite the privation and the bitter cold, I am determined to remain cheerful and to keep up my courage. I teach Italian eight, sometimes ten hours a day, and

I am doing all that I can to help my wife and daughter in our small household.

Thursday, January 1, 1942

Today is the New Year, and it would be a very sad New Year for us but for the fact that we receive a letter from Albert today. This brightens our spirits and strengthens me in my resolve to stay cheerful. Albert writes that he is well. I find it strange that he doesn't complain of the cold. It is so cold here; it must be even worse in the north.

We also receive a package today from Praeger, Albert's friend in Vicenza. He sends us three hundred lire and a generous stock of tinned foods, including a dozen tins of Spanish sardines. Praeger also very kindly sends several old newspapers. These are mostly old issues of local newspapers, which are filled with Hitler's recent speeches and declarations, but any news is welcome, even if one has to read between the lines. German forces have advanced to Leningrad and Moscow, and the newspapers say that the Russian capitals are about to fall. But it is already the New Year, and we have heard nothing about this, so the Russians have certainly somehow managed to stop the Germans short of victory, and the Nazis are trapped and freezing in the open countryside. The winter has been so bitter here; the cold in Russia must be terrifying. The newspapers boast that almost four million Russians have already been taken prisoner. From what we have heard, this may be true, but still the Russians have survived like a barbarian horde, withdrawing into the depths of Asia.

The Jews here in Ferramonti refuse to believe Hitler's boasting. Everybody insists that England and Russia will win in the end. I search the papers for some news from the Balkans, but I find only hints of the violence and repression that the Germans are certainly imposing there. We are all terrified for the friends and loved ones who have been stranded or have chosen to remain in Belgrade under German occupation. We have been so fortunate. The Italians have treated us more as refugees than as prisoners. And they do not hate the Jews. Many families who can support themselves independently have been allowed to leave the camp to confino libero *(free confinement), especially those who lived in Italy before the war and can speak some Italian, which is why I have more students than I can really handle. But newcomers continue to arrive to take the place of those who leave. They come singly and in small groups, almost always marked with desperation, fear, and then relief to find themselves safely behind the barbed wire fences that surround us.*

Friday, January 16, 1942

An inspector from the Ministry of Refugees visited our camp at Ferramonti yesterday. I gave him my petition for Albert's release from prison and transfer here. The inspector was genuinely kind. He promised that he would do whatever he could. We have been impatiently expecting Albert for many weeks. Our hopes have been raised that we may see him soon, but nothing is assured.

Tuesday, January 20, 1942

My friend Dr. Leon Koen has managed to escape Belgrade. He sent me a card from Abazia, which I received today. He tells me that my brothers Bukus and Nisim have avoided imprisonment for many months because they are doctors, but have finally been interned in the camp at "Topovskih Šupa" in Belgrade. Nisim has been operated on for a stomach ulcer, but has recovered from this. Leon has heard nothing about my brother Rafajlo.

Thursday, January 22, 1942

Our financial situation has improved dramatically. The Croat husband of our landlady in Herceg Novi has succeeded in retrieving the fortune of almost 5,000 gold coins that I hid in the frame of a couch there when the Italians took us into custody. He has proven himself a great friend. He manages to send me a substantial sum here in the form of a draft on a Geneva bank. He promises to try to send more as soon as he can arrange it. Of course, there is some difficulty and even danger to him in doing this, but I am compensating him generously and am grateful for his honesty and goodwill. We shall become Selbstversorgers—that is, "self-sufficient," foodwise.

But now that we have some relief at long last, I do not plan to change our life completely. We shall continue as we have, but with a little more food, perhaps a few more discrete comforts and, yes, much more security and some ability to help the most needy among us. There is no question of making a move to try to leave the camp until Albert rejoins us.

Sunday, February 15, 1941

To our great joy, Albert finally arrives at dusk today. His arrival provokes great interest among our friends from Kavaja, who all press around him eagerly to hear his stories of what he has experienced. Only now do we learn about the first few days of the war and the disintegration of his command. Only now do we learn how much Albert suffered after he was captured last April and imprisoned at the makeshift schoolhouse prison, how he was transferred to a German prison camp whose commandant treated him well, and miraculously allowed him to leave. Albert tells the full story of how he reached Belgrade after his release from the German prison camp and what he found there when he arrived. He explains what he did in the city, how the situation there had worsened until finally he had to escape to Albania with his friend Šalom. He tells us how he found us in the camp in Kavaja. He also tells us about the selfish and indecent behavior that wealthy Jewish refugees in Split have shown toward him and in general toward poor Jewish refugees, especially the orphaned and the young, who are nearly starving, while the wealthy worry only about their own comfort. But Albert is careful not to say anything about his experiences in Italy before he turned himself in to the authorities at Vicenza, although, when things calmed down, he tells me privately all that has happened. Albert tells me about the time he spent in Padua, about the cruel weeks he spent in Milan, how he and Šalom failed in their plan to reach Palestine, and also about poor Šalom's fate.

And Albert told me how joyful he is to have rejoined us, that he is at peace with himself now that he knows that it is right that he should remain at our side throughout the duration of the tragic insanity we are experiencing. We have worried so deeply about Albert. Now we are here, all together again, reunited as a family, to face whatever lies before us—together.

A Corner in the Camp. By Albert Alcalay.

13

Reunited

FERRAMONTI WAS A LARGE CAMP BUILT ON A FLATLAND WHERE THE Alluvial plain of the Crati River valley begins to rise into the hill country of northwest Calabria. When heavy rains fell, which was not unusual at Ferramonti, this flatland quickly became saturated and swampy. A fence of barbed wire about five feet high enclosed the camp compound in which ninety-six large white barracks were neatly laid out in rows broken only by the positioning of water towers, latrines, cookhouses, showers, and storage sheds. Each of the barracks was given a number that was painted in large numerals on a sign placed in front of its single door. Fascist militia patrolled the perimeter outside the camp, and agents of the Fascist Ministry of Public Security circulated inside the camp to ensure order and conformity to the regulations by which it was governed.

I found many friends from Belgrade gathered in the camp, mixed with a varied population of refugees, mostly Jewish intelligentsia from Germany and throughout Central Europe. Despite the stark tragedy of the situation, the concentration of so many interesting and vibrant personalities fascinated me, and I reflected that simply observing the behavior of these uprooted people would fully occupy my time. There were doctors of all kinds—many of them specialized in the most arcane fields of medicine. There were literati, physicists and mathematicians, chemists, biologists, zoologists, scientists representing every discipline, and professors accomplished in every area of academic study, classicists, historians, political scientists, and psychologists. There were many merchants and craftsmen, including goldsmiths and furriers. There were civil engineers. And finally, there were quite a few lawyers. The presence of a number of day laborers somewhat leavened this concentration of intellectual talent. But it remained much more possible to

155

consult with a medical specialist, an academic, or a legal scholar than to find a shoemaker or a seamstress. The eternal problem of the Jewish people—too many intellectuals, too few simple tradesmen and laborers—was replicated and amplified in the microcosmic social order at Ferramonti, where a doctor's consultation cost only thirty lire, but the services of an electrician were much more expensive.

Whatever their social rank, these people had all been driven away from their walks of life, their professions, and their homes. Most of them had lost all their possessions, and were penniless. Most of them had been completely separated from their families and were isolated within the camp into small linguistic, cultural, and professional groups. The relatively homogenous group of Yugoslav Jews from Kavaja had been fortunate. They had had a difficult time in the refugee camp there, but the Italians had done what they could for them, and they had been transferred together to Ferramonti, under tolerable conditions. But many of the other refugees at Ferramonti had arrived there like wounded dogs, crippled and half crazed by months of unspeakable hardship and horror.

The camp was a real babel of languages. When I arrived in that winter of 1942, it was mostly German, Yiddish, and Serbo-Croat voices that I heard, but in the months that followed many more Polish and Czechoslovak voices added to the cacophony. Greek and Arabic voices were not rare, and in addition to these, one heard the strains of the Oriental speech of Chinese and Japanese, and even Burmese and Vietnamese refugees. The world had exploded, and these varied shards of the wreckage had fallen and been swept jumbled together into the strange safety of the refugee camp at Ferramonti. There, these diverse people—with such wildly different ethnic, cultural, linguistic backgrounds and psychological orientations—were compelled to live together under Italian law.

With such a diverse mass of humanity gathered into the camp, life there held out every possibility of disorder and confusion, but everything fell under the authority of the camp director and the camp marshal who, together, managed to assure a harmonious regime. Ferramonti was a microcosm of the world. It functioned as a small, independent republic with a parliament and a tribunal, schools, communal kitchens, sanitation and social services, and temples, synagogues, and churches.

The camp director, it must be said, was a caring and responsive man. He willingly granted the Jewish refugees in the camp a wide degree of autonomy in the conduct of their affairs. Even among the Fascist functionaries of the Italian government—and most of these officials were only nominally fascist—the essentially humane character of the Italian people usually shone through. The understanding and kindness they so often showed us filled our hearts with gratitude, for their humanity was indeed the salvation of so many of us who had found a refuge in Italy. Some high officials did display a cold, rigidly Fascist mentality in their conduct, but this was by no means commonly the case, and when high officials ruled harshly, their subordinates usually softened and often entirely diverted the impact of such decisions. They disregarded orders or delayed their implementation, exploited loopholes in the system, bent the regulations, or simply ignored them.

Ferramonti was an oasis of peace, sheltered from the infernal storm whose flames were sweeping across German-occupied Europe. In western Russia, the Nazis had herded Jews together and executed and incinerated them on the open steppes. The Nazis had packed Jews into ghettos from which more and more of them were now being shipped in sealed cattle cars to forced labor and death camps in Germany and Poland—to Auschwitz, Treblinka, Sobibor. The diverse population of refugees at Ferramonti had all fled from the murderous tragedy unfolding in Europe. We were grateful to the Italians for their kind treatment of us. The refugee camp was isolated in southern Italy, far from the front lines, far from the violence. There was no industry in the region, no transportation center, no concentration of military force, nothing of any strategic interest. We were completely isolated. Our lives, protected at least for a time, had been arrested in this place. We never lost hope. We never lost faith in an ultimate Allied victory. We had to remake our lives while we waited in isolation for the war to come to an end.

But even as we felt secure and could sustain hope for the future, we were all aware of the horrors unfolding elsewhere in Europe. Some letters did reach us, and new arrivals brought fresh reports and rumors of horror and disaster. As news filtered through to us, and the reality of the annihilation of an entire people became clear, the anguish that we all felt intensified, and then subsided, only to deepen and become even more intense with each fresh report. Italian officials and representatives of the Vatican would not speak of what was happening. But we could read in their faces and their gestures that they were aware of it. We pressured them to provide us with information, but we received little more than promises. Perhaps this was a form of kindness. We all prayed that the Allies knew, and prayed that they would somehow put a stop to it.

When I arrived in Ferramonti in mid-February 1942, my Belgrade friends and many others in the camp swarmed around me to listen to what I could relate of developments in Belgrade and Yugoslavia. I earnestly reported everything that I knew, but by this time, I had been away from Belgrade for more than six months, and I had no fresh, firsthand knowledge of how the situation there had developed. I described the mass execution of Jewish men that had taken place that summer at Tašmajdan in Belgrade. I told my friends how the Germans had selected every fifth man, and how I had been fourth in the count and had just missed being taken. I explained how we had all spontaneously given the victims of the selection our money and the clothing off our backs. I had given my jacket to a friend. I tried to explain the despair everyone had felt when we learned the next morning that the men had all been executed. I described the feelings of terror and hopelessness that had caused so many among us to decide to flee the city because there was nothing more that we could do there.

My own experiences had been terrible, but my fears and anguish sharpened when I heard the accounts of two young men who had miraculously escaped from the Warsaw ghetto and made their way to refuge at our camp in Italy. They brought reports of carnage throughout Poland, described unspeakable conditions in the Jewish ghetto, and spoke fearfully of forced transports to labor camps. These and other reports of tragedy deeply disturbed everyone in the camp. We were utterly powerless to help our people. We felt guilty in our relative comfort and safety, and we wondered how long it would be before the evil hand of war would reach out to destroy us as well. An anguished resignation infected the lives of the refugees in the camp. Everyone struggled to live normally, and indeed our lives were filled with desires, pleasures, hardships, and day-to-day obligations, but so many

among us were exhausted and deeply wounded spiritually. Many of
the refugees had lost their families. The fabric of all our lives had
been ripped to shreds.

The horrifying news that filtered into the camp through letters, and
with the arrival of new refugees, at first reinforced our feelings of resignation and fear. But a different reaction to the tragic news soon took
hold of us spontaneously. Everyone began to express an extraordinary
desire to live. We felt more and more that giving in to despair would
betray everyone who had been left behind and murdered. More and
more, we felt that it was our duty—a matter both of dignity and survival—to do everything we could to recover our lives. A nostalgic
yearning for our homes and the lives from which we had been torn
motivated many of us. But I am certain that it was a subconscious
ethical force more fundamental than mere nostalgia that transformed
us and gave us new energy and purpose to live positively and to do
everything we could to live meaningfully with all our power, regardless of our circumstances.

And so, an exuberant spirit took hold in every domain of human
activity at Ferramonti. The Italians were not at all repressive, and a
real liberty of expression blossomed within the camp's richly talented
population. Beyond the normal chores of daily life, we were not forced
to do work of any kind. We were simply treated as foreign refugees
who would be interned until the end of the war. Many of us were from
countries that had been at war with Italy. Many of us no longer had
passports, and thus had no officially recognized citizenship. The residents of the camp organized into groups to discuss politics, art, history, and religion. The various religious meetings were very popular,
and the highly animated discussions of religious issues were especially well attended. An informal university developed. Naturally, languages were the most popular course of study, especially English and
Italian, but courses and lectures were offered in a seemingly limitless
range of fields. We organized two coffeehouses where one could sit,
have a cup of coffee, talk, and exchange newspapers, where one could
spend leisurely hours in good company, where we never felt any pressure to leave, and imagined ourselves sitting in a Paris café or a coffeehouse in Vienna or Budapest. Chess became a popular pastime,
and chess tournaments were organized. Sports were also very popular.

Soccer clubs sprang up, and not a day passed without a hotly con-tested match. Many camp residents also enthusiastically joined in vol-leyball and ping-pong matches. I quickly adapted to this situation, and freely participated in many of these activities.

One day, shortly after my arrival at Ferramonti, I was studying a list of all the people interned in the camp and noticed with great ex-citement the name of a painter whose work I knew and admired. This was Michael Fingesten, a renowned German Expressionist painter, who had worked with Otto Dix, and in the *Sezession* (Secession) move-ment in Berlin. He knew very little Italian, only German, so I had to speak with him in that detested language, but I was thrilled when he agreed to instruct me in painting. I was stunned to have such an op-portunity in the refugee camp, and reflected on the odd chances of war. I had little money, and I was unwilling to appeal to my father for funds, so I offered to pay my teacher with jars of marmalade that I had received from the Red Cross. Very soon after I had begun my study of painting with Fingesten, I received a commission to paint the portraits of two very beautiful young children. I was paid five hundred lire when I successfully completed this work. This was the first time that I received payment for my work as an artist, and so I was able to make my first contribution to the support of my family.

And so, the following weeks of winter passed. We were isolated in the camp, but continued to receive fragments of information about the turmoil in the world beyond Ferramonti, and this news periodically provoked fresh anxieties among us, but we had no clear picture of the progress of the war. The Italian authorities left us relatively undis-turbed to live within the camp as normally as possible. The militia who patrolled the camp's perimeter generally looked the other way when local peasants approached the barbed wire fence to sell us the produce of their small farms, although such commerce was officially illegal. We were able to correspond with those who had left the camp, and with those who were interned elsewhere in Italy. We managed to reestablish contact with my uncles in Belgrade, where they were both working as doctors, Bukus at a camp for women in Tašmajdan, and Nisim at the Jewish hospital. We were even able to correspond with my uncles who were being held as prisoners of war in Germany. They told us that they had received food packages from Belgrade.

A Man Who Lost His Whole Family. By Albert Alcalay.

14

Ferramonti

DURING THAT WINTER AT FERRAMONTI, I CONTINUED WORKING ON MY art. I made a few more portraits and made gifts of landscape paintings to the director of the camp and to his secretary, hoping that they would appreciate my initiative and respond to it with good will and a favor when one might be needed. I spent a great deal of my time with Fingesten, observing him closely, thirstily trying to know and understand him, and how his mind and spirit worked. I had never met a more creative artist. Fingesten spoke only German, a language that I spoke poorly and for which I naturally felt distaste, but I was nevertheless grateful to have an opportunity to converse with him. We exchanged a wealth of ideas.

Fingesten's talent and spirit amazed me. Gifted with a rare genius to transform the experienced world into art, the elderly artist projected a tangible aura of power. This personal stature was reflected in the transcendent creativity of his profound and original art. The spiritual dimensions of Fingesten's artistic genius were closely bound with his religious convictions and his belief in a higher divine power but, although he was a deeply religious man, he was not dogmatic. He never tried to impose his views on me. Regardless of how much Fingesten impressed me as a man and an artist, I was skeptical of any religious beliefs. Materialist Marxism was more to my taste at this point in my life. However, although Fingesten made no effort to impose any particular belief and much less any system of beliefs on me, he did have a profound spiritual effect upon me, the seeds of which were planted in our many stimulating exchanges. Under his tutelage, my own sense of the spiritual dimensions of art began to take root in the deep interior shadows of my being. Later, when I was practicing art in Rome, my understanding of the spiritual dimension of Fingesten's work deepened, and my own work burst into an active emulation of my teacher's spiritual genius.

For his part, Fingesten seemed grateful to have such an attentive student in me. My teacher was completely alone in the camp. He did have a son, whom I met after the war in New York, where he had settled to work as a sculptor. I never fully understand how father and son had come to be separated. The camp director recognized that Fingesten was a great artist and had given him an entire barracks for his work. I was intensely conscious of the passage of time, and was thirsty for knowledge. I felt that I had already lost so much of my life to the accursed war. I read voraciously at night. I dedicated almost every morning, and sometimes the entire day, to my time with Fingesten, in his studio. I studied drawing with him, concentrating especially on the art of the portrait. Fingesten worked very productively during this period, and had something new to share with me every day. I was a privileged observer of the artist's enormous creative inventiveness, and I studied his work carefully and analytically. I was always ready with many questions, and was deeply grateful to have such an accomplished and responsive teacher, and I was always able to find someone in the camp who was willing to sit as a model in exchange for a portrait or a drawing. This was a joyful time for me.

One day, Fingesten found me engrossed in a book about quantum theory. He was surprised at this, and angrily told me that the art world is so vast that even an entire lifetime was not sufficient to explore it. If I wanted to be an artist, he insisted, I should not devote any time to the study of quantum theory, which had nothing to do with art. Afterward, I thought a lot about the truth of this observation, but I could not completely agree with it. Only much later in life did I accept that Fingesten was right in principle. Nevertheless, I have always had a wide range of interests, and have always pursued them. In my youth, I was intensely interested in realistic explanations of the social and physical worlds, which led me to investigate a variety of theories ranging from dialectical materialism to quantum physics.

The gray skies and freezing temperatures of the winter of 1942 finally gave way to a blue and mild February, and the camp burst into renewed life and a spirit of optimism. Sports were especially popular. Many of the camp residents participated as players or observers in

One of the Doctors at the Camp. By Albert Alcalay.

soccer and ping-pong matches. There were many concerts, many quite professional. Lav Mirski, a Yugoslav musician and opera conductor, directed some of these. I sketched a portrait of him. The camp director even invited Italian musicians from outside the camp to perform concerts. Despite all the difficulties of our lives confined in the camp, the Italian authorities did not treat us harshly. We found the strength to meet our fate with light hearts, and joked and laughed about everything, especially about the Nazis and Fascists. The camp residents were all more or less bound together to share the same destiny, and the life of what was almost a small Jewish republic, with its own laws and order, continued to flourish.

Just as the weather softened in early February, and life was bursting into this new vitality, news of an extraordinary event spread through the camp: a large group of refugees from the island of Rhodes was soon to arrive. The camp authorities ordered that new barracks be prepared for them. Workers and black-shirted militia hastily set up the new shelters, and the first group of new refugees, around two hundred of them, arrived in the middle of the month. Another group of nearly three hundred arrived before the end of March.

These new arrivals at Ferramonti were mostly young Czechoslovak refugees who had been interned on Rhodes—over which the Italians had taken possession after the Nazi defeat of Greece in the spring of 1941. These refugees had endured an incredible odyssey that had begun in their Czechoslovak homeland in September 1938, when the Allied betrayal at Munich had sealed the fate of their country, and the doors of mortal Nazi persecution had menacingly swung open. The Jews of the country knew that their only safety was in flight. One group of people, their hopes buoyed by the ideals of Zionism, made desperate plans to escape to Palestine.

After an exhaustive search, and lengthy negotiations that ended in agreement to pay its Greek owners an exorbitant price, the Jewish agents had no other choice but to purchase a decrepit paddle-wheel steamship, the *Stefano*, in the port of Braila, in Romania. At the end of its working life and all but ready for the scrap heap, with its side-mounted rotating paddles, the antique ship was similar in design to the riverboats whose use had spread throughout Europe and the United States in the nineteenth century. The Jewish agents set about modifying the ship to receive three hundred passengers. The ship was in such a poor state that it would pass no official inspection, but, after strenuous efforts, anointed with a great deal of bribery, the agents finally succeeded in registering it under the Bulgarian flag, renaming the unsure vessel the *Pentcho*.

The Danube was an international waterway on which passage would be at least theoretically possible through all the countries along its banks. By the time the steamship was finally refitted, the Danube and its tributaries had frozen over. Until the ice cleared the rivers, the ship could not steam all the way up to Bratislava in Slovakia, where all the emigrants had gathered for the journey. The danger of this delay mounted with each passing day. From the first days of their occupation of Czechoslovakia, the Nazis had been rounding up Jews. But the ship finally arrived at Bratislava. Its captain, a tormented and drug-addicted former officer of the Russian Imperial Navy, carried false documents declaring that all his passengers were traveling under a common Romanian visa that authorized their emigration to Paraguay—documents obtained only after dangerous, and extremely expensive, negotiations.

On Saturday, May 18, 1940, without any fanfare, the *Pentcho* steamed away from Bratislava with four hundred passengers crammed into its lower decks. It was to travel down the Danube to the Black Sea, then through the Sea of Marmora to the Aegean, before finally entering the Mediterranean Sea and navigating its way to Palestine, through the British blockade. The ship had been radically modified to accommodate a great many more passengers, its dimensions and proportions so altered that it had become a caricature of its previous self. But with its overwhelming contingent of passengers still one hundred more than even its expanded capacity, the vessel was a death trap, hardly capable of passage on even the calmest inland waters. Overtaxed beyond its capacities, the balance of the fragile *Pentcho* depended on keeping the great majority of its passengers below throughout the voyage. At any one time, only a few of its passengers could come up to the main deck for a breath of fresh air. Even if the vessel succeeded in reaching the mouth of the Danube, it would have almost no chance to successfully navigate the rougher waters of the Black Sea and beyond. But its human cargo was desperate. The choice had been stark—either remaining in Czechoslovakia to face Nazi persecution and deportation to internment camps, or escaping on the all but crippled *Pentcho* in the hope of reaching Palestine.

The passengers on the boat suffered many difficulties even during the passage through Hungary, the first leg of their voyage. Food, water, medical supplies, and even fuel were in short supply. With so many people crowded on the boat, it was extremely difficult to maintain proper hygiene and sanitary conditions and, of course, no one had any privacy. The daily ration was barely adequate. Hunger already stalked the ship. A black market developed on board for basic necessities, and there were incidents of petty theft. Quarrels flared up among the crowded passengers. But in general, discipline remained remarkably tight, and the mood was optimistic. Everyone was hopeful for a brighter future in Palestine. Piety and faith sustained many among the desperate company of Jewish exiles.

When the ship finally reached Yugoslavia, almost three weeks after its silent departure from Bratislava, more than one hundred additional refugees were jammed aboard. The *Pentcho* soon afterward passed Belgrade, where at the time I was working for the Zionist relief organization. I saw the ship and had some contact with its desperate passengers. We collected food and medicine for the refugees. The Yugoslav authorities detained the *Pentcho* at Dobra for six weeks before finally allowing it to continue with an escort through the Iron Gate, the dangerous mountain-bound gorge through which the Danube passes as it flows out of Yugoslavia, coursing between Bulgaria to the south and Romania to the north. At this point, its fuel tanks dry, the progress of the *Pentcho* depended entirely on the current of the river. Neither the Bulgarian nor the Romanian authorities would allow the ship to approach any port. Bulgarians and Romanians took potshots at the ship with rifles and shotguns, holding it far offshore. The passengers, now in a deplorable condition, tormented by hunger, thirst, heat, swarming insects, and the threat of disease, wanted to beach the ship. The captain finally obtained permission to approach the shore where Jewish organizations—notably the American Joint Distribution Committee—were at least allowed to distribute bread to the passengers.

Pushed along by the current, the ship continued down the Danube, conditions worsening and desperation growing daily. Its passengers finally decided to haul down the ship's Bulgarian flag and replace it with a symbol of their hunger, a flag of corn. They hung a large banner along the side of the boat, inscribing the word "hunger" in the many languages of the countries through which they passed. The fishermen and peasants of the remote villages of the Danube Delta—some of whom actually visited the ship—were appalled, and incredulous that its desperate passengers and crew intended to cross the Black Sea and voyage beyond into the Aegean and the Mediterranean.

Miraculously, the ship did finally reach Istanbul, but the Turkish government refused it permission to approach shore, and did not even allow bread and water to be transported to it. The ship limped through the Sea of Marmora and into the Aegean, and managed to reach a small town on the Island of Lesbos, where the authorities allowed it to come to rest and take on provisions. Despite the incredulity of the experienced navigators of the Greek Islands, the *Pentcho* again set out, finally arriving at Piraeus, where it was again able to take on fresh supplies of food, water, and medicine. The ship then continued to the southeast, toward the Italian-held Dodecanese Islands, where it miraculously escaped injury in minefields and was boarded by the officers of patrolling Italian torpedo boats. The Italian authorities sharply questioned the refugees. The Italians, finally satisfied and fully understanding the plight of the ship's passengers, responded—to the amazement of all—with warmth, generosity, and compassion, and allowed the *Pentcho* to continue on its impossible quest to reach Palestine.

It was astonishing that the ship was still afloat, and still more astonishing that the desperation of its passengers and crew had not given way to panic when the ship's boiler burst and water invaded parts of the hold. Barely afloat, unable to resist, the weary ship was gripped by a current that pulled it toward the rocky shore of a nearby, uninhabited island. Fortunately, the ship ran aground on the rocks close enough to the safety of shore to permit its courageous passengers to abandon the ship with almost all of their meager supplies before the *Pentcho* finally broke apart and sank beneath the waves. It was March 1941, just as the Axis powers were mounting their all-out offensive against Yugoslavia and Greece, that this brave group of refugees, now swelled to five hundred, found themselves stranded on the tiny, barren, and uninhabited Aegean island of Kamilanisi. Exhausted and racked with hunger, they managed to set up a rude camp. A few still-resilient young men set out in one of the *Pentcho*'s small lifeboats in search of help. Four days later, the British picked these men up just as they were losing all hope. Several days after that, the Italians sent a ship to evacuate the *Pentcho* refugees to the island of Rhodes, where they were interned.

So it was that the desperate attempt of the brave Czechoslovak exiles to reach Palestine ended. Wartime conditions in Italian-occupied Rhodes were difficult. Food was scarce, disease had spread through the camp, and many young people had died. But after the horrific experiences and dangers of their journey, the refugees were relieved to be again on land, to feel the blessings of the pulse of the sun, and the freshening airs of the Mediterranean breezes. One year later, in the winter of 1942, the Italian authorities moved the group to Ferramonti.

The newly arrived Czechoslovak refugees from Rhodes were a miserable-looking group of people, and their tragic story inspired pity among their fellow Jewish refugees at Ferramonti. We collected money to help them. My father gave twenty lire that he had earned giving lessons in Italian. The new refugees told us that, after the first difficulties, they had lived comparatively well in Rhodes, whose old Jewish community had extended all the help to them that it could. Soon after their arrival at Ferramonti, it became clear that our new Czechoslovak neighbors were an extremely resilient and resourceful group of people. They quickly engaged all of their talents as merchants and tradesmen, utterly altering the dynamics of life at Ferramonti. They were well organized, quickly made connections in the camp, and managed to supplement the belongings with which they had arrived with an amazing array of merchandise of all kinds. The black market that had existed from the beginning at Ferramonti soon expanded dramatically. The Czechoslovak Jews displayed tremendous ingenuity. They built ovens out of gas cans and baked fantastic pastries, which they somehow even managed to garnish with whipped cream! They sold flour, oil, and sugar in large quantities, and at much higher prices than before. Everyone understood that the Italian authorities at Ferramonti also profited from this activity. The black market in the camp became so developed that people from outside came there to buy food, diamonds, jewelry, gold, furs, and other contraband goods.

All the hills around the camp became greener with each passing day as the spring of 1942 arrived. On clear days, we could see the village of Tarsia, once the refuge of pirates, chiseled out of the rock of a distant mountain. In addition to the Czechoslovak refugees from the *Pentcho*, other groups arrived at Ferramonti that spring, including refugees from Greek communities in Libya and elsewhere. The Greek newcomers were pleasant people who kept within their own group. Many Chinese also arrived at the camp, most of whom had worked on merchant and tourist ships, and on European railroads as sleeping-car attendants. These Chinese internees developed a laundry in the camp. Everybody found something to do. Certainly, no one suffered from boredom.

My family's financial situation improved dramatically this spring, when the Italian authorities finally returned to my father the gold that they had confiscated from him at Kavaja. Adanja—a relative who by profession in Belgrade had been a criminal lawyer and who knew how to bribe anyone from a doorman to a company director—confided to us the secret of how to obtain the coveted status of *confino libero*, "free confinement" within Italy. According to Adanja, bribery was naturally the best method. But my father was an idealist. He refused Adanja's advice. Instead, Father sent a petition to the Italian Ministry of Internal Affairs, applying for *confino libero* on the basis of the very real illness of my mother, who was by then very weak. While my father sought to obtain official permission for us to live outside the camp, my sister, Buena, actively studied Italian and dressmaking. I myself was busy painting, trying to maintain a balanced relationship with my teacher, Fingesten.

After word spread that Fingesten had accepted me as his student, others showed up to his studio wishing to study with him. Among these was a young Hungarian woman, the wife of a family friend. The young husband and his wife were from the Kavaja group. They were on their honeymoon when the Italian authorities had arrested them. The young

Hungarian woman was rather plain, but she was well groomed and had an appealing, coquettish sensuality.

It was my great misfortune that my teacher, a man of seventy, became infatuated with this woman and forgot about everything else. Fingesten lived from day to day in this fantasy, and whatever he set out to paint or draw became her face. He became so infatuated with her that there was soon no more sense in my going to him for lessons. Fingesten's obsessive attention to this young woman flattered her, and she encouraged it, finding it very romantic and uplifting that a great man of art had developed such a passion for her. Fingesten nearly lost his mind. He worshipped the woman, regarding her as a divine goddess. Each day he went through the entire camp gathering flowers for her. When she entered his studio, he would light many candles and spread flowers in her path. It was absolutely wild. He never tried to make any advances. It was the last springtime of an old man who was suffering from an enlarged hernia that he always hid behind the newspaper that he constantly carried.

I could not at all understand Fingesten's behavior, and regarded it as highly peculiar and extravagant. A few years later, however, after we had been liberated, I understood perfectly well. By then I, too, had fallen in love. It was a pity that I was caught in the middle of this love affair between the aged artist and his young student. The Hungarian woman confided everything to me. I had lost a teacher, and at the same time I was forced to stand up on my own feet and assert my independence as an artist. Somehow, my understanding of the artistic soul deepened, my commitment to my own work affirmed itself, and my determination to be an artist became more tangible, more concretely real. I became charged up, very strongly charged, at this point, and from then on I thought constantly about the art of painting, and painted as much as I could under the circumstances. Fingesten was taken to the hospital at Cosenza for an operation on his hernia. There, to my deep sorrow, he died.

With the coming of spring that year, I cultivated a plot of land set between two of the camp buildings. I grew tomatoes, onions, and other garden vegetables. Cultivating a garden was one thing. Keeping its fruits was another. The camp was filled with thieves, and one member of our family had to keep watch over it, day and night, especially at night. By May, the weather had grown quite hot. My family lived crowded together in a single room, and it was very hard to move around.

Of my six uncles, three were interned as prisoners of war in Germany, and three were still living in Belgrade. My uncles in Germany all wrote to our family at Ferramonti that they were worried about their wives who had remained in Belgrade, writing that they had received no letters from them for several months, neither from Belgrade nor from anywhere else. Soon after receiving this worrying news, we spoke with a woman who had just arrived with her two daughters from Pančevo, near Belgrade. She told us that she had met my uncle's wives in the camp at Sajmište, where she and her daughters had been interned with them. She assured us that my aunts had been released from the camp. She also told us that my mother's sister Matilda and her daughter had also been interned there. But the woman who brought us this news refused to speak about life in the camp at Sajmište. We also received a card at this time from my mother's other sister, Anula, who reported that she was interned in the camp at Jasenovac in Croatia with her husband and her son. In the end, apart from my three uncles who miraculously returned from Germany, no one else among our aunts and uncles and their families survived the war.

There was another painter at Ferramonti. Like Fingesten, he also had his own studio, but his was much more elegant than Fingesten's had been. His name was Schecter. He was a converted Polish Jew of very dubious character. He wanted to be friendly with me. I tried to be as polite and straightforward as I could, but I was afraid of him. I did not trust converted Jews, most of whom struck me as cowards and opportunists. Schecter was a close friend of the camp director, and I knew that he was connected with the secretary of the camp, who oversaw the black market. Schecter always had all kinds of food in his studio. I always encountered him in the most unexpected places. We talked about art, and I was very direct in telling him what he should do and what he should not do, explaining that there is also something called the "ethics" of an artist. He would take this from me, but not from anybody else. It seemed to me that he felt a need to be reproached—either out of masochism or perhaps because some earlier held ideals still lingered in his consciousness.

Schecter was courting a very attractive young lady from Belgrade. She was the sister of my friend Bubi Alcalay, and was trying to divorce her husband, who was also interned at Ferramonti. It was an entirely hilarious situation. Whenever Bubi came to visit with my family, he would tell us that the only preoccupation of his sister's husband was how best to marry his attractive wife off to someone else. In general, Schecter snobbishly preferred his own company to that of anyone else. Among the first residents at Ferramonti and a fixture in the camp, this lonely, meticulously groomed, and obsequious man almost always gave the unappealing impression that he regarded himself as the founding member of some exclusive club. Schecter did not want to mix with the other internees, apart from Bubi's attractive sister and me. I never saw him with anyone else besides the camp director, to whom he looked with the servile devotion of a dog on a leash. I despised him for that. He was also a bad painter.

Although almost half of the Kavaja group was granted *confino libero* and left Ferramonti for confinement in small towns in Italy, my father's two petitions were rejected. My father met with an industrialist from Milan who often came to the camp to help some of the prisoners. He advised my father that our family was better off inside the camp, where there was a Jewish environment, than outside, where we would be more isolated. But we soon learned that our safety in the camp was not at all assured.

Mirko Davičo was intensely active as a communist, as were his two brothers Oskar and Jaša. They had all been in jail at one time or another. Mirko had been well known among the students in Belgrade. He was a brilliant speaker, and could stir crowds. Early in that summer of 1942, the camp authorities at Ferramonti received an order from the Gestapo to arrest Mirko. When I arrived at the camp, I had been surprised that he was living under his real name. I was sure that the Nazis would be searching for him, and I urgently felt that he should have changed it to conceal his identity. The director was a good man. He wanted to save Mirko, so he ordered him to be injected with typhus and placed in the ambulatory clinic. The camp missionary even appealed to the Vatican to try to keep him out of the hands of the Nazis.

When the Vatican appeal failed, the camp authorities sequestered Mirko at the hospital in Cosenza. We all struggled to find a way to avoid his arrest, but in the end, the Carabinieri had to take him out of the hospital and deliver him to the Germans. His life ended at Auschwitz.

The Gestapo was thorough in its search for anyone who was on its long list of dangerous persons. As a matter of fact, the Nazis pressed the Italians very hard to let them assume control of the entire camp at Ferramonti, but the Italians held firm, and their firmness was decisive in saving the lives of many Jews. Count Ciano, the Italian Plenipotentiary of Foreign Affairs and the son-in-law of Mussolini, told the Nazis, "You torture your Jews; we will torture our Jews." Of course, the situation in Italy was entirely different than that in German-controlled countries. Count Ciano was a genuine supporter and friend of the Jews. The camp missionary went to the Vatican several times to intervene on behalf of the camp's Jewish internees. But the Gestapo kept a sharp eye on Ferramonti and constantly persisted in their attempts to seize control of it. It was a very serious business. It appeared almost certain at one moment that the Italians would yield and turn the camp over to the Germans, but the Nazis were never successful in this. Other events intervened.

I studied English, to be prepared for the arrival of the Allied forces. But in that summer of 1942, unfortunately, the Germans were winning the battles. They had penetrated into Russia as far as the Volga, and were fighting around Stalingrad and in the Caucasus; in North Africa, Rommel had reached the Egyptian border. The Americans had entered the war only eight months earlier, and the Allied forces were not yet ready to attack Hitler. It was a demoralizing time, but we knew that we had to be patient.

Life was seriously deteriorating in the camp at Ferramonti. There were no longer enough peasants in the area from whom we could purchase poultry, bread, and olive oil. Not only had food become scarce, the quality of what was available was sometimes terrible. Even the bread was bad. I was convinced that the time had come to leave the camp. My father continued to believe that it was immoral to bribe the authorities who could grant the status of *confino libero* to our family, but Buena and I reasoned with Father, and finally persuaded him that we should start working on it.

There was a feeling of general slackness in the camp. By late summer, many of the famished internees were suffering from malaria, but the effort to isolate these cases or to care for them was almost casual. The Carabinieri, militia, and other officials seemed to have lost all belief in the war, and were less and less inclined to take their jobs seriously. Discipline suffered, because the Italians had become sick of playing soldier. They had had enough of it. When we went off to swim in the nearby canal, we were followed by the Carabinieri, but they didn't care at all when it became clear that we really wanted to buy fruit from the peasants. On the black market, the price of bread rose to thirty lire, flour cost thirty-five lire per kilo, oil forty lire for a liter.

My father approached the circle of Avramče Mošic, Dr. Munck, and Laub (Bubi Alcalay's brother-in-law), and told them that we were ready to talk to the director. They were all desperate themselves. Although they were good friends of the director and camp secretary, they had not succeeded in obtaining authorization to leave the camp. The director had dismissed their entreaties, lightheartedly offering that they would be better off in the camp than elsewhere. It was not unlikely that it was because they were such good companions and played cards together every day that the director and the secretary wouldn't take the petitions of their Jewish friends seriously.

We all received shots against typhus in early September. Soon afterward, the top man in the black market at Ferramonti was released from the camp to go to the United States. We could not believe it! Everyone wondered how much the black marketeer had had to pay to grease that departure! The whole camp came to the gate to say goodbye to him. He delivered a speech in which he alluded to his work and responsibilities as the chief organizer of the black market, how he had struggled to assure a steady supply of food to prevent starvation in the camp, and so on. The director was present, and also delivered a speech in which he asked the departing black marketeer to carry the message to President Roosevelt that Ferramonti was a Jewish camp that should never be a target for Allied bombs. The riotous scene had the circus atmosphere of a surreal comedy film.

Ferramonti di Tarsia Concentration Camp. By Albert Alcalay.

By mid-October, I was becoming jittery and impatient. I had already been in the camp for ten months. We had survived, and had been well treated for the most part. But I sensed new danger in the air, both despite and because of the relaxed attitude of our Italian hosts, more than from the penury that each day was gripping the camp in an ever tighter vise of hunger. There was no bread to be had at all, and few potatoes. Cauliflower was the only food in plentiful supply. I sent another small painting to the director, and gave him every opportunity to speak to me and thank me for my gift, hoping, of course, that I would then have an opportunity myself to take up the subject that was obsessing me. I finally spoke with the director, who told me that only one possibility remained for our departure. A member of our family had to have a heart condition. So we agreed that my father, who was the oldest and to whom this could most logically occur, should complain to the regional doctor, who would already be prepared for it. But would my father be ready?

My father suffered from a duodenal ulcer that had stricken him during the Depression era when he was tortured with worry and tension over how he would meet all the obligations of his troubled bank. Because he was by nature a scholar, my father studied all aspects of his ailment, and could discuss the topic in detail, even with medical specialists. Father was completely engrossed with the idea of an ulcer and would bring it into any conversation. He was always on a diet, and was always fussing about food, a fussing that tormented my mother. After having several episodes of hemorrhaging, he also had been operated on. So, he had become a real expert on ulcers. Now, we all had to go to the regional doctor, where Father was supposed to complain about his heart so that the doctor could issue a certificate stating that he should not be subjected to the stresses of camp life and should be allowed with his family to go into *confino libero*. So, we went to the doctor's office, where the doctor, coughing a little, said to my father very meaningfully, "Aha, I hear that you have some heart condition."

My father, like thunderbolt from the clear sky, said, "No, I have suffered from my ulcer for the last thirty years."

Thank God I was at his back to give him a nudge and whisper to him that if he would not talk about his heart, we would have to remain at Ferramonti! The interview was finally concluded successfully, and only a few days later we received the coveted authorization to go into *confino libero* in the province of Pesaro on the Adriatic Sea.

We immediately learned that, of our own people, Geza Gedalja and Dr. Gruen from Slovenia were living in *confino libero* in Pesaro. Most of our friends from Kavaja had already left the camp. Only a few remained, mostly singles in Barracks Nine. Many of our people had succeeded in finding refuge in Spain. We had learned too late that the Spanish government would issue passports to Sephardic Jews. The arrival of Himmler in Rome stirred terror among all Jews. It was rumored that he had come to demand control over all the Jews in Italy. We promptly sent a missionary to the Vatican, and he came back and asked all of us to be present at a mass of thanksgiving to God for our salvation. My uncles were writing desperate letters, not knowing what had happened to their families in Belgrade. Partly because of my friendship with Schecter, and also because I had sent a small painting to the director, we had been allowed to occupy two rooms and a kitchen for the last few months, so we had been a little more comfortable. Now we began to think ahead, and prepare for the journey to freedom in the outside world. I made a few new paintings of the camp, of the barracks, of our kitchens, and many portraits of the people who remained in the camp.

Despair and Loneliness. By Albert Alcalay.

15

Confino Libero

My FATHER, MOTHER, SISTER, AND I LEFT FERRAMONTI ON THURSDAY, December 17, 1942. We took a train, via Sibari and Taranto, to Bari and, from Bari, traveled through Foggia to Ancona, finally arriving at Pesaro, on the shores of the Adriatic, almost 150 miles to the northeast of Rome. Our trip was very long, lasting almost fourteen hours. During the southern leg of our journey, the other passengers on the train—crossbred from Moorish (Arab), Albanian, Turkish, and Eastern Mediterranean stocks—did not look at all Italian, and I reflected on what I had heard many Italians say: "Italy ends in Rome, and all beyond Rome is Africa." People boarded and disembarked from the train at the many small stations that dotted the line as we moved up the tip of the peninsula across Calabria, then through Basilicata to Taranto, and across the coastal plains of Apulia, to reach Bari, on the shores of the Adriatic. On our way, we passed through beautiful farm country cultivated with wheat fields, vineyards, and olive groves, and dotted with medieval castles. Although I had thought that I had pretty well mastered Italian, the myriad dialects that I overheard spoken on the train were completely incomprehensible to me. When, later in life, I read Carlo Levi's illuminating book *Christ Stopped at Eboli*, my mind was strengthened with a new understanding of the people I had seen on this journey.

After the Allied Air Forces began bombing Italy's great cities, the Italian authorities ordered the urban population to move to the countryside. This was largely the cause of the great commotion we were witnessing in most of the railroad stations through which our train carried us. There was an air attack on the city of Foggia while our train was standing in the station there, and we had to quickly leave the train and take shelter under the passenger cars until we heard the all-clear

180

sirens. We thanked God that a public security agent was escorting us. Without his help, and that of another agent from Pesaro who joined us at Foggia, we would not have been able to board the train with our belongings and find seats for the continuation of the journey to our destination, Pesaro.

After the bombing raid, our train quickly pulled out of Foggia, to continue its northward progress along a sinuous route, mostly hugging the Adriatic shore. The train made steady progress all the way up to Pescara, and almost one hundred miles farther to Ancona, which was the last important town before our final stop at Pesaro. All along the way, the train, which was always jammed, continued to make many stops. We witnessed confusion and distress in all of the stations, all crowded with displaced persons and with peasants dressed entirely in black, who clambered aboard with livestock and poultry, and cumbersome bundles and baskets and crates of goods. Despite the threat of bombing, the stations jammed with refugees, the chaotic conditions on our train, and all the confusions and tumult of wartime Italy, the train did run on time.

One unfortunate incident, however, did occur during our journey. The police agent who was accompanying us absentmindedly left his wallet in the train's toilet. He recovered it quickly enough, but not before someone had removed 3,000 lire from it—2,000 of which he was holding in trust for an internee who had remained at the camp. The agent thought that one of our group from Ferramonti had stolen the money, although we were not held under any suspicion. Desperate at this loss, and fearful of losing his post, the agent openly broke down into tears. Father tried to comfort him and promised to write to the young Ferber and to Miša Alađem at Ferramonti to explain the situation and ask them to intervene on the agent's behalf. Father wrote this letter that very evening.

We arrived unscathed at Pesaro, and reported to the police station there, where we were told to report the next day to collect our travel documents. We had no great difficulty finding a hotel room to shelter us for the night before continuing on the next day by bus to the small town of Macerata Feltria, which was to be our home under our newly won status of *confino libero*. Although we felt insecure in our liberty, we were thrilled to be free. We purchased a few newspapers and sat in a café, where we met with other refugees, including a pitiful man from Lublin, in Poland, who shared with us alarming accounts of transports of Jews to concentration camps. Father wept openly at these stories. These were the first reports that we had received of mass transports of Jews. We didn't know what to believe.

The next day, I set out with my father to look for a woman whom we were supposed to contact—we had been instructed to shout out *"Pipistrella!"* ("Bat!") in her courtyard—to make arrangements to have our luggage forwarded to our new home in Macerata Feltria. We also went to the police station to obtain our travel documents, since from this point forward no public security agent would be escorting us. At the entrance to the police station, we encountered a heavyset, sharp-featured, clear-eyed man, to whom we indicated the purpose of our visit.

The man inquired, "Why do you need official travel documents?"

My father answered him, "Because we were interned at Ferramonti in Calabria and have just been released into *confino libero*. When I reported here yesterday, I was told I had to request official travel documents for my family to travel on to our new home in Macerata Feltria."

The man fixed his gaze directly at father's eyes and demanded impassively, "Why were you interned?"

"Because we are doubly guilty, since we are both Jewish and Yugoslav," my father answered in an undiplomatically sarcastic and defiant tone.

The man, still impassive, his gaze still fixed on my father's eyes, said, "You Jews and Yugoslavs want to destroy states and religions."

My father answered him back, more softly, "If we want to destroy religion, why is your holy pope defending and helping us?"

"If you talk like that, you are desecrating the Catholic religion," the man retorted, now angry.

"I am not desecrating anything, since this is the truth," my father protested, "and if you don't believe it, you can inform yourself about it. After all, you did not think this way before the war, but only now when you are under the German boot."

At that moment, the secretary of the police appeared at the station entrance and invited us into his office. He was very understanding and polite, and did all that he could to be helpful to us. He gave us our travel passes. Father and I quickly returned to the hotel to collect Mother, my sister, and the little luggage that we had. We were eager to take the next bus to Macerata Feltria. Unsure of what we would find at our final destination, we were all filled with feelings of both tension and hope. On the bus, I was somehow separated from my family and took a seat by myself, way to the back, among a group of Italian passengers. One of these, a man in his early thirties, was entertaining a few women, telling them jokes that were cracking them up in laughter. Before long, this man turned toward me and asked, "And you, Mister, why don't you laugh?"

I replied, "Because I am not in the mood for laughing."

"Who are you?" he asked.

"I am a Yugoslav," I replied.

Then he said, "If you were a Yugoslav, I would eat you alive!"

I answered him, *"Sono un osso molto duro da rodere."* (I'm a hard bone to chew.) He then shut up and left me alone.

A little later, one of the ladies who had been laughing so much at the young man's jokes very carefully asked him, "Why aren't you in the army?"

He replied, "I asked to be a parachutist and am waiting for authorization."

By then, the bus had left Pesaro far behind. We were traveling through a very beautiful part of Italy, the Marche, a somewhat remote, mountainous region that even today is off the tourist's beaten path. It is filled with medieval towns, of which Urbino, the birthplace of Raphael, and the ancient seat of the Duke of Urbino, is the largest and best known, and of which Pesaro, the birthplace of Rossini, is also a fine example. It was a splendidly clear day—not quite yet winter, the 18th of December, only our first day away from Ferramonti.

We finally arrived at Macerata Feltria, where our friend Geza Gedalja was waiting for us. He helped us find lodgings at the Hotel Feltria, the mountain village's only hostelry. We soon found ourselves amid other former internees, including Dr. Mayeron, a lawyer from Ljubljana, Dr. Levi, a lawyer from Genoa, and some women, one of whom was a Jewish woman from Trieste. It came as a great shock to me to find myself in a world so far removed from the indignities, hard-

ships, and privations of life to which I had grown accustomed in the
internment camp at Ferramonti. Suddenly, we were living in well-ap-
pointed rooms with private baths in a hotel in whose dining salon we
were served meals on tables covered with white linen, and in whose
lounge we were welcome guests. It took a few days before I could adjust to civilian life. It was very nice. It felt like a vacation. But we
could ill afford such luxury and, from the outset, searched desperately
for less expensive quarters. Unfortunately, no apartments were immediately available, so we remained at the hotel for more than a month.

The hotel was a large, white, sturdy building. A functional modern
building with no distinctive architectural adornments, it had only recently been constructed. It stood in a new section of Macerata Feltria,
at the foot of a hill on the summit of which one finds the Castello di
Macerata Feltria, with its distinctive belfry and the unusual large
clock whose numerals go from VI to I. It is quite a climb up to the
Castello, along ancient streets lined with houses in brick and stone,
each slightly taller, each slightly older than the previous one, until
one reaches the still much older and much taller belfry, which juts
powerfully into the sky from the summit.

Dr. Mayeron, the Slovenian lawyer from Ljubljana, was a distinguished, kind, and civilized gentleman. Tall, with handsome features
and graying hair, he spoke in grave tones and moved slowly and ele-
gantly. His services as an excellent teacher of English were very much
in demand in our little community of war refugees. Dr. Levi was also
a fine gentleman. A firm opponent of Fascism since long before the
outbreak of war, he had been interned for many years. He and I soon
became very good friends.

We celebrated New Year's Eve in the hotel dining room with Dr.
Levi and his parents, who had come from Genoa for a holiday visit.
We all enjoyed a fine party with a good meal and pastries. Dr. Levi
ordered champagne. At his request, everyone joined in singing *Hati-
kva*, the Jewish national anthem. Our morale had been raised by
Montgomery's recent decisive defeat of German forces under Rommel
at el-Alamein. This was really the first battle that the Allied forces
had won, and news of the victory had fortified our courage and
strengthened our hopes for an early end to the war. We had also heard
rumors that the Germans were in trouble at Stalingrad. The general

atmosphere was so much brighter than it had been for a very long time.

But our good cheer and optimism, even on this evening of celebration, were tempered by the harsh realities and the dangers of our situation in a world at war. The elder Levi told us of the sufferings of his son, whom the Fascists had interned for nine years in various parts of Italy. His other son, who was a physician, could not work because of new racial laws. The authorities in Macerata, especially the major, were helpful to us in everything, but it was impossible to find an apartment. We stayed in one room in the hotel, for which we paid 2,000 lire monthly. Unfortunately, these charges did not include board, so we were quite lucky to have carried with us a good supply of marmalade and olive oil from Ferramonti! Cheese, eggs, and other foodstuffs were easily purchased from the local peasants, so we ate adequately.

As soon as we were settled in Macerata, I began to explore the surrounding countryside—very tentatively, and somewhat fearfully at first. I loved being free in the natural world, which I inspected in search of fine landscapes to capture on canvas. As the weeks went by, I spent more time painting outside. I was somewhat nervous about this. I felt that it was unwise to be so visible. But, despite my fears, this time spent out of doors did allow me to escape the confinement of my family's small living quarters at the hotel, and certainly distanced me from the irritations of my mother's constant supervision, which extended even to my painting!

January passed without any extraordinary events. In early February, a newly interned person, Count Giglucci from Florence, arrived. A very intelligent and good-looking old man, he carried himself with an aristocratic bearing and dressed in an urbane English fashion. The insecurity of his situation clearly frightened him. This was plainly evident from the nervous tension of his manner and his constantly shifting glance. He was doubtless under suspicion because his wife was British. She was a frail creature whose hearing was poor. They were living apart, but she did come to visit the count while we were together at Macerata. The old man fascinated me. I had never seen a count before, and I thought it quite extraordinary to be in the presence of an aristocrat. He was quite reticent at first, but, soon enough, we began to converse. Highly educated in the classics, history, arts, and contemporary affairs, the count could speak about almost everything.

Dr. Mayeron gave us lessons in English, and Buena studied dressmaking as well. With few distractions, and no household to maintain, Mother was bored, nervous, and meddlesome. She constantly disturbed me while I was painting. We did hear encouraging news that February of a German defeat at Stalingrad, and of Allied advances in North Africa, where Allied troops had taken Tripoli, and had pushed the Germans back into Tunisia. We also received a letter from my uncles in Germany, who wrote to say that Isak had had to be operated on for kidney stones, and that David had been hospitalized for his stomach ulcer, although it had finally been decided that he did not need an operation.

That February, a police inspector from Pesaro came to Macerata to check on our situation. He promised us that we could soon move to the small town of Pergola, where we would be able to find an apartment. Not many days later, my parents went to Pergola and found lodgings. My father told us that the secretary of the *municipio* had greeted them courteously, and had been quite considerate, but nevertheless had asked him why the Jews would not embrace Christianity. The secretary said that he considered the Jews to be a very intelligent people. He could not understand why they didn't abandon their religion, which had brought them so much suffering. My father had replied that Christians had been inhumane through centuries of persecution and genocide. Ignoring this, or in an attempt to justify Christian intolerance, the secretary rejoined that my father should accept Christianity as a superior religion, one better than the Jewish faith, which, so the secretary argued, was an archaic and outmoded tradition. My father wisely decided to be diplomatic. He conceded that Christianity was perhaps a better faith, but added that it appeared to be an ideal religion that had little to do with practical life. Father remarked to the secretary that Christians had shown themselves to be intolerant, and had shown no pity even toward innocent children.

On March 15, 1943, we traveled by bus to Pergola. En route, I spoke with some girls on the bus. When I said that I was going to Pergola, one of the girls sighed deeply, closing her eyes, and said, *"Pergola, paese di felicità!"* (Pergola, a land of happiness!) Although I did not really understand what she meant by this, I did not question her about it. I decided to explore and find out for myself.

Pergola was a beautiful, walled, medieval town. Unlike many other towns in the region, it was not set squarely on a hilltop, but arose from a highway on the slope of a deep valley. It was relatively isolated, connected only by bus to the outside world. A small river ran through the town, which consisted of clusters of three- and four-story buildings, colorfully roofed in red tiles. The townscape, punctuated by tall chimneys, was adorned with greenery. The town's most notable structures included several impressive palazzi, a cathedral, and the old town gates. Dominating the main square was the monumental colonnaded *municipio*, the largest and most impressive building in Pergola. The town hall's design was typically Italian, both in its functionality and in its psychologically powerful aesthetic statement of the building's purpose and historical significance. The streets were animated by children at play and adults in conversation or busy with their errands. The post office, the bus station, and the local offices of the Fascio (the local Fascist authority) were located on the main square, along with the town's café.

The town had a pharmacy, grocery stores, vegetable stands, a bakery, a stationary shop, a few wine shops, and a bus station. Most of these shops lined the town's well-kept main street, which led into the square. The main street was paved with large blocks of granite and was quite wide. There were no sidewalks. Every Sunday, the town held a festive procession down this street. The predominantly Renaissance-style, three- to four-story, stucco-covered buildings that lined the main street were well maintained and decorated with window lintels and other architectural elements. Almost all the windows had shutters that could be closed to keep out the sunlight and heat. The narrow side streets were lined with plain houses from which, for the most part, the stucco had fallen away, exposing crumbling facades of brick and mortar. These side streets were almost always in shadow, the high walls of the houses blocking out the direct light of the sun, except at midday. The large portals of the houses were often left open,

exposing their interiors and household furnishings and personal belongings.

My parents had found rooms in a large apartment owned by a
woman named Angelina. Widowed, with one daughter, Angelina had
very little income and resorted to renting rooms in order to survive the
difficult times. She and her daughter were welcoming and cooperative
in arranging the living quarters. The apartment was located in a building on a side street, just off the town's shop-lined principal thoroughfare, not far from the main piazza where the town café and the
municipio were located.

A very old Jewish family lived in Pergola, but, because the rules of
confino libero forbade us to mingle with Italians, we were not allowed
to interact with them. Signor Astore Camerini was the head of this
family. He lived with his wife and two of his four daughters in a large
palazzo in the center of the town. Signor Camerini was greatly respected among the townspeople. He was one of Pergola's signori, a
class of landowners who held *poderi*—allotments of land that the
peasants were hired to live on and cultivate. This arrangement—
called *mezzadria*—was a lingering vestige of medieval feudalism. The
signori and the peasants shared the harvest of the land—crops, livestock, and any other produce—in two equal parts. Both peasants and
signori paid taxes on their revenues. The signori lived very comfortably in their palazzi. They sent their children to the best private
schools and universities. In proportion to their resources, they were
free to travel, and to enjoy many of the uncommon refinements and
pleasures of life. Apart from the signori and the peasants, Pergola's
population was comprised of local officials and administrators, professionals and office workers, shopkeepers and tradesmen, kitchen gar-
deners and part-time laborers. Some of Pergola's residents usually did
not do anything at all except sit in front of their houses or spend time
at the central café, where they drank anisette, played cards, dominoes,
and billiards, and discussed almost everything—and they always
knew exactly what every citizen of the town was doing.

Among our fellow internees in Pergola were two Jewish men: Dr.
Marko Hantwurzel, a young pharmacist whom we knew from Ferramonti; and Leo Birnbaum, from Frankfurt am Main. There were also
three French women. Soon after our arrival in Pergola we also met a

newly interned gentleman, a salesman from Milan, who introduced himself as Aldo Filinić. He told us that he was Czech, but had been born in Trieste. I found it strange that he spoke neither Czech nor German, and I kept him at arm's length, but he was very intelligent and gregarious, a genial man of urbane demeanor and friendly charm that he extended to everyone he encountered.

Among the refugees we came to know in Pergola were the Spurle family—a widowed wife, with her two daughters and two sons, who had arrived from Naples. They were very decent people, but their manners were quite primitive. Although the English-born father of the family had been a teacher of English, the sons knew very little of his native language. Apparently, the Spurles had never traveled outside Naples before their flight to Pergola. The Spurle sisters spoke a heavy Neapolitan dialect, and displayed entirely parochial dispositions. The two brothers were always dressed in formal black suits with ties and stiff collars, and their shoes were always highly polished. They had pale, almost albino complexions, and light blond hair, which they slicked back with generous doses of hair oil. If their hair had any natural sheen, the hair oil dulled, rather than brightened, it. The elder brother was the taller of the two. They could always be seen *en promenade* together, strolling very slowly, almost ceremoniously, always in unison, almost as if they were Carabinieri in civilian attire. The sisters were completely uneducated. They knew nothing about the world, and habitually posed silly, sometimes imbecilic questions.

During our brief stay at the hotel in Macerata Feltria, the atmosphere had been surprisingly relaxed. The Italian official we reported to had even encouraged us to go out at night, to the movies. In Pergola, the rules governing our presence had been enforced much more severely, at least in those first days after our arrival. The officials there had absolutely forbidden us to go out at night, and told us to keep to ourselves during the day. We were free to move about the town, but only to shop for food and other necessities, and to register each day at the *municipio*. We couldn't spend time at the town's animated café. The officials instructed us to keep our contacts with the townspeople to a minimum, and they, in turn, suppressed their natural curiosity and friendliness, avoiding us out of fear, because they knew that we were being closely watched. Fortunately, we had access to the town library's fine collection of books, so we spent most of our time in our first days in Pergola reading.

Nevertheless, soon after our arrival in Pergola, I began to paint outside again. Despite the rules of *confino libero* that forbade contact with Italians, I mingled freely among the young people of the town. Schools and universities were closed, and many of the sons and daughters of the signori were at home. The young men were keeping a low profile to avoid military service. Because I was an artist, well educated and widely conversant, these urbane and intelligent young men and women accepted me immediately. I could see that there were no fascists among them, although most of their fathers had been obliged to join Fascist party organizations.

The authorities soon noticed my contacts with the local youth and warned me not to mingle with them. The secretary of the local Fascist party looked upon me as a personal enemy and was very severe about the matter. I was closely watched for several days and had to abandon any contact with my new friends. I was able to resume these relationships later, although only with the utmost discretion. Despite my unsettling contretemps with the authorities, our situation remained the same. My family, as usual, had to report to the municipio each day to register our presence and to pick up our mail, all of which was censored, and the authorities did not restrict our normal freedom of movement in the town and within two miles of its walls.

We had access to Italian newspapers and, reading between the lines, we could deduce the progress of the war. Some of our Italian friends listened to Radio London and shared solid information with us. By the spring of 1943, it was clear that the Germans and their allies had suffered a devastating defeat at Stalingrad, and were struggling on the Russian front. Hitler appealed to all the countries of the Axis and all German-occupied countries to join in the struggle against Bolshevism, but there was no evidence of any enthusiastic response to his call. In North Africa, German and Italian forces were in retreat. This news heartened us, but it did not change the fact that almost all of Europe was still tightly in Hitler's grasp, and we were sad and grief-stricken with concern for Europe's Jews, about whose fate rumors and reports swirled, in an increasingly heavy cloud of black smoke.

From our isolation in Pergola in the first days of April 1943, we sensed that the war had turned decisively toward the beginning of the end for the Third Reich. But we knew in our bones that Germany would not yield without a ferocious struggle. And we feared that the German persecution and destruction of Jews would intensify, and that its dark hand would tear us from our relative security in Italy. We were determined to save ourselves at any cost. My uncle Jakov, who lived in Lausanne, Switzerland, miraculously succeeded in obtaining passports for all of us to go to the United States, but he was unable to send them to us. We did not know at the time that the Spanish government—as if to wash its hands of an ancient guilt for the injustice and cruelties of the Inquisition—had been willingly issuing passports to all Sephardic Jews who requested them, in order to save them. If we had been aware of this, we probably would have found a way to reach the safety of a Spanish consulate. But our ordeal was to continue for two more years, and we would have to overcome many difficulties and face many fresh dangers.

We quickly adjusted to a quiet life in Pergola. I can still feel the sharp cold and humidity of the climate, and remember that it did not bother me at all. Food was plentiful and good. All of us found something to occupy our time. Although I had to be discrete in my contacts, I made many new friends and spent a great deal of time with them in their homes or in the town park. I was intensely alive to everything. I read voraciously. I thought deeply about my future and worked diligently to improve my abilities as an artist. I visited all the churches in the town, carefully examining their architecture and the paintings in them. With all of this, I felt no loneliness, yet neither did I feel that I had a real friend to whom I could open my heart. My heart was filled with anguish and hope. Most of all, my heart was hungry for affection—hungry to give and to receive.

One fine clear day in early April, I accompanied a group of lovely girls on the road outside the town. I don't remember how—I was somehow carried beyond myself—I approached a very beautiful girl with large dark eyes, dark hair, and a soft voice, and I embraced her and kissed her in front of the entire group. I was astonished that I had done this, and the girl was much more surprised than I was. The girls were completely taken aback, but they understood the moment and retreated, murmuring, so that only this girl remained. Her name was

Vittoria. It was almost a miracle, since I did not know the girls very well. While I was in their company, much of my attention had been distracted by my care at avoiding observation by the Fascist authorities, so I had participated only sporadically in the conversation.

When I later discovered that the girl I had been so powerfully drawn to was Vittoria Camerini, of Pergola's oldest Jewish family, I was twice overjoyed that I had been drawn to her—the only Jewish girl in the group. I did not feel any antipathy for Christians, but my particular situation as a Jewish refugee had accentuated my Jewish identity and had brought forward within myself a poignantly anxious awareness of Jewish angst. I had been educated in the Jewish tradition, and I unselfconsciously emanated a Jewish character, often even in spite of myself. I had suffered and had struggled to survive anti-Semitism. I felt that I shared a common destiny with my people, and I was deeply aware of the desperate plight of Jews in Hitler's Europe. I believe that Vittoria understood me immediately, and that she responded to me in part out of her own need to affirm her own identity, and to express and assuage her own anxieties, although her anxieties were not as acute as mine were. Vittoria was awakening to her own Jewish identity, and she was beginning to feel the dangers of persecution. The Jews of Italy were highly assimilated, but although some Jews had risen to high positions in Mussolini's government, life for many of them had become very difficult since the passage of anti-Semitic racial laws in 1938.

So it was with a startling kiss that a beautiful and fulfilling relationship began. Vittoria and I shared a tremendous need for understanding and empathy. We were both searching for affection. Young in a threatening and uncertain world, we were searching for something in which to invest our hopes for the future. Because the universities in Italy had been closed during the war, Vittoria had not been able to continue her studies, yet she was a highly intelligent and very serious young woman. Well educated and well read, she was an acute and perceptive listener, and was responsive in conversation. She was passionately interested in a host of topics, including history, and Jewish history in particular, politics both contemporary and theoretical, philosophy, the sciences, and literature, art, and music. From the outset, our relationship had a rich intellectual dimension, and I was able to bring to it all that I had experienced and learned. The vibrant intellectual pleasures of our relationship nurtured the emotional bonds that deepened between us in the succeeding weeks, as the love that Vittoria and I shared became more intense. I loved her with all my heart and soul. I did not search for reasons why I loved her, and I don't think she looked for reasons why she loved me. We needed each other, cared for each other, and were protective of each other.

Word of my relationship with Vittoria quickly spread through the town, and many of the townspeople commented about us. Although I was concerned about the possible dangers from the local Fascist regime—to Vittoria, to myself, and to our families—I cared little for what people thought about me. I was a self-confident and resourceful young man, and I knew what I wanted. Because of my self-confidence, because I carried myself with dignity and discretion, and perhaps because the Italians were generally weary of the war and had no desire to strike out at anyone, including the respected Camerini family, I encountered no official trouble, not even from the secretary of the local Fascist Party, who had reacted so severely to my first contacts with the young people of the town. Vittoria's family seemed indifferent to our relationship. I did manage to engage in stimulating conversation with Signor Astore Camerini on a wide range of topics. And when my father came to know the patriarch of the house of Camerini, I was happy to see that Signor Astore accorded him respect and even a degree of friendship. They shared many interests.

Vittoria had three older sisters. Signor Astore's eldest daughter was married to a Roman Jew, Angelo Anav. His second daughter, Renata, had earned a doctorate in biology, and had married a very fine philosopher, Luigi Tagliacozzo. Luigi and I formed a lasting friendship when he arrived in Pergola after the fall of Mussolini in July 1943. He was very supportive of my relationship with Vittoria. Luigi and I had intense discussions about artists and art, poetry and literature, and the creative process. These members of the Camerini family all gathered that summer in Pergola out of fear of bombardments and other difficulties in the large cities of Italy. Signor Astore's third daughter, Helena, was involved with a local young man from Pergola. All of these relatives lived in the large Camerini palazzo.

As the youngest of the four Camerini daughters, Vittoria was most closely tied to home. Signor Astore had great standing in the community and showed graciousness to many, as indeed he did to my family and me. Although he was a very knowledgeable and dedicated person, he was a man whose relationship with the younger generation was complicated by his own traditional values. He was a studious and accomplished agronomist who, from time to time, displayed flashes of pride in his mastery of the arts of agriculture and his skilled management of his *poderi*.

As my relationship with Vittoria deepened, my sense of purpose in life altered radically, and my focus shifted from within myself to our shared experience. My love for her was not a matter of emotion only, but had the effect of transforming my entire being. I remained as intensely active as I had always been, but my actions and sensations were now felt with a degree of peace and serenity that I had never before experienced. I was completely happy wandering with Vittoria through the woods and fields surrounding Pergola. We went often to one of her *poderi*, one of the many parcels of her family's land that was sharecropped by local peasants. We often spent time with the larger group of our friends. Soon after Vittoria and I became a couple, Lucia—her best friend—also found a companion in a young law student named Mario Rossi. As two couples, we enjoyed wonderful times together, meeting almost every day, often for several hours, to explore and observe everything in the immediate vicinity of Pergola.

Week after dreamlike week passed serenely, and my relationship with Vittoria was growing stronger each day. We were entirely comfortable with each other. We argued only once, when one day she wanted to teach me to dance and I refused, arguing stiffly that dancing was reactionary, bourgeois, and a shallow pretext for eroticism. But I did love music, and was gifted with a fine musical pitch and a tremendous musical memory, so I finally agreed and discovered that I very much liked dancing after all. A group of girls from the better families frequently joined us in the park. They loved my mother. One day, they made a song called "Bionda Signora" (Blonde Lady) and appeared beneath our window to serenade her. We met Signor Scandellari, a very nice man from Bologna married to one of the three French women, who was quick to assure us that her husband would become a French citizen after the war. Whenever we heard news of the Royal Air

Force's bombardment of Germany, she would repeat, *"Sehr wenig."* (Too little.)

Even as these peaceful, happy days of spring lengthened and ripened into summer, there were many chilly and rainy days when it was not comfortable to remain outside. On one such day, I offered to make a portrait of Vittoria's older sister, Helena. Helena agreed, which gave me a pretext to spend time with Vittoria at her family's palazzo. Although Signor Camerini had made me feel welcome there, we were all properly sensitive to the danger of any indiscrete contacts, so I had restrained my visits to the Camerini home. Vittoria's mother was quite reserved, barely concealing her uneasiness about her daughter's connections with a refugee in *confino libero.*

By early summer, the atmosphere in Pergola had changed. It was evident that the Italians wanted nothing more to do with the war. The forces for peace within the Italian government were growing stronger, and the alliance between Italy and Germany was nearing the breaking point. The Camerini family became increasingly fearful that German forces might occupy Italy. Reacting to the constantly circulating rumors that German troops were about to arrive in Pergola, Signor Camerini, fearful for the safety of his youngest daughters, often sent Vittoria and Helena to stay at one of the Camerini *poderi* two or three miles away, outside of town. I would rendezvous with Vittoria in the countryside, making my way separately to join her, and returning alone. When it became clear that there was no immediate danger, Vittoria and Helena returned to the Camerini palazzo in Pergola, and Vittoria and I resumed the normal rhythms of our relationship, always vigilant toward the dangers that surrounded us, and the dangers that we all feared were drawing closer.

The Allied invasion of Sicily in July gave rise to a great deal of talk that the Royal Air Force might bombard Rome. These rumors of an impending air attack provoked a sudden exodus from the Italian capital. The Roman side of the Camerini family soon arrived in Pergola to take shelter at the Camerini palazzo, where there was ample room to accommodate them all. The fall from power of Mussolini and the Italian Fascists at the end of the month was generally greeted with a muted excitement that quickly faded to an uneasy state of suspended expectations. Those of us with the status of *confino libero* were the most affected by the change. Doubtless fearful of reprisals, the deposed local Fascist authorities faded immediately into the background. We no longer had to fear them, and, overnight, everyone in the town tried to befriend us.

I was relieved and happy to be able to meet more openly with my many friends. Achille Caverni, who had attended school with Vittoria, was among the closest of my companions. He was studying medicine. His old uncle owned the town's hardware store. One of three brothers and three sisters, Achille came from a large, well-landed seigniorial family. Achille's family was traditional and Catholic: honest, very religious, direct and unsophisticated—largely unaffected by technology and modern mores. Achille was very interested in art, he dabbled in it himself, and I gave him some lessons. He was intellectually curious and had questions about everything, even religion. Although a devout Catholic, he did not uncritically accept the parochial preaching of his family's church.

In late July, after the Allied conquest of Sicily, Italy's king, Victor Emmanuel III, ordered the arrest of Mussolini and charged Marshal Pietro Badoglio with forming a new government. The government decided to continue in the war on the side of Germany. Allied air bombardments of cities on the Italian mainland grew in intensity day after day, creating great alarm among the urban population and swelling the flow of refugees. Everyone now was openly listening to Radio London. The Germans had little confidence in the new Italian government, and were pouring troops into northern Italy. Some of our friends who were interned in the north wrote anxious letters filled with dark suggestions about what was going to happen. But there was still no sign of the Germans in Pergola, and our situation there remained the same. The townspeople continued to be cordial, especially the newly emerged anti-Fascists among them. The police gave me permission to do portraits but, because of their outlandish security concerns, they forbade me to paint any landscapes.

As we had done from the beginning, we anxiously sought news of our relatives we had left behind in Belgrade, but our persistent efforts were now more futile than ever. The Vatican and the Red Cross wrote to us that they could not obtain any information whatsoever. We were beginning to fear that something horrible had happened. We had heard many terrifying stories and had just learned from a Polish refugee that trains had been arriving in Poland packed with Jewish deportees from France and Belgium, many of whom had perished in transit. These bitter revelations tore at painful anxieties that had been with us for many, many months, and I bleakly focused on my memory of a man I had met at Ferramonti. A mournful soul, he had always dressed in black. He had constantly asked if anyone had heard any news about a group of Polish Jews who had been sent to Lublin. The man had made a meager living in the camp as a tea-seller, but one day he simply stopped working, repeating over and over again, "Why should I work anymore? There is no one from my family alive anymore. They killed them all in Poland, so who should I work for?"

I often discussed this situation with Vittoria's brothers-in-law, Angelo Anav and Luigi Tagliacozzo, who were then both staying with their families at the Camerini palazzo. In spite of my intense concern, they could not seriously accept the idea of any real threat from the Nazis. I told them not to have confidence in anybody except close friends, and that they should all be prepared to flee. I underscored the potential gravity of the situation with accounts of my experience of the German occupation of Yugoslavia. I succeeded in stirring up Signor Astore a bit, at least to the point where he began to consider how to save his family. Although life in Pergola remained deceptively calm, everyone began to feel the growing threat of German occupation and the persecutions and hardships that would come with it. We were all tensely alert for any fresh information, interpreting the news that came to us over the radio from London and Rome, and even Moscow, trying to form an accurate picture of what was really happening. Over the British airwaves came insistent demands that the Italians surrender unconditionally; these demands were supported by innumerable Italian anti-Fascists who had been in exile since the now-deposed Mussolini had come to power. The Germans continued to concentrate troops in the north and, by August, in central Italy as well. As the days passed, and pressures mounted, it became more and more certain that the situation was becoming increasingly explosive. The increasing German presence in Italy was a real threat to the Jewish population. I passed many sleepless nights struggling to find a way to escape the calamity that was about to befall all of us. I shared my deepest feelings about the situation with Vittoria, and also with Achille. They were my closest friends, and they shared my alarm—more than did many others among us.

The Allies struck across the Strait of Messina on September 3, 1943. A few days later, Badoglio's government announced an armistice. We received the news with jubilation. Celebrations broke out in Pergola, where the local anti-Fascists ordered the authorities to ring the bells in all the churches. Aldo and Scandellari joined in the celebration, went to a bar, and got intoxicated. Overnight, our official status was completely reversed. We could come and go as we pleased. Local officials told us that we were no longer interned, and that we no longer had to register at the *municipio* each day. But I questioned the durability of any liberty in an Italy that was effectively occupied by German troops, and many of us were soon sobered by our grave appraisal of the immediate consequences of the developments. We knew that the Germans would react soon.

I discussed the situation intensely with Achille, and asked him to help me find a monastery isolated in the mountains where I could seek refuge. I also asked Achille to obtain topographic maps of the region for me, thinking that it would soon be essential to have them. Achille and I set out almost immediately on a two-day journey into the mountains to visit a Carmelite monastery, where I met with the Father Superior, who assured me that I could find shelter at the monastery if I needed it. It was already the middle of September when we returned to Pergola a few days later. The town was in complete confusion. German parachutists had rescued Mussolini, and German troops had occupied Rome. Count Ciano had been placed under arrest, and Marshal Badoglio and King Emmanuel had fled to the protection of the Allies. My father wanted to flee to the south immediately, but my mother would not want to hear a word of that. Vittoria confided to me where she would hide if something happened unexpectedly—with a trusted family of peasants on one of the many *poderi* that her family held—and I consulted with her brothers-in-law, Luigi and Angelo, who were now fully alive to the danger of the situation.

I asked Luigi and Angelo to talk to Signor Astore, to see if he could secure refuge in a convent for the women of the family. I talked to Signor Astore myself, and struggled to convince him that it was urgent to arrange this, arguing that the men of the family would be able to move about more freely if security could somewhere be assured for the women. But Signor Astore was unwilling to take instructions from me. He answered coldly that he would make his own arrangements. If the need arose, he would scatter his family on different *poderi* with his trustworthy peasants, and then decide what to do. I was furious with him, but I now certainly understand how difficult it was for him to accept my advice about how to protect himself and his family from the Nazis. Now, for the first time, their Jewish identity endangered the entire Camerini family.

Confusion in Italy intensified as October approached. After the Germans rescued Mussolini and established control in the occupied north, Italy was effectively divided into two countries at the front line. The German authorities immediately reconstituted the Italian Fascists into a new party organization, now called the Republican Fascist Party, and installed a puppet Italian Socialist Republic under Mussolini. A mood of despair settled over the people of Pergola, as the Fascist authorities moved to reassert their authority. We were again obliged to register each day, but we felt no other changes. Pergola was an isolated town, so we saw only a few Germans, and there was no official German presence there during this period.

Throughout the tense weeks of late September and early October, everyone listened intensely for news from the front lines. Naples was liberated and, in mid-October, we heard that Marshal Badoglio's Italian government-in-exile had declared war against Germany. The Allied forces quickly consolidated their hold in the south, but the Germans checked them along a line that stretched from a point to the north of Naples across the Apennines to the mouth of the Sangro River, almost one hundred miles to the south of Pergola. As October dwindled, and the first days of November fell away, we strained to hear news of a fresh Allied advance, but we received no such news, and our hopes frayed and our desperation mounted.

I slept little during this turbulent time. I jumped out of bed at the sound of each passing truck. We received news that Jewish-owned shops had been looted in Rome. From London came warnings over the radio that Jews should flee or take to hiding. It was then more dangerous for many to travel than to remain where they were, so the flow of refugees to Pergola slowed, but refugees from the fighting at the front and other points of danger were still arriving to seek shelter in the town or to transit through the town in search of safety elsewhere. We received a small group of Yugoslav internees into our home for a few days. They had fled from Arezzo to the west. When the local authorities learned of this after our guests had departed, a Fascist official came to our door and chastised us for our charity, sternly instructing us never again to take in refugees. We dutifully acknowledged his warning, happy enough not to be thrown into prison for our kindness, but just as ready to help the next people in need we might encounter.

In early November, Signor Camerini sent Vittoria and the other women of his family to the relatively safe shelter of the Camerini *poderi* scattered around nearby Montesecco. I continued in my efforts to find a more secure refuge for Vittoria and a safe harbor for my family. Achille brought me any map he could get his hands on. I studied all of them carefully, making notes, measuring distances, marking the locations of houses, churches, and other landmarks. I reconnoitered nearby villages to see if I could locate a house or a stable or any kind of secure shelter to rent. I failed to find anything, but I was successful in mapping out several different routes of escape. I did everything I could to prepare for a sudden departure, should that become necessary. I bought a flashlight, a compass, a knife, and a few other useful tools, and told my mother to gather the most essential belongings— shirts, socks, warm pants—and to sew knapsacks in which we could carry them and any other necessities, so that our hands would be free, allowing us to move more quickly if we had to flee. Always keeping one ear trained to a radio, I was preoccupied with these preparations for several weeks, successfully completing them by mid-November, which proved to be just in time.

The mood in Pergola that November was depressed and sullen, the sky low and gray. We had written in October to our friend Geza Gedalja in Macerata Feltria to see what his intentions were, but we had received no answer. By November, we could feel the danger in the air and in the fearful and downcast eyes of the townspeople. Some people suggested the idea—both ridiculous and deplorable—that only Italian Jews would be persecuted, and that we would be left alone. There was no comfort for us in such thoughts.

Sometime after the middle of the month, we received the first dreaded word of impending trouble from Miša Adler, whom we were surprised to stumble upon in the streets of Pergola. Miša was fleeing from the nearby town of Urbania, where for many months he had resided in *confino libero*. He told us, breathlessly, that an order to arrest all the Jews had been received in Pesaro. He did not know if this order also extended to refugees in *confino libero*, either Jews or any others. Miša was traveling under forged travel documents that Geza had obtained for him for one hundred lire. He urged us to move toward Rome, even without authorization, arguing that it would be easier to hide in a large city. He bade us farewell, and hastened furtively away. This encounter left us deeply sad and bewildered. We simply did not know what to do, whether we should flee and, if so, in what direction.

More disturbing news came to us very early the next morning, when our friend Aldo rushed excitedly over to our apartment to tell us that an order to arrest all the Jews had just been broadcast over the official Italian radio. But it was still unclear—to Aldo, to all of us—if this order included refugees. I raced off to Montesecco to see how Vittoria was. She was astonished that we had not yet left Pergola. She begged me to flee immediately. I embraced her, and quickly returned home. That very afternoon, Signora Mikoulis—I did not know her, but she had some connection with my mother—came to tell us that we were in great danger, and that we had to leave as quickly as we could. The atmosphere was charged with tension. Shaken, I was gathering myself to try to reach a decision, when Aldo arrived to play cards with my father, as he customarily did every afternoon. Compared to his excited state earlier in the day, Aldo was surprisingly nonchalant. My father, however, was not in a relaxed frame of mind, and quietly excused himself from the game. Soon afterward, himself undecided as to what we should do, my father went for a walk with my sister. In the last light of a gray afternoon, they encountered our fellow internee, Mr. Spurle, who told my father that he had learned from an unnamed lady that the town police had received official notice over the telephone that they were to arrest all Jews. The police were expecting written confirmation of this order within a day. My father asked Mr. Spurle if he would talk to his landlord, Massaioli, to ask if we could rent his villa in the nearby village. He promised that he would do so.

My father returned home deeply disturbed. There would be no time to rent villas. Only a half hour after my father and sister returned home, a young girl I did not know came to our door with a message from Vittoria's elder sister, Helena, telling us that we had to leave immediately. It was clear that the time had come to depart, but we were still frozen in indecision, until Lidia Buccellati arrived early that evening with news from her father, the town postmaster. He had received a telegram that he was supposed to deliver immediately to the Carabinieri. He had bravely decided to hold it overnight to give everyone a chance to escape. The telegram was the expected written confirmation of the order to arrest all Jews and foreigners. It also contained instructions to deliver them to assembly points where they would be loaded onto trains and shipped to the north. The meaning was clear—we were to be placed in German concentration camps, to perish or to endure whatever bleak fate awaited us there.

In the autumn of 1943, we knew nothing about the "Final Solution." We did not know that the extermination of the Jewish people was the policy of the German state. But we knew it in our bones, and we knew that we had to avoid falling into German hands, at any cost. As soon as night and sleep had fallen over Pergola, we would leave Pergola behind—"*Pergola, paese di felicità . . .*"

16

In Flight and Hiding

NIGHT HAD FALLEN OVER PERGOLA BY THE TIME LIDIA BUCCELLATI
brought us the final warning that we must depart immediately. As soon
as she had left us, I declared to my family that we would have to leave
within a half hour. Everyone in the town would by then have retired
for their supper, and we could make our escape unseen along the
route that I had planned. We hadn't yet had supper ourselves, but
nobody cared for one. As we were frantically preparing to depart,
young Marko Hantwurzel came to our door—we had first met him at
Ferramonti—and he too wanted to leave Pergola, but he had no idea
how to leave or where to go, and he was penniless.

It didn't take us long to gather the necessities for our escape. We
had anticipated that we might be forced to flee Pergola, and everything was well prepared. We had to leave most of our belongings behind. I entrusted the most valuable of these to Capanoni, the town
druggist. He lived just across the street from us and had earlier agreed
to safeguard anything that we would have to leave behind. In less than
thirty minutes, we were gathered in a silent knot at our door. Before
we set out into the night beyond our darkened threshold, I told my
parents and sister to follow quickly and silently behind me along our
escape route—down darkened alleys and side streets, cutting through
narrow backyards, until we reached the cluster of poor houses at Birarella, just beyond the town wall, where we could somewhat slow our
pace. Marko Hantwurzel departed with us. He was a sullen and un-
congenial young man, but I recognized that we were all in the same
boat, so, with some prompting from my father, I grudgingly accepted
that he had joined us.

We reached Birarella without incident and were soon skirting along
the margin of the road to Montesecco, a road that I knew well, having

so many times taken it with Vittoria. It was a clear night. We walked in silence, always keeping as close as possible to the cover of brush along the roadside, each of us deeply immersed in thought, each intensely alive to the dangers of the moment. We were afraid of being captured by the Carabinieri, who were likely to be patrolling the outskirts of town. We had taken no time to eat, but no one complained of hunger. The road was gradually becoming steeper, and I heard the quickened breathing of my parents as we climbed away from the town. All of my senses were sharpened, alert for any noise or signs of movement in the dark. As we continued up the steep incline, I suddenly became aware of something behind us. Silently motioning everyone into the cover of bushes in a field beside the road, I looked out, half-hidden, down into the half-light that scarcely illumined the ribbon of dust that led out of Pergola. I soon distinguished the shadowy forms of three men walking bicycles uphill. At first I thought that it was a patrol. But, when one of them called out in a muffled voice, "Alberto, Alberto!" I instantly recognized them to be men of the Camerini family.

Signor Astore had finally decided that the danger to his family was real, so, earlier that day, before the warnings of an impending roundup had spread through the town, he had set out with Angelo and Luigi to seek out secure shelter for the Camerini family, even considering the possibility of hiding the women in a convent. When they returned that evening to Pergola, they had found the Camerini palazzo closed, dark, and empty, and learned of the order to arrest all Jews and foreigners. They set out immediately for Montesecco, where they assumed the women of their family had taken refuge. Luigi knew that I had intended to take the Montesecco road out of town, and it was probably he who spotted and recognized us just before I signaled to our group to hide. Our brief roadside reunion was quiet and grim, but we were relieved and happy to see each other. I told Signor Astore that he had to move his family from Montesecco immediately. Everyone in Pergola knew the locations of the Camerini *poderi*, and the Carabinieri were sure to search for them there as soon as the following morning. After our muted consultations, we wished each other good luck and safety. Luigi, Angelo, and Signor Camerini were soon swallowed by the night, as they went on toward Montesecco. I led our group of five down the road and took a fork to the right, toward the tiny village of Sterletto.

Thanks to the kindness of a peasant who dwelled in a house on this same road, we found shelter for the night. We told the peasant that we were from San Lorenzo, and were going to Pergola. My mother and sister shared a rude peasant bed. Marko, my father, and I bedded down on some straw in the stable. The night had grown very cold, and I shivered sleeplessly in the frigid stable. Thus began, in that December of 1943, an exile within an exile inside wartime Italy—almost two years of hardship for my family and me. We no longer had the status of even refugees. When we crossed the darkened threshold of our home in Pergola that night, we became fugitives. Stripped of any civil rights, we could depend only on the kindness of strangers, and the limited purchase of our purse. We had to avoid any contact with authorities. We could not enter any city, town, or even a village. We could not use any kind of transportation. We could not even walk openly on the roads, because they were constantly patrolled.

We were confronted with complete uncertainty, and our lives were in danger. I was torn with anxiety, as well as with feelings of sorrow and grief. I was also suffering a broken heart, since the fork in the road to Montesecco had not only marked a rupture with our life in Pergola, to which I had so well adapted, but also the end of the idyllic relationship between myself and Vittoria, a relationship that had brought to each of us so much joy. Even if Vittoria and I were to survive the ordeal that now lay before us, we were destined to endure it apart from each other, and would be so marked by it that we might never again be able to recapture what we had now lost. The war and a shared sense of the destiny of our people had brought us together, and it was the irresistible force of the war that was now tearing us apart.

But I had never lost hope for life, for an intensive and positive life, and for fulfillment in which I could find the rewards of satisfaction. I believe now that my early education in the Jewish movement had given me the strength that I needed to make the difficult passage that was before me. My friends and I had grown up with the ideal of transforming the Jewish people, reaffirming our roots in the soil as a primary source of life, becoming heroes of the land, content to live the collective life of the kibbutz, and to raise a new generation that would be freed of the historical burden of our people. Although the circumstances of life had infinitely distanced me from participation in the realization of this ideal of transformation in Israel, I deeply felt the moral force of my education and ideals as an independent strength within me, as if a new Israel had already been built within my heart. I was also supported by the dialectical perspectives of my intellectual training—my knowledge of the historical process, economic issues, and political forces, the very structures of society. Thus, the strength that I drew from my moral and intellectual education reinforced the blessing of a psychological capacity to transcend the difficulties of the moment, and afforded me the strength, courage, and vision to meet the challenges of uncertainty and the mortal threats that shadowed our fugitive lives.

Moreover, I was not alone. If I were not sufficiently strengthened by inner character, my responsibility to protect my family certainly focused my resolve to survive. I had an older father, an ailing mother, and an adolescent sister with me, and I had to care for all of them. We had already survived so much. If we were entering the darkest period now, I could and did reason to myself, it must mean that we were at the midpoint in the dark tunnel of our passage through the war. We would simply have to move forward, in any way that we could, until first a pinprick, and then a small circle of light would grow into the bursting sunlight of light, and hope, and life itself restored.

The next morning, at dawn, we said good-bye to the peasant of Sterletto. We thanked him warmly for his hospitality and expressed our hope that we would see him again. None of us had been able to sleep at all, and my mother was complaining, as usual, but there was nothing we could do for her. Despite all that she and our family had already endured, it would yet take a long and bitter time before Mother understood and accepted that no one could help her, that no one could make the situation better. We first took a small road—I always had my maps at my hands—and continued to walk. But of course we had to avoid the roads, so we soon took a much harder and slower passage across broken ground and muddy fields, clambering over fences, and pulling ourselves up slippery embankments. Our caution was hardly extreme—we had already seen two cars packed with Carabinieri on patrol. Although there was no certainty that we could find shelter there, I was leading my family to the family homestead of my best friend, Achille Caverni. It was situated on the outskirts of the village of Caudino, about twelve miles away. The house where Achille had been raised stood empty there, with only a peasant caretaker, a miller, and their families living in separate quarters on the ground floor.

Our march toward Caudino was difficult. Although it was a clear, crisp December day, my father and mother were perspiring heavily, and had to stop every hundred yards or so to catch their breath. I understood that my parents could not take much walking across the countryside, and that we would have to find suitable shelter without delay. I hoped that Achille's house would offer the safe refuge that we needed. We were advancing slowly, but safely, toward our goal. I had fixed its location on one of my maps—it was just over a mile past Caudino, at the base of a line of sparsely populated, forested ridges dotted with isolated houses, tiny settlements, small farms, and pasturage. As we skirted Caudino, the sun gleamed on the summit of Monte Sant'Angelo, which rose only a couple of miles beyond the village. Although the Caverni homestead was half-hidden, situated some fifty yards from the road, I remembered its location well. Achille had pointed it out to me several times, and I had marked it on my maps. Even cutting through the countryside away from the road, I was able to guide my family to it. As we approached the house across a field that stretched behind it, I easily recognized the impressive three-story stone building and quickly stepped forward to meet a group of peasant boys, who accompanied me to the house. My family and Marko followed in my tracks, arriving only minutes later.

The peasant caretaker, who occupied the ground floor of the house, was a simple, good-natured man named Santino. A blond, tobacco-stained mustache hung over his mouth, which was always fixed in a warm, and rather merry, grin. He was very polite, and he wanted to help us, but he did not have the key to the upper floor, and, besides, he did not have permission to admit us to the apartment. Santino invited us into his home, and seated us in a big kitchen with a large fireplace, which also served as a stove. The kettle hung there, and it was the center of the household. Santino and his wife had only one child, their daughter Annetta. An animated, pleasant girl of sixteen or seventeen, she was surprisingly well spoken, certainly more articulate than her parents. I sent one of the young boys who had accompanied me to the house—it turned out that he was the miller's son—to Pergola on his bicycle, with the charge of finding Achille and delivering to him a letter that I had quickly dashed off. While we waited for Achille's reply, Santino gave us a bit of wine and some cheese, and provided my mother a place to lie down and rest. The miller's son returned that afternoon with Achille's regretful reply that we could not stay at the house, because it would be too dangerous. One of his cousins—an Italian officer who had deserted the army—was hiding there. Achille feared that the police, who were searching for deserters, might look for him there, and would then also find us. He enclosed a thousand lire with his note—as payment for a portrait that I had painted of his small niece.

For the Italian peasant at this time, the local priest was the first person to seek advice from or to consult in the making of any decision, so Santino suggested that we call Don Domenico, the priest of the nearby village of Caudino. After some brief hesitation, I agreed to this, and off again went the miller's son to call for him. Don Domenico came immediately. A direct and energetic young man, he was not a priest who hid behind the sacramental roles of his office. We told him that we were Yugoslav Jews who had fled from Pergola because of the order issued by Mussolini's newly German-installed government to arrest all Jews and foreigners. Before his overthrow and subsequent return to power, Mussolini and Count Ciano had protected the Jews in Italy. But now, Count Ciano had already been executed, and Mussolini was merely a puppet in the hands of the Germans. Despite the clear danger of helping refugees, Don Domenico did not hesitate to extend a helping hand to us. He advised us to go to the peasant Boccanera, whose house was perched on top of the hill. The priest instructed us to tell Boccanera that he had sent us, and assured us that he would look into other places where we could take refuge. He promised that he would be in touch with us as soon as possible.

By the time we received the disappointing news from Achille and had visited with Don Domenico, the mid-December sun was already sinking toward the horizon. There was no time to lose if we were to reach the home of Boccanera before nightfall, so we bid farewell to Santino and his family, and to the village priest who had so kindly come to our aid. We set out for what we hoped would be a sure refuge. We climbed the country lane steeply snaking up the hillside. It was painful for me to see my parents struggle, panting and perspiring heavily in the chill of the oncoming twilight, pleading constantly that we stop to rest. I had earlier slung my mother's pack on top of my own, and I now offered to take father's pack as well, but he proudly refused. Marko moved ahead, offering no help, and looking impatiently back at us. I was proud of my sister Buena, who struggled forward without complaint. But I had to pull Mother along, as she wept at her own reduced state, too weak to climb the steep hill unassisted. We moved very slowly, but the sun was just setting when, finally, exhausted and soiled with the effort, we arrived at Boccanera's door.

But our hopes for food and shelter were again disappointed. Despite our desperate condition and our pleadings, despite even the authority of Don Domenico's word, Boccanera would not take us in. He had no room for us, he insisted, because he was already sheltering masons who were enlarging his house, and he didn't have enough room even for them. He was resolute in his refusal, and sent us to his neighbor, Anselmo Bucci, who lived at least two miles away. So, we started numbly downhill in the direction that he pointed, through a plowed field, the mud caking heavily on our shoes, so that our descent became very difficult, even for me. In addition to the load I was carrying, I had to support and pull my mother along. She no longer had energy for tears, but she groaned with each heavy step. It was such an abrupt change for her, leaving behind our relatively comfortable and secure life in Pergola to face such a painful and dangerous ordeal.

We were still trudging through cultivated fields when the last gray twilight slipped away. We could hear dogs barking from time to time and also, occasionally, the sound of passing vehicles. Night had completely fallen when we arrived in front of Bucci's house. I stretched the truth when I told him that Don Domenico had sent us, but Bucci welcomed us warmly when he heard this introduction. Bucci was a prosperous peasant. He was a widower, but he did not live alone. His household included his eldest son, Riccardo, and his wife and their three small children, as well as Riccardo's two younger brothers and a poor young village boy, who tended Bucci's sheep and goats. I immediately opened a conversation with them all, explaining that that we were traveling from the north. But it was late, and Bucci, seeing that we were famished and exhausted, offered us some bread and cheese and wine, which we gratefully accepted, while he decided upon our sleeping arrangements. Mother, Father, and my sister Buena collapsed into the bed that the two younger brothers normally shared with the young shepherd. Displaced from their bed, these young men slept beside Marko and me in the kitchen in front of the fireplace. The house was soon quiet. I slept deeply that night. I think we all did.

We awoke the next morning, somewhat restored by our sleep, but quite sore from the hardships we had endured. Bucci was all cheer. He was jubilant and proud at the thought that Don Domenico had sent us to him, interpreting this as an expression of the priest's confidence in him as a man of Christian virtue and kindness. I did not explain to Bucci that Don Domenico had originally recommended us to the kindness of his neighbor Boccanera, and that it was Boccanera, who may not have had quite such good standing with Bucci as the priest, who had sent us on to him. But I was confident that Don Domenico would be happy to learn that we had found shelter, and that the good priest would grant to Bucci the honor that so seemed to please him, without betraying that this had not been his first thought. I immediately started to try to determine the best way to let Don Domenico know where we were, but I needn't have been concerned about this, as the village priests had their own very effective ways of knowing everything that was going on in their parishes.

If the kindly peasant Bucci was pleased with the honors of charity, his son Riccardo was not quite so friendly. He didn't complain about our presence, but, unlike his carefree father, he gave no evidence of being happy about it. After breakfast that morning, Bucci accompanied me to the property of another, even more prosperous, peasant named Paoletti, thinking that he might be able to help us. But Paoletti refused us outright, declaring in an arrogant voice that he saw no reason to take anyone in. When I offered to pay him well, he dismissed me, shrugging: "What can you pay me? I have eighteen *poderi!*" Confronted with this hostile response, I recognized that it was useless and degrading to speak further with the man. I had never seen an Italian behave so harshly. Troubled and disappointed, Bucci and I returned across the fields to his house.

My mother was suffering terrible stomach cramps and was confined to the bed. We talked with Bucci's family—Riccardo's little daughter called my father *"Omo!"* (a child's rendition of *uomo,* or "man") and my mother *"Donna!"* (woman)—with what energy and enthusiasm we could muster. Apart from my abortive visit to see Paoletti, we remained indoors to avoid being seen by other peasants. We certainly wanted to avoid drawing any attention to our presence there—or bringing any danger to our hosts and to ourselves. But it was likely that the entire village was already aware that refugees from the north were staying at Bucci's house. Doubtless, neither Boccanera nor Paoletti saw any reason to keep our presence secret, and even if they hadn't spoken about it, I was sure that the news of our arrival would quickly become commonly known in the village community, just as naturally as water flows downhill. The danger to us all—including our hosts—was real. Every moment was precious, and the need for shelter anywhere had to be calculated carefully against the risk of discovery and capture.

That day happened to be a Catholic holiday, and when I heard that Bucci was thinking of going to church, I encouraged him to do so and to speak with Don Domenico, who was at this point our surest friend and would certainly praise Bucci for his kindness, and perhaps encourage him to shelter us until we could find another place of refuge. Soon after Bucci's return, I asked him if we could stay for another few days, at least until my mother's condition had improved. Despite the danger of the situation, Bucci kindly agreed, his kindness perhaps fortified by Don Domenico's praise—although I never learned if Bucci had spoken with the priest.

And so, we stayed at Bucci's house for an entire week, until one morning, Riccardo's wife, Armanda, returned with the news that peasants at the village church had told her that we were from Pergola, and that the police were asking for us and knew that we were in the area, and that they had telegraphed arrest orders to the police command post in Arcevia. Bucci was a fine human being, full of empathy and understanding. He had been aware of the danger, but he had allowed us to stay, despite Riccardo's harder appraisal of the risks of this kindness, and the sullen disapproval of our presence that had mounted in the younger man with each passing day. But now it was clearly time to move on. The Carabinieri could appear at the door at any time to arrest us, and to punish the Bucci family as well. When Father gave Bucci five hundred lire for his trouble, Bucci returned a hundred lire to him, explaining that five hundred was too much.

I decided that we would head for Sassoferrato, which was quite far from Bucci's house. Bucci warned us to avoid the Fascists at Cabernardi, a sulfur mine by which we had to pass. Bucci instinctively offered to transport us in his ox-driven cart, but Riccardo discouraged him from this, and I told the kind old widower that we appreciated his offer of help, but that we did not want him to expose himself and his family to any more danger. Don Domenico came to Bucci's house just as we were preparing to leave. He gave us the names of priests at San Giani and at Santo Stefano who might be able to help us to find lodging. I thanked him warmly for this—we were all so grateful to him for his help and friendship. Taking the priest aside, I asked him if he could obtain false documents for us, explaining that we could not go on like this for very long. Don Domenico promised to do all that he could for us, and instructed me to contact him in ten days. I thanked him again, and told him that I would find a way to reach him, if we survived, adding that if my family could obtain false papers, we would take a train for Rome and hide there in the anonymity of the big city.

We set out from Bucci's house only hours after Armanda returned with the news that the police were closing in on us. We walked the entire afternoon across muddy fields and broken countryside without seeing a single soul or even a humble dwelling. I didn't force the pace, and Mother and Father and Buena held up bravely through the ordeal of the day's march. Marko was uncomplaining, at times even helpful. I studied my compass and maps, and kept our path in the direction of Sassoferrato. Apart from seeking suitable shelter for the night, I didn't have any specific destination, although I did intend to follow Don Domenico's advice and seek help from the priests at San Giani or Santo Stefano. Late in the afternoon, we spotted a house perched alongside a country road, and decided to seek shelter there. Completely exhausted, our shoes heavily caked with mud, we went straight to the door and knocked. I requested hospitality from the woman who opened the door, and immediately offered to pay her for her kindness, but as quickly she refused us, telling me that she had no room at all.

She looked suspiciously at us, as I turned to my parents and sister and told them to huddle together for warmth and to try to rest while I went with Marko to speak to the priest. When the woman heard this, she was perhaps reminded of her Christian duty. For whatever reason, she relented and invited my parents and sister into the kitchen to warm up, while Marko and I went down the road to speak to the local priest.

Soon after Marko and I had set out, the woman's husband appeared in the kitchen where my family had wearily taken seats beside the stove. The woman explained that she was not refusing us *per cattiveria* (out of orneriness), but because she had no room. My father was so numb with everything that had happened to us within such a short time that it took him several minutes to explain that we were from San Lorenzo. Seeing our heavily mud-caked shoes, the husband expressed his surprise, noting that the roads were dry. My father explained that we had taken a wrong road on our way to Macerata, where we were hoping to stay on the *podere* of a doctor and friend. Because we had lost so much time, we had attempted to make shortcuts through the muddy fields. Finally, Marco and I returned, having had no luck in finding anything with the help of the priest, who was less responsive than Don Domenico had been. The husband, whose name was Gino Friscott, said that he would help us to find some kind of lodging. Just after nightfall, we did find a bed for my father, mother, and sister with a woman named Teresa Rosa, and Marko and I were allowed to bed down on the floor of her kitchen.

My family had experienced eight days of harrowing hardship and disappointment since the night we had fled Pergola. None of my plans had worked out. My hope of finding refuge at Achille's family homestead had been disappointed, and Don Domenico had not yet been able to find anything for us. I spent the next two days stealthily combing the surrounding countryside to find a refuge for us, studying my topographical maps for houses as isolated and as far from roads as possible, but all my efforts yielded nothing. I knew that we could not stay long at Teresa Rosa's. She had not welcomed us out of kindness, but rather, I believed, because she saw an opportunity to profit from our misfortune. We had stayed at Teresa's for three days, and were preparing to move on, when a peasant woman related to Teresa came to her house declaring excitedly that word had spread that five Jews were hiding somewhere in the area, and that they were willing to pay a great sum of money for shelter. The woman said that the Fascist authorities were looking for us, and that they would kill us.

The woman's words of alarm sharpened desperate anxieties only allayed by our weariness, and we were torn, unable to decide whether it would be safer to remain at Teresa's or to expose ourselves in the open countryside with no clear idea of where we were going. Teresa seemed to be ready to negotiate to let us stay, but I didn't trust her. I believed that she would willingly betray us, if she could find a way to profit from turning us in. On the other hand, she had already put herself in some danger by allowing us to remain for the three days that we had spent in her house, and if she judged that it was safe enough to let us stay, in exchange for whatever payment she felt she could extract from us, then perhaps it was best to remain there.

Because we felt that we would be at greater risk if we didn't move on, we left Teresa's house, but we were filled with apprehension for what might strike us next. We set off toward Santo Stefano, in hope of finding help from a priest there whose name Don Domenico had given me, but we didn't go far. Mother was in pain, and I grew more and more anxious that something terrible might happen to us if we continued. I knew that Mother could not endure travel across the rough countryside, but we would be too exposed if we remained on the roads. We took a risk and asked for help at a house that looked promising, but the peasants turned us away. I realized that we could not go on. Simply asking for help exposed us to fresh dangers, so I said that we would have to return to Teresa's until we could find a better path to safety. There was little debate about this—we all knew that the Fascist authorities were looking for us.

And so, only a few hours after our departure, we were again at Teresa's door. Although I didn't trust her intentions, we had no viable alternative. I explained to her that we were waiting for word from Don Domenico, that our friend the doctor was at Sassoferrato, and that it didn't make sense, after all, to move on until we were assured that the doctor was there to receive us. Teresa agreed to let us stay, but only if we would pay one hundred lire daily for room and board, and if Marco and I would sleep in the storage area. Given the risk that Teresa was running in taking us in, and because we had no other choice, we accepted her terms in an anxious spirit of gratitude and suspicion. We settled back into the house. We didn't know what our next move would be. My tortured thoughts cast in every direction for an answer to what we should do. We were painfully alert to any noise. The sound of approaching cars especially excited our anxieties. But we did have a roof over our heads and would have enough to eat. Mother and Father could rest and recover some strength. Perhaps the police would not be too energetic in their search for us. Teresa had not extorted too much payment from us. And Don Domenico might yet find a more secure refuge for us. For the moment, we were surviving.

With winter almost upon us on the twelfth day of our flight from Pergola, we felt somewhat settled, at least for the moment. Father decided that it was time to strike a festive note to cheer us all. He bought a large turkey for two hundred and forty lire, and we enjoyed a real meal in which Teresa, as well as her husband, daughter, her brother, and a neighboring peasant woman joined us. But our fare was meager in the days that followed. Teresa provided us bread and black coffee at breakfast—without sugar. We dined at noon on a thin vegetable soup or spaghetti with bread. Each evening, Teresa set out a few apples for her husband's supper and went off with her daughter to visit a friend. Fortunately, we were able to purchase some ham and cheese, and we shared these provisions with Teresa's husband.

A week after our return to her house, Teresa announced that she had found a local man who would be willing to take us to Macerata in his truck. This would have made it possible to reach the estate of our doctor friend at Sassoferrato, but we didn't yet know if he would be there to receive us, and we were afraid that such a journey would be too risky, so we decided not to leave immediately. We needed more time to consider other possibilities, so I explained to Teresa that we had to visit the priest at Caudino to see if the priest there had received word from our friend. Marko and I set out immediately. As we headed toward Caudino to contact Don Domenico, we explored the surrounding area for suitable lodgings, still hopeful, despite my earlier failed efforts, to discover any alternative that would be safer than Teresa's house. We would be able to move on, but only if Don Domenico had been able to procure the identity documents that we needed. It would still be dangerous, but with papers we would have a much better chance to avoid being detained.

As it turned out, Don Domenico had learned that we were at Teresa's. The good priest had not forgotten us. While Marko and I were off to Caudino, he arrived at Teresa's, on a motorcycle, like a goggled Flying Dutchman in a curiously futuristic movie, his black vestments flapping in the dust behind him as he sped down the unpaved country road. He comforted my family and assured Father that he was doing everything he could to find a safe refuge for us, explaining that he had looked in Arcevia and Sassoferrato, but had not yet found anything.

Our progress toward Caudino was slowed by the care we had to take to avoid being seen, a care that we had to take even more scrupulously as we approached the small village. When Marko and I failed to find Don Domenico there, we went on to visit Bucci, who received us warmly with his gentle smile. I told him that it was dangerous for us, that we really didn't know where to go, and asked him if he could take us in one more time. He regarded me kindly and replied that he was willing to shelter us, but he didn't want more quarrels with his son Riccardo, who wanted nothing to do with the situation. The police had not come to Bucci's house in search of us, as Riccardo's wife Armanda had warned they would, but sheltering us would still be very dangerous. I thanked Bucci for his kindness, and said that I would speak with Riccardo, to see if we could reach an understanding.

Taking Riccardo to one side, I asked for his help and understanding. I acknowledged the danger that we brought to his household. Yes, we were fugitives, but we were not criminals. My father was an important figure. After the war, he wouldn't forget who had helped us. The Fascists would not stay in power for long. But Riccardo had good reason to refuse us. He explained that he wanted to help us, but he had to protect his own family. The Germans and Italian Fascists had posted warnings everywhere, instructing the population that anyone aiding or sheltering Jews and anti-Fascists would be executed and their homes would be razed. Riccardo looked me straight in the eye, his features fixed in grim lines. He told me that he had three young children, and that he was a quiet person who did not want to get involved. I answered that I understood his fears, and that I admired his devotion to his family. I passionately told him that I recognized that we were all at risk, that I deeply appreciated everyone's help, especially that of Don Domenico, who was also courting danger in his efforts to help us survive the difficult passage. I told Riccardo that we would only need his help for a short time. We were waiting for instructions from an important authority, and would soon move on and leave him in peace. My mother was not well. She could barely walk, and would not survive the hardship of exposure to winter in the open countryside. My father would compensate him well for his troubles now, and after the war would compensate him even more. I understood the risks, and I respected him, but I was also trying to protect my own family, and I was asking for his respect, and for his understanding and help.

Finally Riccardo relented, but only reluctantly. He said that he would accept in silence our return to his father's house, but only if we stayed for no more than ten days, and only if we remained hidden indoors for the entire time. Riccardo insisted that my family would have to leave Bucci's house immediately at the first sign that the police suspected that we were being harbored there. This troubled me, but I assented. I thanked Riccardo and Bucci for their understanding and kindness, and told them that I would return with my family the next night under cover of darkness.

So, Marko and I headed back to Teresa's house at Sassoferrato. We were grateful to have any shelter, but our past week there had been difficult, and I wanted to leave. As Marko and I stealthily made our return, I brooded on Riccardo's reluctance to accept my family at his father's house. My nerves were drawn tight, and I was very sensitive to any rejection, and, however well I understood and respected his anxieties, I couldn't help resenting that I had been forced to plea for Riccardo's help, and that he had placed so many conditions on it. I wondered if it was wise, after all, to lead my family back to Bucci's. The situation was dangerous for everyone. Could I trust Riccardo not to throw us out? He was right to be afraid. But did he have the moral courage to resist his own fear?

When Marko and I finally returned, unseen, to Teresa's, late in the afternoon, Father told me of Don Domenico's visit, and that the priest had not yet found a place for us. I gave Father a full account of our day, telling him that I was really undecided about returning to Bucci's. I simply did not know if we could rely on Riccardo. In such a dangerous situation, how could we trust a man so riddled with fear? Riccardo might overreact to a rumor and, in panic, order us out of the house. Worse, it was even possible that he might turn us in to the authorities, if he believed, rightly or wrongly, that this was the only way to save himself and his family. But I could see no safe alternatives, and none of us wanted to remain where we were.

I examined the situation from every angle, in search of a solution that would promise the greatest security to my family, but much of my thinking was really pointless speculation on hypothetical situations, which left me with no real rational basis upon which to arrive at a sound decision. I ultimately realized that I would have to rely on my instincts. Self-aware, I knew that my instinct would be to move forward, to change the situation, but even my instincts were confounded, because a return to Bucci's would be moving in a circle, and not at all taking a bold new direction. My father was tormented and repeated over and over: "Where now, where now?" I tried to both calm him and encourage him, saying that we had already survived so much, and that we would surely find a way to go on. My mother had suffered a hemorrhage of her uterus and was bedridden. She would barely be able to walk. All the roads were now completely controlled. The Fascist authorities had now even officially organized the flow of refugees from the large cities into tightly monitored truck convoys. We were afraid to move on.

But we recognized that we had to move on. Teresa had treated us with harsh disrespect, and had offered only paltry meals to us. She knew that we were Jewish refugees and wanted to be rid of us, unless she could draw some real advantage from our continued stay. She was irritated that we had not decided to hire the local man to transport us to Macerata in his truck. She didn't seem to be afraid of the police, but she had no particular compassion for Jews and foreigners. Our way of speaking the Serbian language among ourselves annoyed her, and she was offended that Buena had refused to go to church with her and her daughter. She disliked Marko intensely. Although he spoke the best Italian among us, his behavior was surly and sullen, and he spent all his time smoking cheap, malodorous cigarettes, in silence.

Teresa, who had unsympathetically witnessed our tortured indecision, finally broke in abruptly and told us to decide what we wanted to do. For her part, she continued, she would allow us to stay in the storage shed attached to the rear of the house. She could provide us with two beds, and we could somewhere find a woodstove so we could cook for ourselves. She added scornfully that she would also agree to give us a cup to share among ourselves. I barely resisted an urge to shout out angrily at her for the sake of human dignity. I could see in her eyes that she wanted to profit from us, and at the same time to degrade us. My mother, who is of a choleric nature, was the first to lose control, and burst out sharply to her that she should have more heart in these uncertain times. Teresa answered her that the heart was only one organ of the body. My father moved to calm my mother, and asked Teresa how much he owed her for the ten days that we had stayed in her house. When she demanded one thousand lire, my father protested, saying that he had paid more than two hundred lire for the turkey that we had all shared together, and that Teresa had given us so little food, and also that Marko and I had been absent from the house for two days of our stay. At this, Teresa went into a rage, and shouted menacingly, "Greedy Jews, out of my house!" Her husband—a friendly man, who was fond of the Jewish legends of the Bible, especially the story of how Samson, armed only with a donkey's bone, had killed one thousand Philistines—tried ineffectually to quiet Teresa, but she continued to scream and swear at us.

Teresa's outpouring of anger and hate shocked all of us. My father tried to motion for calm, raising his arms before him as if to deflect Teresa's blows from the family. Marko silently continued to smoke, taking in the scene with his customary sullen passivity. When I had heard enough from Teresa, I stood straight in front of her and shouted directly to her face, yelling angrily that we would denounce her to the police for harboring us, if that's what she wanted. Obviously, she knew that we were Jews, and she was ready enough to practice her own private scheme of extortion against us! What would the authorities think of that! We were Jews, and we were proud of it! My people had not harmed anyone, but our homes had been bombed, our friends and families had been tortured, imprisoned, and assassinated, and we had been forced into exile, and had finally been driven to seek shelter at such places as her house. As Jews, we were no strangers to the values of compassion and understanding. What was she as a Christian? Who was she to treat us in such a degrading manner? If we had had any choice, we would not have looked to her for help. Regardless of the dangers outside, we had too much self-respect to remain in her home. I would not hire her to clean my shoes. I shouted to her that my father was an important banker. I yelled that we would return after the war to search out people like her who had practiced extortion on people in distress.

My indignant rage caught Teresa off guard and reduced her to silence. Her stance was still defiant, but, with my harsh words still reverberating in the room, I had stripped her of her arrogance. I had had the last word. Teresa no longer had any power over us. My entire family was astonished at the vehemence of my speech. Everybody was completely silent. Teresa's husband looked sidewise at his wife. A good man, of quiet disposition, he had witnessed her self-serving and overpowering arrogance over many years, and doubtless had suffered directly from it himself. I thought that he was smiling quietly inside—I was sure that I read tacit approval in the crinkling of his eyes—for this may have been the first time in his life that he had seen someone face his wife down. I wouldn't say now that Teresa was an evil personality, but the pressures of the war did transform bad natures into worse ones and sometimes into evil ones, just as, in so many cases, it challenged and uplifted many good natures into better ones, and sometimes to saintliness. The silence hung in the room, until I calmly broke it with a simple declaration: "We will give you seven hundred and fifty lire, and you had better be content with it."

Thanks to whatever providence watched over us, a tempestuous storm beat down furiously on the house that night, and we were all confined inside. If Teresa had been tempted to denounce us to the authorities, she could not act on it. By dawn, the storm had calmed to a steady beat of cold, driving rain. I remained sleepless, as I had the entire night, to keep a watchful eye on Teresa. The rain slackened late in the morning, when Father and I helped Mother out the door, and Buena and Marko filed quietly after us, to set out for the long, difficult walk to Bucci's house, which we expected to reach after nightfall. I was apprehensive about returning to Bucci's. I was still mulling over my doubts about Riccardo. But any thought that we should remain at Teresa's had been completely extinguished, and I judged that we would be safer closer to Caudino. The police didn't seem to be looking for us there—it was too close to Pergola, perhaps, and we had already been gone for almost three weeks. Besides, Don Domenico would be close at hand. I believed that he sincerely wanted to help us, and his help still promised our best chance to find a safe refuge. Perhaps he could send word to Achille in Pergola to see if he could help in some way. Perhaps Achille would be able to send some news about Vittoria.

My thoughts never strayed far from Vittoria during those difficult days. I thought about her during the wakeful nights, and when I slept, I dreamt of her, and she was vibrantly present in the borderland between waking and sleeping that was my usual state in the earliest hours of those bleak December mornings. Dreaming or awake, Vittoria was a palpable presence that brought love and peace to my soul. It was Vittoria's presence within me that cradled hope, like a child with the promise of a brighter future. As each difficult day collapsed seamlessly into the next, Vittoria's presence grew stronger and became a sustaining light to me in my personal struggle to survive and to assure the survival of my family. When the inhumanity of our situation became too oppressive, when I felt worse than a homeless dog, Vittoria's presence lifted me and gave me the physical will to go on. Her presence was real to me—it was more than a dream, more than an idealized image, more than the conception of brighter times past or future—and it gave me the strength to transcend the real dangers, the utter uncertainty, and the physical hardship that challenged us every day. I believed that I was similarly present within her spirit, and that I was similarly a source of strength to her. These feelings were not romantic, at least not in a conventional sense. I did not think of Vittoria in possessive terms. Our communion was rather one that palpably reunited a sundered destiny, of which she carried one half, and I the other. And so, as we left Teresa's house behind, Vittoria's presence eased my troubled mind and gave me the strength to move forward and survive. My thoughts became clearer and my resolve stronger, as I measured each difficult step as a step toward Vittoria, and peace, and happiness.

As our small band made its way toward Bucci's house, the cold drizzle of rain built in intensity to a steady downpour, which soaked all of us to the skin. I was worried about Mother and Father and

Buena, who were all shivering violently in the cold, but no one complained, not even Mother, supported by Father and me at her sides, as we continued stoically forward. The fields were utterly impassable seas of mud, so we had to travel on the country roads, but we encountered no traffic or any other signs of life along the way, and I didn't feel that we were in any danger of discovery. Everyone, including Teresa, I felt assured, would remain housebound on such a day. The roads themselves were muddy under the pelting rain, but we made good progress, and I soon realized that we would arrive at Bucci's house before nightfall, which would be too early.

Early that afternoon, we came upon the small village of Camerano. We took shelter in a peasant home, where we warmed ourselves and dried our clothes as well as we could. Our pause there served a double purpose. Cold, drenched, and exhausted, we needed to rest, and we also needed to delay our arrival to Bucci's until after dark. Although we had passed through Camerano only two weeks earlier, none of us had any memory of having been there, so we were astonished when our hosts warmly took us in, saying that they had wondered what had become of us. They were fine fellows—two brothers. An exploding mine had stricken one of them blind. I quickly developed a strong rapport with the other, a fierce anti-Fascist, with whom I dashed off to a neighboring house, where we listened to Radio Moscow. This sympathetic company, and the opportunity to hear reports of events in the outside world, constituted a rare tonic for me. When the brothers offered us shelter for the night, we were sorely tempted to accept, but despite the harshness of the weather, I reluctantly decided that we should try to keep our appointed rendezvous at Bucci's. So, barely two hours after our arrival, we set out again.

Our brief stop at Camerano strengthened my faith in humanity and put me in a brighter mood, so I felt optimistic as we set out in the gray half-light of the tempestuous winter afternoon for the last leg of our day's journey. The downpour, which had continued unabated during our pause, beat down on us even more intensely as we struggled down the steep grade of the mountain road toward Caudino. The steady rainfall had turned the road into a treacherous river of mud, so we stayed to the side as much as we could, grasping, whenever possible, the branches of trees and shrubs for support as, step after step, we pulled our feet out of the mud. After almost an hour of bitter struggling and painfully slow progress, we realized that we would have to seek any kind of shelter that we could find. When we came upon a peasant homestead beside the road, I decided to ask if we could take shelter in the stable until the rain stopped. A kindly old peasant named Mastucci greeted us. He was appalled that we were traveling on such a rude day, and quickly invited us into his home, shaking his head and saying that we could not possibly continue on the muddy roads.

Mastucci headed a large household of almost twenty children and grandchildren, all members of one big family. We had hardly entered the house when the family crowded around us to help us out of our sodden overcoats and to settle us as comfortably as possible before the hearth to dry off and chase the chill out of our bones. Mixed with this warm reception was a chorus of wonder that we should be traveling on such a day, but the Mastucci family did not pepper us with questions about who we were or where we were going. This did not mean that they were not acutely curious about our sudden appearance. They observed us closely, but their polite restraint and discretion was characteristic of the Italian peasantry, who passed their lives with a certain reverence for city people, and especially for the signori on whom they depended. Without demanding explanations, they quickly understood well enough who we were, a daughter of the family later confiding to me that they knew that we had stayed at Bucci's almost two weeks earlier. Even as they observed us with respectful discretion, the family told us in joyous unison about themselves, proudly declaring that they had received a prize from Mussolini because their family had farmed the same land for nine hundred years. I was astonished to learn this, and reflected admiringly how deeply the people of Italy were rooted in the land. We also learned that Mastucci had lost a son in the war.

We were all arrayed around the hearth in the Mastucci kitchen, which was the principal room of the house. A huge blackened kettle hung over the fire. As conversation ebbed and flowed around us, I looked to Father and Mother and to Buena, who had remained silent, apart from a few brief responses and wan smiles of gratitude. My father had wrapped his arm protectively around Mother, who was rocking gently, staring into the flames and drinking up their warmth.

Marko was crouched on his knees at a corner of the hearth, absorbed in the task of drying his diminished stock of cigarettes, which he had lined up like soldiers on a board that he held to the fire. Mastucci quietly attended to the details of hospitality, instructing two of his sons to sleep in a neighboring house, while his wife attended to supper, mixing ingredients into the black kettle, which she tended with a long wooden ladle.

Our supper was a mush of cornmeal called polenta, a dish commonly eaten in the north of Italy, especially in the Veneto. As soon as his wife signaled that it was ready, Signor Mastucci called everyone to table. The cheerfully discordant music of benches and chairs being pulled across the stone floor mixed with laughter and a babbling of voices old and young as everyone—almost two dozen souls in all—gathered around a large rectangular expanse of hewn wood polished with many decades of constant use. With no setting of any kind—no dishes, no glassware, nothing—the table was completely empty, but the smiling and expectant faces of the Mastucci clan, each with a wooden spoon in hand, was a sure sign that this would soon change. One of the Mastucci daughters gently herded us to our places and handed each of us a spoon. I was puzzled. Seeing everyone clasping a spoon, but with no other evidence of supper on the table, I thought that we were about to witness some kind of traditional spoon ceremony or game. But, at that moment, Signora Mastucci, with the help of two of her grandsons, lifted the heavy kettle from the cast iron arm that held it over the hearth and hauled it to the table. She then gingerly upended the hot kettle and evenly spread the steaming polenta in a half-inch layer over almost the entire surface of the table.

After Mastucci intoned a prayer over this provender, the entire family, with our group tentatively following their example, dug into the polenta with their spoons, each spoon pushing toward the center of the table. There was plenty to eat, and the simple meal was surprisingly good and warming. No one spoke. There was only the sound of the spoons hitting the table. The only movement was that of the circular motion of the spoons from table to mouth, the motion of the spoons becoming elliptical as the polenta at the margins was consumed and the remaining portion receded to the center of the table. It was an unforgettable spectacle. Within ten minutes the table was clean, and all the spoons at rest. Mastucci then set upon the table an enormous bottle of wine, encased in woven straw—it must have been a ten-liter bottle—and brought out three glasses. And so we ended our supper, with our stomachs filled and warmed with the polenta, and with the warmth of the wine coursing through our veins.

Our experience at Mastucci's was a revelation to me. Although by this time my experience of Italy—and my sense of its ancient civilization—had become broad and deep, I had never anywhere before that evening had such a profound sense of the past living within the present. Filled with a sense of well-being after our simple meal at his table, I absorbed everything in Mastucci's home and reflected on the utter absence of anything modern there. My eye and spirit cast over every detail of the household, and every gesture of its occupants. I savored how much of the archaic past was reflected in the way of life that I was privileged to witness, and in the hospitality my family and I were so grateful to receive. Here, I reflected, was the real strength of Italy, the real identity, the real support, the backbone of the Italian nation. It was in the homes of the peasantry that a national identity had been for countless generations preserved and passed along from one generation to the next. I felt, that evening, that I was, unforgettably, experiencing the purest expression of the core of the Italian spirit, an essence that had persisted through the slow evolution and all the regional variations of customs over centuries, the shifting shapes of language and song, building styles, and the myriad aspects of human life and culture. Italy's history was a rich tapestry that mixed the vibrant colors of Roman imperial triumph with the violent shades of conquest, occupation, and subjugation at the hands of so many peoples, from the Goths of Alaric and the Vandals of Odacar, to the Germans and the French, and now—to Hitler's Nazis. Italy had risen to modern nationhood through the tumultuous competition of papal authority, city-states, and invaders. But for me, on that evening, the tumult and pageantry of history counted for nothing, as I sat, warmed with good Umbrian wine, as a privileged guest at Mastucci's table. For those moments, at least, the vanities and madness of what is so often mistaken for civilization were held at bay by something truer, something that seemed more ancient than history itself.

Late in the afternoon of the next day, the time came to move on to

Bucci's. After expressing our thanks, and after a prolonged exchange
of warm farewells with everyone in the enchanting Mastucci household, I led my family and Marko away. The rain had ended before
dawn that morning, but the roads and fields were still deeply choked
with mud, so our progress toward Bucci's was extremely difficult. No
vehicles could move on the roads, and we encountered no one apart
from a few lonely shepherds who observed our tortured pilgrimage
from a distance. Our shoes were sucked into the mud with each step,
and we had to stop constantly to catch our breath and gather our
strength to go on. As a chill twilight settled over the still countryside,
we had to turn off the shoulder of road and cut across a plowed field
to approach Bucci's home unseen. This final passage was almost impossible. Halfway across the field, Mother and Father sank helplessly
to their calves in the mire, and I had to dig, and push, and lift their
legs free. We then struggled forward together, with me between
Mother and Father, my arms wrapped around their waists, lifting them
forward step after painful step, as I exerted myself beyond any
strength I had ever known myself to have. We finally reached the other
side of the field, where Marko and Buena, ghostly shadows in the last
little light of the day, were silently waiting for us. We were very close
to Bucci's, but we remained hidden in the brush for another hour,
until night had completely fallen.

When I tapped lightly on the door of Bucci's house that night, it
was the third week, almost to the hour, since our flight from Pergola.
My parents, whose strength was entirely spent, could barely make it
up the few stone steps to the house, and could barely raise their heads
to smile their relief and gratitude when Bucci shepherded us through
the door into the dimly lit front room. My parents suffered even more
from shame than from their utter exhaustion—shame at the sight we
made after three weeks of moving around without regular sleep or
food, and without any opportunity to bathe. We indeed made quite a
spectacle, our damp and filthy clothing slathered with mud and hanging misshapen on our gaunt, exhausted frames, as we stood inside the
door, unsure of our welcome. Bucci stood before us, his arms half
open in welcome, and half open as if to question us. I shot a glance at
Riccardo, who was standing back in the shadows, his face impassive,
and his posture rigid.

The House of Bucci. By Albert Alcalay.

My mother's sobs broke the silence of the room, and it was Riccardo's wife, Armanda, whose soft voice uttered the first words spoken, as she moved to comfort her. Armanda told Mother that a bed was already prepared for the family, that we should take some warm soup and bread, and then that we should sleep. Armanda said that she had been worried when we had not arrived the previous night when we had been expected. She guided Mother and Buena into the small room that we were all to share, and, giving them coarse woolen shifts, gently told them to shed their soiled clothing. She then rushed to the kitchen, reappearing moments later with a large basin of steaming water, and two hand cloths. Gathering up the discarded clothing of my mother and sister, she laid them in a heap on a bench beside the kitchen table, and returned to Mother and Buena with two large cups of soup and some pieces of bread. Armanda then directed my father, Marko, and me into the kitchen, where she also gave us soup and bread. She then filled a basin with scalding water from the kettle over the hearth, set the steaming basin down on the table beside a few neatly folded squares of cloth, and turned to Bucci and Riccardo, quietly issuing firm instructions to them. She then bade us good night. Riccardo and Bucci gave fresh shirts and trousers to Father, Marko, and me, and told us that we should sleep together in the room with my mother and sister, telling us that they had laid out pallets of straw there for Marko and me. I knew that Mother wouldn't like sleeping in the same room with Marko—she had developed a real animosity toward him—but we were all close to collapsing, and there was already enough tension in the air, so I chose not to add to it with any quibbling about sleeping arrangements. After Father, Marko, and I had eaten, washed, and changed, we filed into the room, where Mother and Buena were already curled up and deeply asleep.

We slept late into the following day, and awoke within minutes of each other, the men first to leave the room for the kitchen, where we found Riccardo and Bucci seated at the table, and our freshly washed and boiled clothes permeated with wood smoke, but dry and folded on a bench set in front of the kitchen hearth. The house was quiet. There was no sign of Armanda and her three small children, nor any sign of Riccardo's two younger brothers, or of the young shepherd boy who lived with them. Bucci gently motioned to us to join him and Riccardo at the table, and solemnly offered us some wine and bread and cheese. With Riccardo seated silently at his side, Bucci explained that he understood the difficulties of our situation, and that he wanted to help, but he could not shelter us for more than the ten days that we had agreed upon. It wasn't a matter of money. It was simply too dangerous for his family, and for us as well. Riccardo then reasserted that we would have to stay inside the entire time. Too many people in the village knew that we had stayed there. The police had not questioned them, but this could happen at any time. And if there were any sign of trouble, we would have to leave immediately. Marko left the table while Riccardo was speaking and crouched in front of the fire, from which he lit one of his battered cigarettes. Father and I thanked Bucci and Riccardo for their help, and assured them that we well understood the situation, and that we would move on at the end of ten days. I admitted that I didn't know where we would go, but said that I was hopeful that Don Domenico would soon find shelter for us. Father insisted that Bucci accept the thousand lire that he pressed into his hand. Soon afterward, Armanda and her three small children shyly appeared in the kitchen, followed moments later by Mother and Buena. That night we ate well, very well, at Bucci's table, after Bucci's family returned from the church in Caudino, where they attended a Christmas Eve mass given by Don Domenico.

The ten days passed so quickly. Despite the fear and tension that our presence brought into their household, Bucci and his family treated us kindly. Mother remained almost constantly in bed, but it was clear that she was regaining some of her strength. And, after a few days of rest, Father had recovered a measure of his dignity and appeared to be well. We celebrated the New Year—1944—with the Bucci family, enjoying a fine feast together and toasting our hopes that the war would end by Easter. Almost three years had passed since the German invasion of Yugoslavia had uprooted our lives. In April 1941, my parents and sister had fled Belgrade under German bombardment. In early June 1941, I had managed to return to the city under German occupation, and had narrowly escaped it the following August. We knew that the Germans would eventually be defeated, but with Italy now under German occupation, the prospects for the survival of our family seemed never to have been worse. Don Domenico came to the house by night a few days after Christmas. He told us that there was a promising prospect that Don Nicola, the priest of Costa near Arcevia, could provide us with shelter. He urged us to be patient and to trust in providence. But we had heard nothing more from the priest, when, on New Year's Day, Bucci reminded us, with resigned firmness, that he expected us to leave within the next two or three days. And, after the New Year, Riccardo made no effort to restrain his bitter impatience to be rid of the danger of harboring us.

From the first day of our stay at Bucci's, I tortured my mind to determine what we should do next. I knew that we could not stay there longer than ten days, and I became more and more discouraged and desperate as each day melted through sleepless nights into the next. Constrained to remain inside the house, I could not reconnoiter the surrounding area for other shelter, and I realized that, even had I been free to do so, there would be little or no chance of finding anything. I considered returning to Camerano, to request shelter of the two brothers there. I even considered returning to Mastucci's teeming household, where perhaps we would be welcome. But I knew, in my heart, that we would have to find a place of hiding more discrete than these would prove to be. Don Domenico, who offered us our best hope, and who, I had no doubt, had worked earnestly to secure a safe harbor for us, had had no success. Without identity papers, which Don Domenico had not succeeded in obtaining for us, we would be detained immediately if any authority stopped us on the roads. And even if we had such papers, I was sure that the Nazis had tightened their grip in the cities, where it would now be more dangerous to seek refuge, even lost in the anonymity of the crowd, even if we could reach a large city, and even if we could clear or somehow bypass the many checkpoints on the constantly patrolled roads. I could see no way that we would be able to remain near Caudino. Our presence in the area was widely known, and if the authorities had not succeeded in capturing us, or had not even made any real effort to do so, they had certainly succeeded in spreading fear among the local population that it would be extremely dangerous to harbor us. Everywhere I turned, I came up against impediments. Numb with self-doubt, my mind paralyzed, I had only Don Domenico's kind counsel to rely on: not to lose hope, to keep up my courage, to trust in providence. But, with no real solution in sight, the good priest's encouragement meant less and less to me as the days passed away, and tension mounted in the household. I watched Riccardo day and night, fearing that he might snap and denounce us.

I finally decided that, when we were forced back into the open, I would try to lead the family across the ridges beyond Caudino, to the higher reaches of Monte Sant'Angelo. Perhaps I could hope to find shelter for the family in that relatively remote region, and Marko and I could join the partisan Resistance that was centered there. Perhaps! If we were destined to perish, then I could at least die fighting. But I never really believed that this was a real choice for us. I could see no promise in such a plan for the survival of my parents and my sister. The journey, difficult for anyone, would almost certainly be impossible for Mother. And Marko had given me no reason to believe that he would be willing to join in any struggle. But the desperate idea of joining the partisans—even with the probability that they would not welcome us, and the certainty that there would be no place for my parents and sister among them—was the least impossible of the impossible choices before us, and it gave me something to present to Riccardo to demonstrate to him that we did not intend to stay beyond the ten-day limit of our welcome. I made arrangements with one of Bucci's younger sons to guide us, at least part of the way. I hoped against hope that a surer path to survival would somehow open to us. I knew that my plan had no chance of success, and I was already contemplating the bitter prospect of abandoning my family and going on alone.

Hoping that Don Domenico would succeed in his efforts to find us secure shelter, we lingered at Bucci's as long as we could. After dinner, on the tenth night of our stay—this was the evening of January 2—Riccardo told me coldly that we would have to leave the next day. I simply said that we would set out after dark the next night, toward Monte Sant'Angelo. I turned to one of Bucci's younger sons, who had agreed to guide us to the partisans there, and told him that we wouldn't need his help, though we were thankful to him for his willingness to accompany us, just as we were thankful to the entire family for all the kindness that they had shown to us. My father then stepped in and gave each of Riccardo's three children a coin, telling them to keep our secret, to tell no one that we were going to Monte Sant'Angelo. My first reaction to my father's gesture was that it was pointless at best, and at worst that it would endanger us. When he impressed upon the children's young minds that our destination was a secret, he assured that they would remember it as something important, making it all the more likely that they would share it with their young friends in the village, despite their father having forbidden them to mention us to anyone at all. But I then reflected that we would be long gone before the children would have any opportunity to say anything to anyone outside the family, and, if they did, it would hardly matter. Our plan to join the partisans was a desperate gambit anyway—one that we would probably not survive. If we were to survive, some other solution miraculously would have to present itself, in which case the rumor that we had gone to join the partisans could serve our interest. After all, Don Domenico and Father and I had agreed that we would act as if this was our only plan, desperate as it was.

Don Domenico's advice to trust in providence proved wise, for a heavy snowfall on the night of January 2, and well into the morning of January 3, blanketed the countryside with more than three feet of snow. Until it melted away, it was impossible to leave Bucci's house, and the authorities could not reach us there to arrest us. Despite the snow, Riccardo was furious when we did not leave the house. There was nothing that we could do. We remained huddled in our room for another week. This miraculous reprieve caused me to wonder if some providence was watching over us after all. I felt that we had been spared from a sentence of death, just as I had felt in Belgrade, when I narrowly avoided being counted among every fifth man—I was counted fourth—in the Nazi lineup of Jewish men who were selected for execution as reprisal for a Resistance attack on German soldiers. But Riccardo's glowering rage, and his determination to expel us as soon as possible, embittered this period of reprieve. We were completely isolated in the household during our final week there, and we knew that we would soon have to move on.

As the protective shield of snow gradually melted away, tension in the Bucci household mounted. On the seventh day, the temperature dropped sharply, transforming the landscape of mud and melting snow into an icy wasteland. Riccardo would not speak to us, so it was Bucci who sadly told us that morning that we could no longer remain in his house. We would have to leave immediately. He said that we could stay for another day or two in a barn some fifty yards behind the house, but warned that Riccardo had threatened to denounce us to the authorities as vagrant Gypsies if we lingered any longer. Mother was in tears at the frightening prospect of leaving Bucci's home. Father and Buena were mute with fear. Marko retreated even more profoundly into his sullen passivity. It was left to me to gather our few possessions into our backpacks and herd our group outside into the cold. Bucci, Riccardo, and Armanda witnessed our departure silently, with Riccardo's two younger brothers in the background behind them. There was no sign of the young shepherd boy or of Riccardo's three young children. Marko, Buena, and my father were the first to file out the front door. Our eyes were downcast. No words were exchanged. Just after I had helped Mother, still weeping, climb down the icy front steps, Armanda darted forward and managed to press a package of food into my arms before Riccardo angrily pulled her back into the house and slammed the door shut.

We stood for a few moments, paralyzed in horror in front of Bucci's house. I then led the family across the frozen yard to the cold barn, where I made a bed of straw for my mother and father and sister in an empty stall between the meager warmth of two stabled cows. Marko, who had dropped his sullen mask for an expression of weakness and fear, looked at me with dumb expectation, which I met with a bitter shrug. Ripped with remorse, I paced the barn, half resolved to abandon my family and to go on alone to join the partisans. Barely an hour later, when every hope seemed finally to have been exhausted, and I had almost decided to set out on my own, a miracle occurred. My friend Achille appeared at the door of the barn. Achille had learned through Don Domenico that we were in hiding at Bucci's. His appearance at the door of the house had caused a bitter outburst of anger and argument between Bucci and Riccardo. Achille's visit sharpened Riccardo's fears that our presence at Bucci's had become too widely known, and Riccardo had shouted to Bucci that he wanted us off the property altogether. Achille's timely visit stunned all of us and renewed a faint hope that perhaps, with his help, we could find a way to survive. I shared my despair with Achille. Shocked to see my parents and sister shivering on their bed of straw in the filthy stall, he was

In the Field of the Bucci Family. By Albert Alcalay.

saddened to hear the chronicle of what we had endured and alarmed at the utter precariousness of our situation. I couldn't bring myself to tell Achille that I had almost decided to abandon my family. I told him that we had to leave that night or no later than nightfall of the next day, and that I would lead the family toward Monte Sant'Angelo, where I hoped against hope that I would be able to find a way for them to survive, and where I planned to join the partisan Resistance, as that was all that was left to me to do. Achille did not linger. He told us to remain where we were until the next morning. He said he would visit Don Domenico immediately, but he made no promises. When he left us in the barn that afternoon, I didn't believe that I would ever see him again. I have never felt more lost than I felt during the long, bitterly cold, and sleepless night that followed, but I had resolved to stay with my family, at least for one more day.

Don Domenico came to us at first light the next morning. He had managed to communicate with Don Nicola, the priest at Costa. As a last resort, Don Nicola had appealed to his niece to take us in, but she had refused. But Don Domenico came with better news than this. His eyes warmly gleaming, he pressed a large iron key into my hand. This, he told me, was the key to the upstairs apartment at Achille's family homestead near Caudino, where a month earlier we had first sought shelter. Don Domenico explained to me that Achille's cousin had moved on, although he didn't offer any explanation of why he had left—or where he had gone. After contacting Don Domenico in Caudino, Achille had spoken with his parents, and then met with Santino, the peasant caretaker of the property, who had told him that there had been no sign of police surveillance. The priest passed along to us Achille's firm instructions that we should tell absolutely no one where we were going, and, once we had arrived, that we should keep out of sight and live as quietly as possible, so that the upper floor that we were to occupy would appear to any observer to be uninhabited. Don Domenico told us to enter the apartment that night, without disturbing Santino or his family. Only Achille, the priest, and Santino and his family were to know that we were there. Achille would supply us through Santino with all the provisions that we would need. Don Domenico said that we shouldn't expect to see him soon. Santino would keep him informed of how we were doing. He promised to visit us

later, after the situation had calmed and the awareness of our presence in the region had been obscured by rumors that we had gone on
to Monte Sant'Angelo and had not since been seen. Before leaving,
Don Domenico went to Bucci's house, doubtless to calm Riccardo
with his assurance that we would be gone in the night. The priest returned to us with a bottle of wine, some cheese, and some meat, and
a large flagon of water, and then disappeared.

After Don Domenico left us, we saw no sign of Bucci, Riccardo, or
anyone else, apart from the shepherd boy who visited the stable early
in the afternoon to attend to the cows. It was so cold. Mother and
Father and Buena hugged each other for warmth in their bed of straw.
Marko seemed to draw warmth from his cigarettes. Even in the dim
light, we could see our own breath and that of the cattle. The waiting
was difficult. Toward the end of the day, we shared our meager provisions in the empty stall. As soon as night fell, after reassuring my family that I would return in less than two hours, I set out with Marko to
scout the best route to our destination. The Caverni homestead was
not far—I estimated less than an hour's walk for Marko and myself. I
wanted to make sure that the way was clear, and I wanted to test the
key in the lock before leading my family there. Marko and I quickly
crossed Bucci's yard and made our way along a country lane to a goat
path that crossed it less than one hundred yards ahead. We had used
this same path more than two weeks earlier, when we had traveled
from Teresa's to see Don Domenico. The goat path snaked down a
steep ridge to the main road, which led past the old homestead of
Achille's family and beyond toward Caudino. The path was treacherous with ice and loose stone. As Marko and I rapidly clambered down
the bare face of the ridge, our footsteps resounded in the still night,
and our silhouettes stood out in the bright light of a rising full moon.
I should have been more cautious, but I was impatient to reach Achille's house, and the countryside was entirely deserted on this frigid
night so, unheard and unseen, we scrambled down the barren ridge in
less than half an hour, and then followed the main road toward Caudino.

Achille and I had passed by the Caverni homestead several times
while reconnoitering around Pergola, and he had once or twice spoken
of it as a possible place of refuge for my family, but he and I had never

stopped there, and Achille and I had never made a formal plan that my family could take shelter in the house. Nevertheless, in the desperation of our flight from Pergola, I had led my family there in the hope of finding shelter, at least temporarily. So, it was only on that brisk afternoon in early December that I had met the peasant caretaker of the Caverni homestead, Santino, and his family. Santino had greeted us kindly, but he had to turn us away. The house itself was a large three-story structure of stone, covered in mustard stucco. Santino, his wife, and his sixteen-year-old daughter occupied the lower level; its large central doorway opened from the back of the house into a large room with a huge fireplace and a floor of packed dirt strewn with straw. It was into this room that Santino had welcomed us on our first visit. Adjacent to this room were stalls for the stabling of Santino's animals, which included a mule, two cows, and a perhaps as many as a dozen sheep and goats. A large poultry shed was attached to the rear of the house. A peasant, who operated the humble mill across the yard behind the house, also lived on the ground floor of the Caverni house, in separate quarters with his wife, and their two hearty young boys.

Marko and I soon reached the cart track that led from the main road to the Caverni house. We approached the house cautiously. As it loomed into view, starkly silhouetted in the moonlight, I felt a rush of conflicting feelings, as fear, joy, anxiety, and relief pulsed through my every vein and nerve. We were startled by the barking of a dog from inside Santino's quarters on the ground floor, but the dog fell silent almost immediately, and there were no other signs of life in the yard, which was utterly still in the moonlight. I led Marko up the stone steps, to the door of the apartment on the second story. I shuddered, almost in fear, when I saw the strangely animated pale images of a ruined fresco and broken frieze-work on the side of the house, ornamental elements that bespoke its prosperous past. The key turned unwillingly in the lock. I lifted the ancient, heavy latch, and pushed on the massive door, which opened with a groan of protest and a gust of stale air.

Marko followed close behind me as I entered the house. I quickly shut the door behind us, leaving us in the spectral semidarkness of a manorial entry hall. All of the second-floor windows were shuttered and heavily draped, but the hall was dimly illuminated by a ghostly

light emanating from a large room directly beyond. I struck a match
to the stub of a candle that I carried in my pocket. Holding the candle
before me, I tentatively advanced toward the mysterious light. The
tomblike entry hall—furnished sparsely with a few antique high-back
chairs and a large wooden chest—was everywhere shrouded with cob-
webs. The floorboards creaked and groaned mercilessly with each
step. The strangely lit room beyond the entry hall appeared to be a
cavernous kitchen and common room. It was flooded with moonlight
that filtered through a large glass skylight set high above in the ceiling. I lingered there less than a minute, only long enough to inspect
its main features. Flanked by tall, shuttered double-windows, a heavy
door was set into the back wall. This door opened onto a flight of stairs
that led down to Santino's yard in the rear of the house. Directly below
the skylight, a heavy oak table and an odd collection of chairs and
benches dominated the center of the room. A large fireplace occupied
the wall to my right. A kettle hung over the hearth. An ample stock of
wood was stacked neatly in the corner beyond the fireplace, to the
right of the rear door, along with several casks of water. Along the wall
opposite the fireplace, I saw first an empty corner, then a door, and
then, stretching almost to the limit of the far wall, a battered credenza
topped with shelves, on which were displayed an assortment of goods,
kitchen utensils, and tableware. I later learned that the door led to a
room that had been closed since the death of Achille's older brother,
who had died there. I took in all of this in less than a minute, and
turned back to the entry hall, from which two facing doors led to two
large bedrooms, each furnished with two large cast-iron beds, massive
armoires, chests of drawers of crudely carved wood, and old, heavy
chairs, their worn upholstery stained with humidity and decades of
use. A flight of stairs led from the entry hall up to the third floor, but
the door at the top was padlocked and, throughout our stay, we never
ventured there.

Marko and I arrived back at Bucci's sometime after nine o'clock
in the evening. Bucci's house stood completely mute and dark in the
moonlight. Marko remained in the shadows outside the stable, while I
slipped inside to retrieve the family. Mother, Father, and Buena were
anxiously waiting for me, shivering in the dark. Everything had been
prepared. Within a minute of my reappearance, we gathered up our

backpacks and noiselessly left the stable. I let Marko take the lead
along the route that we had already traveled that night. I followed behind him, at Mother's side to help her along. Buena followed me, and
Father, like a shepherd with an eye on his flock moving in front of
him, filed after Buena. We quickly reached the goat path, but our passage down the steep face of the bare ridge was slow and difficult,
eased only by the light of the moon. Marko scrambled down the path
in front of us, while I remained at Mother's side to help her navigate
the ice and treacherous loose stones on our trail. Despite our care and
cautious pace, Mother lost her footing several times, and I barely managed to save her from a dangerous fall. With no help from Marko,
Father and Buena followed behind Mother and me. We found Marko
waiting for us, crouching at the side of the road at the foot of the ridge,
smoking a cigarette. We paused for a few minutes to catch our breath
and then, without exchanging a single word, proceeded down the center of the deserted road.

When the Caverni homestead came into view fifteen minutes later,
I motioned our tiny column to a halt. The yard in front of the house,
scarred with shadows cast by the setting moon, was completely still.
After only a few moments, I led my family to the house, up the front
steps, and into the haunted atmosphere of the entry hall. Communicat-
ing by touch and gesture—we whispered not a single word—I led my
family by candlelight to the bedroom to our left, where Father eased
Mother down onto one of the beds and lay down beside her. Stumbling
over a chest at the foot of the bed, Buena instinctively moved to the
other side, and stretched herself out. Only moments later—by that
time I had already found blankets in the chest and was unfolding
them—Mother, Father, and Buena, still wearing their overcoats, and
gathered into a tight knot of exhaustion, were already soundly asleep.
I felt their arms mingled and their bodies drawn together against the
damp cold of the night, as I gently drew the covers over them, and I
thought what a blessing sleep was.

Exhilarated with relief that we had found a safe harbor, I was hardly
aware of my own exhaustion and of the bitter cold. I motioned to
Marko to follow me into the kitchen, which by then was in shadow, no
longer illumined by the direct light of the moon through the skylight.
I turned my candle toward the table, to make a small pool of molten

wax into which I set the candle. Marko stood by passively, while from the woodpile by the door I gathered kindling and hauled several logs to the hearth and set them alight with the stroke of several matches and an ancient bellows of wood and cracked leather that I found hanging beside the fireplace. The fire quickly built to a warming blaze of light, in the circle of which Marko joined me. I was oblivious to Marko, to everything around me, while my body, my bones, hungrily drank in the heat, and I stared into the dancing flames, and fell into a trance. My trance in front of the fire that night was only disturbed by fitful memories of what we had witnessed and endured in almost three years of war since my waking on an April morning in 1941. The hissing of the logs, the crackle and spit of the fire, the sudden blue flaring of the fire consumed all memories of our lives before the war. Such memories were no more alive to me than the white ash that accumulated in the hearth, and our future was dark behind the curtain of flame. When the candle had guttered out on the table, and the flames had finally subsided into embers, I shook myself alive. Marko had collapsed into sleep beside me. I nudged him half-awake, and drew from my pocket a second candle stub, by whose light I led him to the second bedroom. He numbly clambered onto one of the cast iron beds. I covered him with several blankets and then crossed the hall to the other bedroom where my family was bundled in sleep. My own exhaustion washing over me, I held the light of the candle toward them as much in a gesture of benediction as in an effort to see their breathing forms, and then, after a minute of tender and reverent reflection, returned to the kitchen, to the dying fire, which I replenished with another offering of wood.

At around five that morning, a cold wind moaned and gusted at the house, bringing in its train a mix of rain and sleet that whipped, sheet-like, at the shuttered windows and the old, stone walls. The wind calmed with the pale arrival of dawn, and the sleet and rain subsided. Inside, the kitchen night gradually yielded to a pale light that reached in through the skylight above, and I began to make out the features of our new home. The house showed signs of past prosperity—it was the homestead of the Caverni, and I thought I remembered Achille having told me that his own father had been born there—but even in the dim light of our first morning there, I felt a sadness in the house, as I observed how much it had suffered from abandonment and the passage of time. Achille's older brother had lived in isolation there, but his term of residence was already many years past, and the apartment had since rarely been occupied. There was such emptiness in the house. It was like a tomb from which even the ghosts had departed, leaving behind the worn relics of past joy and lives long gone.

With the first light of dawn, I again checked on Mother, Father, and Buena, whom I found still asleep in their cold, dark bedroom, huddled together on the bed under their blankets. When I returned to the kitchen, I was tempted to open the back door to look at the outside world, but I respected Don Domenico's detailed instructions that we should remain hidden inside the house, as quietly as possible, until Santino told us that we could come out. In the gathering light of day, I could clearly see several casks of water just inside the door beside the ample pile of firewood that was stacked all the way to the far right-hand corner of the kitchen. Set against the right-hand wall, between the woodpile and the fireplace, I noticed for the first time a large wooden bin filled with heavy chunks of black charcoal. I laid several pieces of the charcoal on the embers of the fire—remembering that Don Domenico had told me that we could burn charcoal by day, but we could have wood fires only by night, for fear that a plume of wood smoke would betray our presence in the second-floor apartment. I quietly drew a chair up to the table and silently absorbed my surroundings, my heart filling with inexpressible gratitude. As the sounds of a new day rose in the household beneath me, with the stirrings of animals being fed and the sounds of voices rising through the floorboards, I meditated on the fresh rhythms of the renewed life that Achille had opened to us.

I was approaching the limits of my strength. I knew that I would soon have to sleep, but I also knew that I had to be certain, before I rested, that everyone understood the rules of our new household. The coals in the fireplace gave off much less heat than the wood fire, but everyone would have to understand that we could not burn wood during the day. Everyone would have to understand that we had to live as quietly and invisibly as possible. We wouldn't be able to go outside during the day unless Santino told us that the way was clear. We would even have to be mindful of our movements inside the house, taking care to make as little noise as possible. We could only speak in low voices, and we quickly learned the new skill of walking in our apartment without making the old floorboards creak and groan with each step. Rising from the table, I tried to open the door in the wall opposite the fireplace, but it was locked. I then turned to inspect the credenza and the shelves mounted above it. The shelves were laden with a dusty array of old oil lamps, discolored glasses and chipped

My Family in the Caverni Kitchen. By Albert Alcalay.

cups, earthenware and dishes of porcelain, and table service, crockery, cooking pots, and utensils—an impossible mixture that only a century of accumulation could produce. I was happy to find a large wheel of salty peccorino cheese under a cloth on the sideboard, and a large battered tin filled with pasta. I also discovered, within the credenza, at least three dozen large bottles of wine and freshly filled bins of potatoes, onions, and apples. Rounding out this provender were at least a dozen jars of tomato, vegetable, and fruit preserves, a large glass jar filled with olives, and a large earthenware flagon of olive oil, even a basket of dried herbs, tarragon, bay leaves, and thyme, and a cluster of garlic cloves. To my amazement, I also found stocks of pepper, salt, and even some sugar. I searched for coffee and tea among all these riches, and was rueful when I found only an empty canister that smelled of coffee, but I was not disappointed. How could I be? There was no stove, no plumbing in the house, and no electricity, but it was clear that we had all the provisions that we would need, and that we would have coal for heat and cooking by day, and by night the comfort of wood fires in the hearth.

With only the charcoal for heat, the kitchen had chilled, but the discovery of our ample provisions had warmed me with hope. I took an apple from the bin, cut myself a wedge of the almost frozen cheese, and filled a cup with water from one of the casks. After consuming this simple meal, I took a small lamp from the shelf, filled it with oil, and lit it, adjusting the wick to produce a low, even light. Lamp in hand, I moved carefully across the entry hall to wake my parents and my sister. Entering their dark bedroom, I could see clearly for the first time, in the gentle light of the lamp, the form and disposition of the massive old furniture and the heavy drapes over the shuttered windows. When I set the lamp down on the chest of drawers, I saw my own ghostly image staring at me, strangely corroded in the oxidized plane of an old cracked mirror. Before waking my parents and Buena, I opened the double doors of the armoire to discover shelves laden with old blankets, towels, and age-yellowed bed linens and pillows.

After coaxing them awake from the warm security of their beds, I guided my parents and Buena, and then Marko, to the kitchen, and gathered everyone as quietly as possible around the table, in order to explain, before I myself collapsed, the regimen of our new life. Everyone, even Marko, was astonished at our provisions. I impressed upon everyone the need to be as quiet as possible, never to speak above a whisper, and always to move along the walls of the corridor to avoid causing the loud groaning of the old floorboards. I explained that we could burn coal during the day, but we could only make wood fires in the evening. Before leaving the kitchen for my bed in the room that I shared with Marko, I told everyone that we would be able to go out at night, and even during the day, but only when Santino called on us to emerge. As soon as I felt assured that everyone understood well the rules that would govern our lives, I left them in the kitchen. I gratefully collapsed into my bed and slept under a thick pile of blankets until nightfall.

When I awoke ten hours later, I was completely disoriented in the total dark of the cold room. Long minutes passed before I focused my mind on where I was, and hauled myself out of bed to make my way to the kitchen, as gently and silently as a moth drawn to the faint glimmer of the oil lamp on the kitchen table and the glow of the fire that Marko and my father had built in the hearth. Marko was seated in front of the fire, smoking his acrid tobacco. My mother and father were at the table, playing cards in the small circle of light cast by the lamp. Buena was seated beside them, quietly sewing. None of us said a word, but I exchanged smiles of greeting with my family, and I looked over toward Marko, who continued to smoke and stare into the fire with no acknowledgment of my presence. I was ravenously hungry, and swung myself silently into a chair at the table, reaching immediately for the remnants of sliced lamb that Mother had saved for me. In front of my plate she had set a bowl of potatoes, which she had boiled in the kettle over the coals. Also before me on the table were a cruet of olive oil, a pitcher of water, and a basket into which she had piled all that was left of the bread that Armanda had given to us only the day before—only the day before in a world that already felt so far, far away. Mother had even found the salt, a small portion of which she had spooned into a dish. And as I poured the rich green olive oil onto the plate, and was gratefully tearing into the bread, potatoes, and meat, Buena set a glass of wine at my side.

So began our voyage in the ark of Achille's family homestead, our refuge from the mad storm that was raging in the world beyond. Santino surely knew that we had arrived. I didn't doubt that he had seen us approach the house, and that his sharp ears had since heard a muffled voice, or a creaking floorboard from the apartment above, but we saw nothing of Santino during our first days in the apartment. It was as if we did not exist at all. We adapted to our new home, while life below went on as it had gone on for many, many years. Early each morning, if often from our beds, we could hear the world below us come to life, with the crowing of a rooster, the cackle of hens, the braying of the donkey, the bleating of sheep, the bark of the dog, and the voices of Santino, his wife, and his daughter. From time to time, we also heard the voices of Antonio, the miller, and of Sophia, his wife, and, above all, of their youngsters, Sergio and Rotiglio, two strapping young boys, whom we had first met when we visited Achille on that first day of our flight from Pergola. And these voices, and the sounds of the animals, and the cacophony of daily life were like music to us, a music whose rhythms we quickly became accustomed to, as we expectantly waited each day for the sounds of waking life that always began with the restless stirrings of the animals in their stalls, signaling their impatience for their morning feeding, and the sound of Santino's rich peasant tenor as he greeted them with fresh hay and perhaps a few apples, and some oats for the donkey. We heard the sound of Santino's wife, Menga, calling her husband to breakfast, the infectious laughter of Annetta, and the chopping of wood. At noontime, there was a crescendo of sound and activity as the two families joined together for the most important meal of their day. And then there were the quieter afternoons, punctuated by the sounds of the boys at play in the snow, and the barking of the dog, and occasionally a scolding voice. And then, in the evening, came the gentler sounds of a world going to sleep, always announced by the piercing sweetness of the Angelus that rang out from Don Domenico's church and reached us even a mile away, even through the stone walls of our refuge, as if to remind us each evening that, even with the fall of night, hope could touch us in the notes of its song.

We listened to this music for three full days—from our beds and from the kitchen where we spent most of our waking hours together— before we saw Santino. We had developed our own rhythm of life, rising late in the morning and remaining in the kitchen until ten or eleven at night to draw comfort from the fire we could build in the hearth after dark. At eight o'clock, on the fourth night of our stay, we were startled when we heard three knocks at the back door. Recognizing this as Santino's signal, I reassured everyone—we were all gathered silently before the fire—and I opened the door to our peasant host. Santino urged me gently toward the hearth, where he joined our group in the warming circle of light. The flames illumined his worn face, accenting the kindness and wisdom engraved in his weather-coarsened features. Santino told us that no one in the community had any notion that we were staying at the Caverni house. There had been talk about us, of course. People were wondering what had become of us. But the commonly accepted notion was that we had headed back across the ridges to join the partisans at Monte Sant'Angelo. He reminded us to continue to live quietly and cautiously, but said that we could begin to come out at night—he would give a signal that the way was clear by tapping three times on the beams beneath our kitchen floor, generally at around eight o'clock.

Santino then said that we should attend to certain practical matters immediately. Marko and I refilled three casks with fresh water from the well in the yard. Finally, Santino and I replenished the coal bin, while Marko stood aside. These chores were to be a regular part of our routine over the coming months—and a source of friction between Marko and me, because Marko always had to be prodded to do his share of the work, and he sometimes refused. With Santino's help, our tasks were quickly done. On Santino's sign, I led Mother, Father, and Buena down the stairs and into the yard for a bit of exercise and fresh air. Buena immediately exclaimed her awe at the beauty of the rising of the almost full moon and the brilliant carpet of stars that was strewn across the clear night sky, and we had to remind her to be quiet. The night was very cold, and the ground was frozen. While Santino, Marko, and I worked, Mother and Father strolled, arm in arm, back and forth, along the length of the back of the house, with Buena timidly following them, in a mute and regal promenade beneath the canopy of the heavens. This was the pattern that they were to follow in their outings on most of the succeeding nights. Only many days later, when they felt more assured, were they willing to step more than a few paces away from the house.

Complaining of the cold, Marko was the first to reenter the apartment, where we found him a few minutes later, smoking a cigarette in front of the fire. Santino followed us deferentially into the kitchen. Father pressed some money into Santino's hand—I didn't know how much—and Santino then quietly told us that he drove his oxcart into Pergola once every week to trade and buy supplies for the household. He explained that Achille had told him to contact him for anything that we might need. We were well provisioned, Father pointed out, we could hardly ask for anything more, but Marko interjected that he needed more tobacco. After an embarrassing pause, I thanked Santino, and told him that we were grateful for the provisions. I added that my parents and sister would be grateful for tea or bouillon, if that would be possible.

Santino was quick to supply us with bouillon and tea, and the tobacco. I don't know where Achille could have obtained the tea—it made a strong, dark brew—which pleased Mother and Father enormously. Our life followed its prescribed pattern in the following days. We remained in our beds until midmorning. I was always the first to rise. I went straight to the kitchen to ignite a coal fire in the hearth and to heat some water. On most mornings, I cleared the hearth, quietly shoveling the ashes of the prior night's fire into a large bucket that I would empty into a ditch behind the house after dark. Father would be the next to appear. Each morning he filled a basin with hot water, which he carefully carried to Mother and Buena. At around eleven, Mother and Buena would appear in the kitchen and immediately begin preparing the day's principal meal. I often helped them with such tasks as peeling potatoes, but there was really little for me to do—Mother and Buena were jealously protective of their work—so I bid my time in listlessly leafing through the volumes of an ancient popular Italian encyclopedia, which was the only literature I had found in the apartment. Marko invariably showed up at noon, just before Mother and Buena served our dinner. Sullen, entirely withdrawn into himself, he would invariably settle in front of the hearth as close as he could to the warmth of the coals, often careless about the noise he made. Never showing any regard for my mother and Buena, who patiently worked around him, and never offering to help, he would light a cigarette, pour himself a glass of wine, and glare moodily into the embers.

After our noon meal, we would spend the entire afternoon in the kitchen, clinging to the little light of the winter days. With only the heat from the charcoal in the hearth, it was quite cold, even in the kitchen, so we usually wore our overcoats. Mother and Buena cleared the table, rinsed the dishes and eating utensils in a bucket, and dried and arranged each item with reverent care. On some days, Father and I each enjoyed a glass of wine while Mother and Buena were working, but only one small glass each. When everything was done, Mother made tea and sat diagonally across from Father at the end of the table, where they played cards until twilight. Buena sat away from the stove, on the other side of the table beside Father, with her sewing. In addition to mending our worn and torn clothing, she fashioned heavy double socks for all of us—even for Marko—to keep our feet warm.

Toward the end of each afternoon, Mother needed to lie down. Despite the frigid cold in the bedroom, Father and Buena would join her there. We were able to heat the beds with a contraption called "*il prete*" ("the priest") that we had found in the kitchen and whose use had at first puzzled us. *Il prete* was a clever device, an oblong wooden frame, about five feet long, and perhaps three feet high, in the center of which a covered porcelain pot hung suspended. Before my parents and Buena retired to their bedroom each afternoon and each evening, Father or I would fill the porcelain pot with glowing chunks of charcoal from the kitchen hearth. We then put *il prete* into the bed between the covers. So, before my parents and sister climbed into their beds, our "priest" had made the bedding toasty warm, a delicious sensation that Mother, Father, and Buena relished. Climbing into a warm bed became one of the high points of their days. In the evening, I often heated my own bed with *il prete*. Marko never took the trouble to use the device, and that was one thing that none of us felt any obligation to do for him.

After their afternoon siesta, my parents and Buena would reappear in the kitchen well after dark. Mother and Buena prepared the evening meal, which we always ate in front of the fire I had built in the hearth after nightfall each evening. Our supper was always a simpler affair than our noontime dinner, but the time we spent together in front of the fire was the best time of the day, usually punctuated by the pleasure of stepping outside on those evenings when Santino signaled that the way was clear. As soon as we heard Santino tap three times on the ceiling beam below, I launched eagerly into the chores of emptying the cinder bucket and refreshing our stocks of wood, charcoal, and water. I had to goad Marko into helping me with these tasks. He did not share my relish for the exercise. I would happily have worked alone, but I needed his help to get all the work done in the little time that we had to accomplish it. Marko's attitude infected me with anger. I wondered if he had ever had any consideration for others around him, if he had ever had anything resembling a "social consciousness." I couldn't understand how anyone could be so completely selfish.

After mid-January, the weather turned bitterly cold. The ancient stone house was like an icebox. The daytime sky was generally overcast, with only a bleak, gray light filtering into the kitchen through the skylight, which was often glazed over with sleet and light flurries of snow. Although we had neither requested nor really needed anything, Santino showed up at the door earlier than usual one evening with fresh provisions from Achille, including fresh pasta, a block of larded pork, and three precious lemons. Packed with the foodstuffs were several rolls of coarse toilet tissue. I had grown so unused to even the concept of toilet tissue, that it seemed an absurd luxury, laughably exotic, but Mother, with no comment apart from the most resolute grimace of possession, instantly gathered the rolls up and took them into her bedroom.

We felt more secure as the days passed but, even during these bleak January days, there were often visitors to the property, and it remained important to remain hidden and as quiet as possible, especially during the daylight hours. On most nights, Santino would signal with three taps of a broomstick on the ceiling of his rude home below, and we would gingerly file down the stairs in the bitter cold for a little fresh air behind the house. Santino was almost always at the foot of the stairs, his cap in hand, to greet us with the traditional deference of the Italian peasant. We saw very little of the other members of Santino's household during the weeks of winter, and almost nothing of the miller Antonio and his wife and two sons, but all members of both households knew that we were living upstairs, and we had to trust their bond of secrecy.

Don Domenico finally appeared at our door one night in late January. We had been at Achille's for almost three weeks, and I had become quite anxious to see him. Don Domenico sternly cautioned us not to relax our guard. The danger to everyone was mounting. Partisan activity in the region had intensified, and the Fascist authorities were putting renewed pressure on the Carabinieri to round up anyone alien to the area. Although local authorities had generally ignored instructions from their superiors, they were beginning to react to their increasingly shrill, and increasingly menacing, demands. Don Domenico did not yet feel any direct threat to himself—he was quite sure that he was not yet under surveillance—but he knew that in some quarters he was regarded with suspicion.

The priest regularly visited us after this night, generally once a week, although the intervals between visits were sometimes longer. He always came to the house well after dark. He would join us in front of our fire and share news of the progress of the war. It was evident to me from the outset that Don Domenico was receiving reports from Radio London. There was nothing exceptional about this. Any Italian who still had access to a radio could receive such reports, and most who could receive them did so, despite the danger of being caught and the Nazi attempts to jam the broadcasts. As time went by, I also began to sense that Don Domenico was directly involved with the Resistance. The partisans were ranging with increasing boldness across the countryside, especially in the area surrounding Monte Sant'Angelo. Many splinter groups among them, especially the Communists and other leftist elements, used their arms against the wealthy signori, looting the houses and storage sheds of the rich. What these partisans didn't need for themselves, they distributed to refugees and the poor, often through priests like Don Domenico. Although Achille and Santino were already providing well for our needs, I think we ourselves received some of the partisan booty, from the hands of Don Domenico. Soon after he had begun to visit us regularly, he delivered a hundred-pound flour sack. Not many days later, he arrived with a large, delicious, smoked ham.

Although I privately wondered about Don Domenico's involvement in the Resistance, I did not question his kindness. We depended on him, and we were deeply grateful for his help. But I wondered about him, nevertheless. Don Domenico puzzled me. I didn't understand him. He was unlike any priest I had ever met, and I had already met many priests during my time in Italy. He showed few, if any, of the traits that prevailed among the Italian clergy, or even, I imagine, any traits that currently prevail in the Italian Church. He seemed to be a rebel by nature, a personality free of any religious dogma, a man more suited to being a fighter pilot than a priest. I could visualize him on his motorcycle much more easily than I could imagine him in the pulpit. I could not picture him in any sacramental role, in any mediation of communion with God through the doctrine of the Holy Ghost, or whatever. His character displayed something of the prankster that I had known in popular German fairy tales. I couldn't decide whether he was the Pied Piper or Peter Pan, Saint Peter or Saint Paul. Perhaps he was all of these. His behavior toward us only displayed the purest charity, even if his manners were more those of an Errol Flynn, and if his manner was playful and frankly irreverent, he was, at heart, I came to know, a deeply serious man. He was universally respected, even revered, in his parish community, and by all the reports I heard from the peasants of the region—and, I can assure, in matters of the Church, they were connoisseurs of their own expectations—Don Domenico held his pulpit with great dignity and authority. I never did understand him, but I always enjoyed his stimulating company, and I largely owed, and shall always owe to him, from those first bleak months of 1944 right up to the moment of liberation, my family's survival, and my own. What was almost as great a gift to me at the time was Don Domenico's role in the revitalization of my intellectual life, and the beginnings of my interest in Christianity. He brought many books of theology to me, and I was thrilled to set aside the ancient Italian family encyclopedia for the more engaging study of the papacy, the history of church dogma, and a kaleidoscope of theological issues.

We had been at the Caverni homestead for exactly three weeks—I remember the date precisely: January 25, 1944—when Achille's brother Mario arrived to see to the payment of the family's vineyard workers. He told us that only a few days earlier the Allies had landed at Anzio, about thirty miles to the south of Rome. Our hopes soared.

We were all convinced that the Allies would occupy Rome immediately. We reasoned that the war would be over in Italy as soon as the
Nazis had been expelled from the Eternal City. We would be liberated! This was the first positive news of progress in the war that we
had heard since leaving Pergola. But day after day passed, and our
expectations clouded as we heard no further news, until one day, in
early February, we learned from Don Domenico that the Nazis had
contained the Allied beachhead at Anzio, and the main Allied forces
were still bogged down, as they had been since the prior October, before the mountain defenses of the Nazi Gustav line, more than 120
miles to the south. But we did not lose all hope. There were other
signs that the end for the Nazis was coming soon. Around the middle
of February, we heard an enormous roaring in the sky. Unable to resist
our desire to see what it was, we cracked open a shutter of one of the
tall double windows in my parents' bedroom. The sky was filled with
what must have been hundreds of Allied bombers directed at a target
to the north. A few days after this, Don Domenico confided to me—
without inviting any further questions—that the partisans were gradually taking control of the region, and that they were protecting us.

    In the first days of February, Mother suffered an internal hemor-
rhage. She remained confined in bed for most of the month. We were
distraught with concern for her, but we could do little more than comfort her and pray for her recovery. We could not call a doctor to the
house. Father spent all of his time beside Mother in their frigid bedroom, hand-feeding her tea and broth, tending to all her needs. I developed a hideous cold and was miserable for almost two weeks. Don
Domenico obtained medicines for Mother and me. The medicines may
have helped, but it was only time that mended us. Mother slowly recovered her strength. After a few weeks, she was able to join us in the
kitchen in the evenings. My cold was devastating, but I continued to
force myself out of my bed each morning, shoveled the ash from the
hearth, and ignited a fresh coal fire. I tried to concentrate on the books
that Don Domenico had given me. In the evenings, I built the fire in
the hearth and attended to the chores, sometimes with Marko's unwilling help, sometimes on my own. Buena was a real source of strength
to the household throughout this period. Uncomplaining, almost
cheerful, she quietly assured the orderly progress of each day, prepar-

ing meals and attending to every task in the world of the kitchen. When her tasks were done, she sewed and mended and sewed some more.

The daily life of the world below and around us continued, but its rhythms and sounds now grated discordantly on my depressed spirit. The winter was endless. Even the days seemed to be shorter and sadder under the lowering skies and the constant pelting of sleet and snow against the skylight. Don Domenico's visits lifted me somewhat, but he brought no fresh news of Allied advances, and I sensed a new tension in his manner. We had seen little of anyone, and had direct contact only with Santino, who we saw only fleetingly in the evenings. He had not since entered the second-floor apartment, although he continued to provision us with the little that we needed—more tobacco for Marko, a little more tea, and plucked hens, from which Buena fashioned Mother's broth—and he often helped me haul coal, water, and wood up to our door. My cold did clear away—for a time I thought that I would be stricken with pneumonia—but my mood grew darker and more pessimistic. I struggled with this, but could not overcome it, and my ill humor infected the entire household. My mood worsened when Don Domenico grimly told me that the authorities were aggressively shipping all the Jews in Italy to camps in the north, and that pressures were mounting locally. I was desperate to act, but I could do nothing. Don Domenico assured me that we were secure, as long as we continued to live quietly and invisibly. Grateful as I was for this, I was sometimes unmindful of our good fortune, and bitterly felt the burden of our confinement. Where were the Allies? Would the war ever end?

Bitterly cold and gray, and marked with several heavy falls of snow, February was a cruel month for all of us. Yes, we were relatively secure, and our provisions were ample, luxurious by any standard we had experienced during the war years. Although the apartment was freezing cold, we did have the cheer of our evening fires, and—with the help of our marvelous *il prete*—the warmth of our beds. We were astonished and grateful that we had survived. But after weeks of confinement and enforced inactivity in the apartment, the darkness and cold of the season ate like acid at our moral courage. No longer engaged in a daily struggle to escape the Fascists and simply to survive, each of us was left—in the vacuum of our confined and hidden lives—to wrestle with our own spirits. Mother's illness was the greatest blow to our morale during this difficult period. In those first weeks at Achille's house, Mother had regained her central role in the life of our family, a role that had been lost to her since the family's flight from Belgrade, and had never—until our arrival at Achille's—been fully restored to her, when suddenly her hemorrhage shattered the peace and harmony of our daily dinners and the winter afternoons and evenings that we spent together in the kitchen. We were horrified that we could do nothing to help her when she hemorrhaged, and watched powerlessly while she struggled for life. Happily, the bleeding stopped, and the threat of her sudden death receded within a few days. But it never entirely disappeared—we constantly feared the eruption of a new crisis—and Mother's confinement to bed broke the happy rhythm that we had established in our makeshift lives.

With the world closed in around us, we were forced into a tight, painful knot of intimacy. Hidden from the world, there was nowhere to hide from ourselves, and we were forced to expose our naked humanity to each other in a way we had never done before. With Mother and Father sequestered in the bedroom, Buena took refuge in her household responsibilities. Marko, who at his best was an irritation, was completely useless. I felt isolated, and I was deeply disturbed that I could do nothing for Mother, and nothing at all to improve our situation. I plunged, day after day, into despondent introspection. I could not shake myself free of this. My introspection was itself hopelessly circular. I already well understood what my values were. I already had a hard-won understanding of the historical, social, and psychological forces that shaped the lives of men. I was tired of dwelling on my own hopes and fears and dreams. I didn't care to linger over fading memories of happiness. Don Domenico's books failed to hold my interest. I even turned away from thoughts of Vittoria. The habits of study and self-examination that had always been my most reliable source of strength in times of stress no longer offered any convincing nourishment or affirmation. I could find no rational use for any of it, and, because of this, I began to lose any sense of rational meaning in life, or any purpose in suffering. I had always responded to despair with a spirit of resolve, and had always seen the challenge of any obstacle or threat as an opportunity to become stronger in overcoming it. But the literal truth of our situation—that inactivity and silence were the tools suited best to meet it—paralyzed me, leaving me vulnerable and empty of any purpose. There was nothing—nothing!—that I could do. I could only wait for others. I could never accept this.

Torn with worry about Mother, tormented with self-doubt, unable to sustain any real intellectual or artistic passion, chafing at my own impotence to act, I could not conceal the disarray of my spirit. Father understood me better than anyone. He was experiencing the same profound frustration, but he had mastered it better than I had. The example of his quiet strength and steadfastness helped me come to terms with our enforced inactivity. By the end of February, I gradually began to accept the facts of our situation, and my depression and bitterness slowly began to dissipate. With my father's constant care, Mother's condition improved, but she was consumed with guilt, half-deliriously blaming herself for the position that we were in. Although I did my best to conceal it, I could not hide my despair from Mother, and I sometimes heard her choking on her tears, and crying, "It's all my fault! Why didn't I let him go to Palestine? It is all my fault!" Father comforted Mother with his love—not with words or arguments, which he knew were in vain, but with gentle, reassuring murmuring and caresses.

From the time of our first meeting at Ferramonti, I had never liked Marko. Only my father's kindness had assured him a place among us. I had made a real effort to accept him, but his behavior during the bitter weeks of February turned my dislike of him to a cold hatred. Marko made no pretense of any concern at all for Mother, or for anyone other than himself. At the outset of our flight from Pergola, he had attached himself to us solely in terms of his own needs. This withdrawn, pitiful, parasitic creature had gradually transformed into an opportunistic, surly, threatening monster. By February, if he even took the trouble to answer me when I asked for his help with the daily chores, it would be only to snarl that it was too cold. As soon as the coal fire was lit in the morning, he would show up in the kitchen and rudely take a place in front of the hearth, impatiently waiting for a meal and constantly smoking his foul cigarettes. There was not the least element of decency in his character. He took whatever he wanted without asking: food at our table and wine from our rapidly diminishing stock. He was Jewish, but would gladly have denied this if he could. Underlying his arrogance was the real threat that he would betray us to the authorities. The threat of blackmail was his payment to us for our kindness. His bitterly offensive presence among us infuriated me. I wanted to beat him to a pulp. Only Father's infinite patience maintained the most fragile veneer of peace. I could only wait for that sweet time when we would be rid of him.

In the first days of March a break came in the bitter cold, with high winds and heavy rainfall. As the sky gradually cleared, and the days perceptibly lengthened, life in the apartment became more bearable. Mother reappeared in the kitchen at noontimes, and a family life was restored to us. We had survived two months of confinement, and the difficult passage of February. I had learned to ignore Marko, no longer even acknowledging his presence, which seemed to suit him well enough. Mother retired to her bedroom after the noonday dinner, leaving Buena to clear the table and do the dishes, but she rejoined us almost every evening, when we gathered around the fireplace to reminisce and tell stories. Sometimes we sang together softly. I knew hundreds of Hebrew songs of all kinds—plain folksongs, love songs, hymns, songs of sorrow, of joy, dancing tunes, songs of social protest and revolution. Sometimes I sang to the family—always in a low voice, almost a whisper, my singing infused with melancholy, as I thought of my youth, my friends, and ideals. As I serenaded my family, tears often welled up in their eyes, and in my own. In the sweet sorrow of our tears, we recaptured a part of our souls that had been lost to us, and, with the oncoming spring, a rebirth of hope.

On fair days, Santino signaled to us with the welcome pounding of his broomstick that the way was clear for us to climb down the steps from our kitchen to spend a little time in the yard behind the house. Santino was always at the foot of the stairs to greet us, bowing humbly, his cap in hand, and watchfully alert for anyone approaching the house. Santino's wife Menga, and their daughter Annetta, as well as the miller Antonio, his wife Sophia, and their two sons Sergio and Rotiglio all knew by then that we were living upstairs, and they were keeping our secret well—stern words from Don Domenico no doubt having reinforced their discretion. There was little risk in coming out

at night, but I was uneasy within myself at the openness of these afternoon outings. Nevertheless, we all yielded to the pure happiness of
the little freedom that this afforded us—the taste of the afternoon air,
the piercing blue of the sky, the welcome warmth of a ray of sunlight
were all blessings and rare pleasures to us.

We spoke little to anyone apart from Santino, whose local dialect
was often very difficult to understand. Father tried to speak to Santino
about farming matters, but the barriers of language and culture were
too high for any fluent conversation between them. Santino's wife
Menga always greeted us with respect. I could tell that she was very
curious about us. A heavyset woman who dressed entirely in black,
she would regard us intently from the shadow of the door into her poor
home. As the days passed, we did have minimal contact with everyone
from the two households quartered on the ground floor of the Caverni
homestead—contacts marked with the same discrete and respectful
curiosity that we had experienced at Mastucci's remarkable home, but
with nothing of the personal spontaneity and gaiety that we had experienced there. Antonio's two lads were trusty young men, with frank
and open faces, and firm, respectful handshakes. They helped their
father in the mill. Antonio spoke with an educated diction, and was
surprisingly urbane. Both the miller and his wife were well dressed.
His wife's manner was more muted, but she displayed a warm graciousness. Annetta, Santino's vivacious and pretty daughter, spoke
and laughed constantly. I was uneasy with her loud banter. It had an
almost desperate quality, and was somehow forced, as if she felt herself to be onstage and lacked confidence in her ability to play her role.
Her gestures sometimes startled me. Despite her gaiety, her behavior
struck me as fearful, as if she felt that a threatening supernatural force
was watching her closely.

I was the only one among our group who actually entered Santino's
home during this period, and only on one of those March afternoons.
I hardly recognized the large common room where Santino and his
family had greeted us in the bright light of a clear late autumn afternoon, almost seven weeks earlier. The texture of Santino's home was
radically different from anything that I remembered. I realized that
the shutters had been flung open on that now distant day of our first
visit. The room had been flooded with sunlight, reflecting the blue sky

and the burnt umber soil and the yellows of the harvested fields, and the animals had all been at pasturage. Santino was a poor peasant, who governed a poor household, but it didn't seem poor to me in the moments that I lingered within it on that March afternoon. The entire life of the homestead seemed concentrated in its one large room, which was receiving hall, kitchen, workshop, and bedroom all gathered into one. The air was thick with the smell of animals stabled on the same floor, only a few yards away, but it was a happy odor of well-tended beasts, mixed with the sweet aroma of dry fodder and apples, accented with the pungent tang of aging cheeses. Mixed with these intoxicating scents were the earthy exhalations of old stone and worn leather, wood smoke and wool, tallow and oil, and the seductive allure of freshly baked bread. These intoxicating scents blended into a kind of music that harmoniously reflected the music of the life of the household that rose each day through the floorboards to our quiet refuge above.

The March rains washed the vestiges of the February snows from the landscape, and the sunshine that followed dried the muddy roads and fields. Mother had almost completely recovered. She rejoiced in the brighter days and warming temperatures, as she fully resumed her role in the kitchen. My father was happy to see her vitality restored, but he became quite nervous whenever she forgot to observe our rule of silence. Mother would bang the pots and pans on the grill that we had rigged in the hearth, and often spoke so loudly in her rich, sonorous voice that we had to shush her up. One day my father appeared in the kitchen with a sign hanging around his neck. He had lettered the sign in block capitals *SORDO/MUTO* (Deaf and Dumb). Unfortunately, this did not have the desired effect. My mother shouted at him anyway, even as he mutely gestured at the sign, and wildly pantomimed that he could neither hear Mother nor speak to her. It was really very funny, but Mother failed to appreciate the humor of the situation and raised her voice even higher, demanding to know what Father was doing. Before the situation got any worse, Father removed the sign and calmed Mother down. Mother was finally made to understand that she would have to try to be quieter. Father explained that no one wanted to challenge her spirit, which had become quite buoyant with the onset of spring, but it was all the more important with the change of season to maintain our caution and vigilance. Few had passed near the house during the snow and sleet of the cold winter months, and fewer still had visited there, but friends and neighbors now often stopped to visit with Santino, Menga, and Annetta in their home below our creaking floorboards. Any signs of life above would lead to unwanted questions.

As it was, questions were already being asked, and at least some of Santino's visitors came with sharpened ears, and more than a glance at the shuttered second story of the old Caverni house. Just as naturally as water flows downhill, so had knowledge spread through the community that Santino was possibly sheltering a group of refugees. Apparently, no one believed that it was my family that Santino was harboring, and although many still spoke of us and wondered what our fate had been, most accepted the idea that we had disappeared across the ridges and had perished near Monte Sant'Angelo. The source of the first rumors that Santino was protecting anyone had probably come from someone in the local Resistance, which since February had kept a discrete eye on our security. A secret shared among comrades could become a confidence shared in a family, and then would become that most valuable commodity of peasant life, and of human life almost anywhere—gossip. And gossip seeks its own confirmation, and is embellished with rumor, as it is put to its use, which most often is either to promote or deflate the reputation of a person or group.

Don Domenico assured us that only a few in the Resistance knew about our presence at Santino's, and no one knew who we were. He was also certain that neither Santino nor anyone in his or Antonio's family had said anything. The region was awash in rumors, he explained, but none of these had focused on us. Looking back on what happened, I think that our friend Don Domenico would have been wise to be more mindful of the Lord's Prayer: "Deliver us not into temptation, but deliver us from evil," for it was a kind of temptation that opened the door to our exposure and led to the end of our tenancy at Achille's. Among the subjects that generated the most intense discussion in those early days of the spring of 1944 was the fate of one of the most prominent and certainly the wealthiest Jewish families in the region, none other than Vittoria's family, the Camerini of Pergola. Naturally, I had myself earnestly questioned Don Domenico about this. The priest assured me that he knew that all the Camerini had found safe refuge, but declared that he knew nothing beyond that. He firmly resisted my attempts to learn more about them, always insisting that he knew nothing, and pointing out to me that it was best that no one should know anything. I had to agree.

Everyone at the Caverni homestead remained loyal to our secret. They all denied that anyone was occupying the apartment above. Of course, Santino insisted—to anyone who dared to suggest it—that even he had no right to open the apartment on the second floor. It was empty and sealed, and would remain so, until one of the Caverni family chose to open it. But when one of Menga's companions suggested to her that it was perhaps in her home that the Camerini had found refuge, the good woman could not help herself but to swell at the thought she had received such important signori. And that, I think, may well have been the beginning of the end for us at Achille's. Menga certainly said nothing, but a smile, however slight, or a posture suddenly more erect with pride at the thought of the possibility of having received such prestigious guests, was the only confirmation needed for rumor to turn to gossip and gossip to feed upon itself and achieve the status of "fact." And once the "fact" of the presence of the Camerini family at the Caverni homestead had been established, it was only a matter of little time before one of Annetta's young companions had pried the secret from her, that indeed there was a family staying at their home, a noble family, with whom she had spoken, and that we were, indeed, the Camerini.

Don Domenico heard the gossip that the Camerini were residing at the Caverni homestead as soon as word of this began to spread through the homes of his parish. He came to speak with us about it immediately. The family Camerini was greatly respected in the region, and Don Domenico reasoned that no one was likely to denounce their presence at the Caverni homestead, but the rumors nevertheless posed a real danger, and we would probably soon have to move on to another place of hiding. And so it happened that, only a few days later, on a fine spring day in late March, in the first flush of new green leaf and bloom, Don Domenico came to us with the news that it was no longer safe for us to remain where we were. Fascist patrols in the area were becoming more frequent by the day. It was only a matter of time, he told us, before they came to inspect the Caverni home, and it would soon become nearly impossible to escape with all the roads more and more intensively controlled. On that same day, Achille's brother Mario arrived from Pergola to tell us that we had to leave immediately. He warned us that the Germans were preparing to comb the whole region in a campaign to repress increasing partisan activity and to interdict British airdrops of weapons. As a matter of fact, the Russians had parachuted two experienced women guerrilla fighters into the area to help the partisans organize resistance, and Don Domenico told us that partisans were intensifying their activities. They had just sacked the house of Broschelli, the richest signore in the region, and had taken away booty of more than 600,000 lire. Don Domenico suggested that we move to one of the abandoned Broschelli houses, then into an abandoned mill, then get in touch with the partisans, and, eventually, escape to Monte Sant'Angelo.

We were alive. Mother had finally recovered a measure of her health and strong spirit. Father was prepared to follow Don Domenico's advice that we should try to join the partisans. Buena would bravely follow us wherever we decided to go. And I was in despair. In my view, there was even less reason for the partisans to accept my family and shelter them than there had been three months earlier, and I thought it would be all the more foolish to join them just at the time that they would be under the most intense pressure from the Germans. I knew one thing for certain, however. Although, even as late as the spring of 1944, I knew nothing definite about the Nazi "Final Solution" for the Jewish people, I knew that above anything else we had to avoid falling into German hands. And I knew that we had to leave immediately. One good thing did arise from the renewed danger of our situation, at least as far as I was concerned. Marko decided to abandon us. My father even gave him some money and wished him good fortune. Perhaps Marko planned to cross the front and join the Allies. I didn't care. We never saw him again.

The House of Attilio. By Albert Alcalay.

17

Final Refuge

PERHAPS IT WAS THE CHANGE OF SEASON THAT EASED MY ANXIETIES. THE weather was beautiful at the end of March. Perhaps it was Marko's departure that brightened my mood. In any event, my black mood of fear and despair quickly yielded to a calm acceptance that we had to move on. Father was as concerned for the safety of the Caverni family as he was for our own security, and he was determined to leave. I had to agree with him, although I was still skeptical of the idea that our family could find safety with the partisans. Where to go now? Despite all the efforts of the Fascist authorities to control the roads and the flow of refugees, the situation had become chaotic, with the onset of spring and expectations of renewed fighting to the south. The roads were filled with families fleeing the front and the bombing of the cities. I thought that we might have a chance on the open road, even without papers. If we traveled freely and boldly, and avoided attracting any suspicion, we might pass unnoticed among the refugees. It was evident to me that Don Domenico was troubled by complex worries beyond the scope of my knowledge, and he was unable to point us in any direction other than to seek shelter with the Resistance, but he spoke reassuringly to me. "Don't worry," he said: "the Lord will provide, somehow." I wanted to believe him. What else was I to do?

Santino was in the kitchen with Father, Mario Caverni, and me on the day that Mario came to tell us that it was no longer safe for us to stay in the apartment. Santino, who believed the rumors that my father was Signor Astore Camerini, told us that Mother and Buena could stay in his home on the ground floor, and that Father and I could stay in the miller's house. Father had no success in his efforts to convince Santino that we were not Camerini, but he did make the kind peasant understand that we would have to leave. After all, both Mario and Don

Domenico had told us all that we were now too exposed to danger at the Caverni homestead. Once Santino had accepted that we had to move on immediately, he told us about a place not far away where he thought we might find shelter—in a small house on property occupied by his neighbor Attilio Elizabetini. Seizing on this possibility, Father and I set out early the next day to speak with him.

Attilio lived little more than a mile from the Caverni homestead, a walk of less than half an hour, and a pleasant walk on that fine spring morning. Following Santino's clear directions, Father and I crossed the fields to a footpath about two hundred yards behind the Caverni house. Roughly parallel to the main road, this footpath ran along the lower slopes of Monte Sant'Angelo. When we reached the path, Father and I turned to the right and followed its gentle curve around the side of the mountain until we came to a small village, or rather a settlement, of widely separated houses built on each side of the path. A little farther down the path, we found Attilio's house, just as Santino had described it. We soon found Attilio himself, hoeing rows in his garden. After introducing ourselves as friends of Santino and Don Domenico, and after the long discussion that followed, Attilio led us behind his home and sixty or seventy yards up a stony slope of ground, to a small house hidden behind a copse of trees. The simplest of houses, it was a solid two-room structure of white limestone, with a flat, beamed ceiling, plank flooring, a door of heavy oak, and four windows fitted with sturdy shutters of weathered wood. The door opened into a large room dominated by a large fireplace and furnished with a table and a few benches and chairs, and a single bed in the corner. Adjacent to this simple kitchen was a smaller room, in which we found an oversized armoire and two antique cast-iron beds, each with a weather-stained mattress of straw. Isolated far from the main road, the house was in an ideal position. If the Germans did thoroughly sweep the countryside for partisans, we knew that we would be forced to flee up the mountain, but we reasoned that we would at least have some advance warning. Father and I quickly concluded that the house would be our best refuge, at least for the moment, and we agreed to rent it. We told Attilio that we would return late in the afternoon with Mother and Buena and our few belongings.

Mother and Buena were elated when we told them that we had

Attilio's Home and Garden. By Albert Alcalay.

found a new home not far away. Father and I spoke with Santino and the miller. There was no point in trying to hide from them where we were going. They already knew, and we knew that we could trust them completely. Nevertheless, we reminded them that it was in everyone's interest that no one should speak anything of our winter passage in the upstairs apartment, or of our newfound home farther around the foot of the mountain. We thanked Santino for his good counsel in finding our new refuge. He was very pleased, and offered to help us move our belongings there. I refused this kindness, but asked Santino if we could continue to rely on him for help in obtaining provisions, if and when we might need them, and also to let Don Domenico know where we were. He readily agreed to these things.

We needed little time to gather our few possessions, and, with Santino's help, to close the upstairs apartment. After exchanging warm farewells with Santino, Menga, and Annette, and with Antonio and Sophia, and their two boys, Sergio and Rotiglio, we crossed the fields to the path and made our way to our new home. Despite our sadness at leaving our friends behind, our hearts were light and joyful in the warm sunlight of a beautiful day. We felt so free. We found Attilio waiting for us when we arrived. He had already filled casks of water from his well and stacked a supply of firewood in the kitchen. As humble as our new dwelling may have been, Mother surveyed it with the enthusiasm of a duchess inspecting a new palace. She spoke enthusiastically of charming alfresco luncheons in the warm sunlight of the coming days. Father arranged to purchase provisions and a few basic household goods from Attilio, who had already provided rough woolen blankets for the beds that Buena and Mother and Father were to take in the bedroom, and for me in the kitchen. We were well settled in our new home by sunset that evening and enjoyed our first meal there, happily gathered around a warm fire. There was still quite a tang in the night air of early spring.

Attilio Elizabetini was a sharp and intelligent fellow, an uneducated man, but one of natural intelligence. Attilio wondered who we were. He entertained the idea that we were members of the Camerini clan, but also thought that my father might be a well-known politician, perhaps a senator, who might rise to a position of power after the war. I am sure that he also suspected us to be who indeed we were—Jewish refugees from a distinguished family from some other land. Father told him that we were from Gorizia—to the north, on the border of Italy and Croatia. Soon after dark, on our first night in our new home, Attilio appeared at our door to see if we had everything that we needed. On that first night, he addressed my sister in Croatian. *"Laku noć, Gospodićna,"* he said, which can be translated as "Good night, Miss." We were shocked to hear this—we had decided that we would not speak Serbian in the presence of Attilio or any other of our new neighbors— but we tried to show no reaction.

We adapted very quickly to a completely new life. We spent most of the time outside. At first, we did not move very far from the house, which was a very pleasant, shaded place. The mountain air was scented with lovely, fresh perfumes emanating from the trees of the nearby forest. Within a month, we became very friendly with Attilio and his family and neighbors. Attilio worked in the sulfur mine at Cabernardi. The land on which he lived was actually the property of his brother-in-law Archangelo Monti, who lived with one of his daughters in Cabernardi, where he was also a miner. Both Attilio and Archangelo were very polite to us, and displayed the same intense but respectful curiosity about us that we had experienced elsewhere. Archangelo was convinced that we were Camerini. Attilio peppered us with questions. Did my mother or father have land or houses? Was their country forested? Did they raise cattle there? Did they cultivate the vine? Attilio had seen military service in Gorizia. He knew that region better than my father, who had never been there. Archangelo asked Father if he was a merchant. He even directly asked Father if we were relatives of the Camerini. Attilio asked my father if the word "Jew" offended him. Both Attilio and Archangelo wanted to know why we didn't have ration cards for food, why we were avoiding people and living such an isolated life. My father always answered circumspectly. Attilio finally gave up questioning him altogether. But Attilio trusted us. After all, Santino had sent us to him, and, even more importantly, we knew Don Domenico. Attilio's good opinion of us became highly respectful when he saw that Don Domenico visited us regularly. He was especially impressed when the priest brought us two sacks of flour that the partisans had confiscated from the signori.

We met many of the peasants who passed Attilio's house on their way on the path up the mountain, where they harvested trees and prepared charcoal. Attilio thought that some among them might be Fascists, and warned us to be careful. He did not tell us that he sometimes went deep into the woods to join the partisans. I have never known a man who worked harder than Attilio. He was extremely poor, but he seemed unaware of his poverty, and was unscarred by any jealousy toward those who were more prosperous. Attilio worked almost all day in his garden and in the fields. I wondered when he slept, because he also worked the night shift in the sulfur mine, which started at 8 PM. He took his supper at about 6 PM and then left the house and walked for nearly two hours to reach the mine five miles away, sometimes under torrential rain. This man had such a very hard life, but he always seemed content. He was filled with natural wisdom. He knew many proverbs and even some rhymes from Dante's *Inferno*. After we had been with him for a few weeks, Attilio told me that he had decided that he did not want to know who we were, or why we were hiding, but that he would be very sorry if we didn't tell him after the war. I promised him that we would, as soon as we saw the first Allied troops.

Attilio's family included two healthy daughters, Adda and Vilma, his small son Giani, and his faithful dog Friano. Attilio's wife Maurina was in motion throughout the entire day. She never stopped working. She was always barefoot, and her feet were harder than the soles of my shoes. Her cheekbones stuck out, leaving her eyes as two vivid deep holes in her face. Deep creases already surrounded her mouth, since she had almost no teeth, although she was not more than forty years old. She had the heart of an angel and would do anything to help anyone around her who needed help. Vilma, a big, husky peasant girl already in her twenties, with red cheeks, black hair, and very large hands and feet, always went barefoot, too, and she smiled all the time. She always had something to say, was always ready to gossip or to speak about almost anything, just to hear herself talking. Adda was younger, perhaps sixteen years old or so. She too was big-boned, but she was much slimmer than Vilma, and she was fair and not so quick in thought or speech as her older sister. Adda's dresses had been handed down to her, and their sleeves had grown short with wear. The girls were often singing—at least when Vilma wasn't talking. They did

Maurina and Her Young Son. By Albert Alcalay.

most of the household chores and worked with the family in the fields
and in the stable, where they kept hens, pigs, and sheep. What a simple life they had, and yet so fulfilling! I observed these two girls for a
long time, and I somehow came to envy them. They sighed, laughed,
fooled around, and seemed not to begrudge any part of their hard days

of work. They ate only in the morning and in the evening, and they almost never ate meat, or only rarely a bit of chicken. I was amused to see them dressed to go to church on Sunday, when they had to wear shoes. They were simply unable to walk in shoes, so they carried them, walking barefoot the couple of miles to the church in Palazzo, a village not far from Caudino. The girls put on their shoes before entering the church, and took them off immediately after the mass.

One day in late April, my sister Buena woke up with acute pains in her side. We immediately feared that she was stricken with appendicitis. When she began to vomit, we became even more alarmed. We knew that we had to do something quickly. If her appendix broke, the resulting peritonitis would quickly kill her. I sent Vilma to call Don Domenico. He came immediately, and told us to call the doctor from Palazzo. He, too, came promptly. He examined Buena and confirmed that she had acute appendicitis that urgently required an operation. He then told us not to call him again, because two Fascist agents were closely watching him and tailing him. He added that the authorities had transferred all the Jews remaining in Pergola to Palazzo, and that he was certain that the Germans would soon launch a *rastrellamento*, a "combing" operation of the entire area to clear it of the partisans who had seized effective control of the countryside and were boldly preparing to openly celebrate the First of May, Workers' Day. Then, abruptly, he left.

Don Domenico was alarmed about Buena and wanted to call for a surgeon to operate on her immediately. But the very idea of this was absurd to us. My father declared that he would take Buena to the hospital, regardless of the consequences. I argued furiously against this, pointing out that Buena was in no condition to be moved, and certain that Father and Buena would both be arrested or even killed if they left our place of hiding. Maurina also opposed the idea. Speaking through her toothless mouth, she told me about a local wisewoman who might possess some other remedy. She asked my permission for Vilma to take her bicycle to fetch her. I had never felt more desperate, not even when Mother had hemorrhaged. I had absolutely no idea what to do. I told Maurina to send Vilma, but I also asked Don Domenico to try to obtain documents for us, so we could take Buena to the hospital for an operation, if we ended up being able to move her.

Don Domenico left to try to obtain the documents. I tried to calm Mother, who had already fainted twice. Buena's condition remained grave. Vilma finally returned. Out of breath, gasping to speak, she told us that the wisewoman was coming behind her on a bicycle. Although a peasant, the wisewoman had perhaps once been a nurse; she knew how to handle a syringe. I did not even have time to be shocked at the absurdity of the situation, as she gave Buena a shot to calm her down. I tried to find out what she had in the syringe, but it was useless. I don't think that the woman herself knew. Was it some kind of folk medicine? Why the injection? I stood there paralyzed with astonishment. I didn't even know what the woman was doing and, now, looking back, I can't recognize myself in that moment. But my sister calmed down, and she regained her normal good health in the days that followed. I never learned what medicine she had been given, although it was clear that the medication led to her recovery. If I had not witnessed the episode, I never would have believed it. I felt a tremendous obligation toward Maurina, and wondered how I could repay her when we resumed our lives after the end of the war. After the war, when my sister finally had her appendix removed, I told the surgeon what had happened. He was surprised. He surmised that the peasant woman had given my sister morphine, or some other tranquilizer.

At the end of April, the partisans based on Monte Sant'Angelo intensified their activity. Despite all the talk of German plans to mount a campaign to exterminate them, the partisans operated with no real opposition through the first weeks of spring, and they became increasingly bold. The Fascists no longer had any real authority in the countryside, and could no longer patrol the roads without fear of ambush. We began to see the partisans during the daytime. They sometimes entered Attilio's house. They knew about us, and gave signs that they were protecting us. I even met one of the Resistance organizers whom the Russians had parachuted into the area. She was an extremely impressive figure, a muscular, big-bosomed woman who went by the name of Natasha. She looked like a steelworker. The partisans looked up to her as a legendary heroine. It was said that she was capable of shooting two machine guns at the same time. Later, I heard that she had survived the *rastrelamento,* but had become pregnant and died

Vilma Preparing Supper. By Albert Alcalay.

giving birth to an infant fathered by an Italian. Mother Nature's ironies are sometimes astonishing!

On May 3, Don Domenico brought a great sum of money to my father. Achille's father sent this money as a loan, with the understanding that my father would repay him later in gold. The money gave us the means to survive for many months. At the same time, Don Domenico finally brought us false documents that listed us as Christians. This was a comfort to us and we felt more secure. Don Domenico told us that the marshal of the Carabinieri in Cabernardi had confided to him that the Germans would soon launch raids on a grand scale. We had expected this news, but it alarmed us, and we wondered if we should move on once again. Don Domenico tried to reassure us and told us not to panic. To ease my mind, he invited me to begin painting his portrait the following day. I accepted his kind offer.

May 4, 1944, was probably the most important day of my entire life. Continuous rifle fire on the mountaintop awakened us at dawn that day. We speculated that partisans were testing new weapons that had been parachuted overnight from British planes dropping arms to the partisans at that time. That morning, I was preparing to depart for Caudino to begin the portrait of Don Domenico, as I had agreed to do. I was checking my paint box, and collecting my easel, turpentine, and canvas. While I was busy with this, Attilio went a little way up the mountain to see what was going on there. He also believed that the partisans might be testing new weapons. The shooting continued without interruption. My father was against it, but I set out for my appointment in Caudino. At about 7 AM, Adda, the younger daughter who was working in Caudino, came racing home to report that the Germans were attacking the partisans on the mountaintop. My father sent her immediately back to Caudino to call me back from Don Domenico's house, where I was preparing to paint his portrait. I rushed home with Adda as fast as I could. I told my father that I was considering Don Domenico's advice that I flee toward Sterletto. But Attilio said that the Germans would see me from the top of Monte Sant'Angelo and shoot at me. "What should I do?" I asked. The turn of events had completely surprised me. I couldn't assess the situation. I didn't know where the Germans were. Were they only on the mountaintop, or were they all around us? Of course, because they were looking for young men to draft into the army, I had to hide. I ran into a small forest at the base of the mountain, but I realized that this was not at all a suitable place. I was too exposed there, so I returned home. A general panic and fear showed on everyone's face. Even poor Friano was terrified.

Attilio was frantically rummaging through his house for a place to hide his rifle. Suddenly he shouted out to me. I ran to join him inside. He pointed under the window of his bedroom to a small space hollowed into the wall. Attilio asked me if I could squeeze into the space. I immediately bent down and, with a little difficulty, folded myself into it, completely bent in two like an Indian fakir, my knees touching my chin. Attilio then pushed a heavy chest of drawers in front of the hole to conceal it. When Father came three minutes later, calling out for me at the door of Attilio's house, Attilio helped me out of my new hiding place. My arms and legs were already numb. We were all so fearful. Mother had taken refuge in her bed as if she were ill. Her blond hair always drew attention, and she couldn't keep herself from talking when she was frightened. All of us were terrified at what might happen. My father had hidden our old documents and our money and other valuables under a loose floorboard in the bedroom of our little house. My sister had disguised herself as a peasant girl, removing her shoes and wrapping a kerchief around her head. My father sat silently, trying to read. Attilio took up a position hidden in the tall grass to watch for any movement.

The hours passed. The sun advanced to noon. Nothing happened. None of the neighboring peasants appeared. At around two o'clock, Attilio observed soldiers coming from the mountaintop toward the house. He rushed back to warn us. I squeezed into my hiding place in the wall of Attilio's bedroom. I was cruelly cramped in my position there, but I told myself that I would quickly become numb to the pain of it. Attilio pushed the chest in front of the hole. We waited. Seventeen German soldiers soon came into view. They were heavily armed for attack, with machine guns, grenades, and pistols. It was a hot day, and they were sweating and carrying their helmets. Attilio welcomed the soldiers with a salute and displayed his documents to them. The doorway of the house was wide open, but none of the soldiers tried to enter. They all sat and squatted in the front yard, smoking cigarettes. One of the Germans spoke Italian. He interrogated Attilio. Why wasn't he working? Did he have any weapons? Had he seen any partisans? Who lived in that other house in the back? Attilio calmly replied that he worked on the night shift at the mine, and that he had no weapons. He told the German that he had never seen partisans in the area, and that another family lived in the other house.

Attilio offered the soldiers some wine, but they demanded water. He asked the German interpreter what the soldiers were doing in the area. He told Attilio that they had killed forty-six partisans on the mountaintop. The soldiers then entered Attilio's house to search for weapons, and turned everything upside down. Cursing and joking, they paused for what seemed an eternity to search the drawers of the chest concealing my hiding place. I heard their fingers scratching on wood as they rifled the drawers and threw clothing and papers to the bedroom floor. I remained dead still. I clenched my teeth to prevent them from chattering in fear, and I clasped my hand tightly over my nose to prevent myself from sneezing. My lower body was now completely numb. The soldiers seemed to remain in the room forever.

British airplanes suddenly roared overhead. The Germans flew out of Attilio's house to the shelter of the shade trees in the yard. From my hiding place, I could hear them counting off the airplanes: *"Ein, zwei, drei . . . zehn"*—and I heard other comments in German. The soldiers then searched the stable and inspected the grounds around the house. But they strangely didn't bother to enter the house that sheltered my family. Eventually, another soldier arrived, probably a sergeant. Passing the open door of my family's house, he, too, didn't take the trouble to check inside.

This soldier finally yelled, *"Haben Sie alles gesehen?"* (Have you checked everything out?).

"Jawohl!" (Yes!) the soldiers barked back.

"Schnell! Vorwärts!" (Quick! Get moving!), he said.

With that, all the soldiers got up and moved off. Attilio accompanied them as far as the brook.

We could begin to breathe again. Attilio was emotionally overwrought when he returned, and began to weep with relief. He then sighed, *"Il grande pericolo è passato."* (The great danger has passed). My father embraced him, and he embraced my parents. Only then did Attilio come to move the chest away from the wall and to extricate me from my hiding place. He had to support me. My legs were completely numb and paralyzed. Everyone massaged my muscles, which very slowly came back to life.

Peasant neighbors came to the house a short time later. They told us that the Germans had found a young man hidden in a house nearby, and that they had torched it and killed the entire family sheltered there. Only when I heard this shocking news did I fully realize the danger that had threatened all of us, and how fortunate we were that the danger had receded, at least for the moment. Losing control of my emotions, I began to shake and sob hysterically. I had not cried for many years. Our narrow escape from danger triggered the release of enormous grief and sorrow pent up within me. No one could soothe my tears. Everyone wept with me. I didn't cease weeping until that evening. Although twice before the Germans had threatened me with death—in the early days of the war in Yugoslavia—my experiences that afternoon stand out as the most harrowing of my life, and each detail of that terrifying day remains indelibly vivid in my memory. Later that day, just as the sun was setting, we noticed more movement on the road in front of the house, as the local peasants began to stir from hiding. Some of these came to the door to tell us that the Germans had evacuated the area and left for Arcevia. They had taken with them two sons of our neighbor Spazzone. We later were relieved to hear that the Germans released these young men that same night. So ended May 4, 1944.

I stayed in Attilio's house that night and slept beside my hiding place in the bedroom. Adda was working in Caudino. Friano barked at any stranger, so I would be immediately alerted if anyone unknown to the house approached it. Dear Maurina offered me eggs, which was the peasant medicine for everything. They would take a raw egg, make a little hole in the eggshell with a pin, and then suck the yolk and the white out of it. By the next morning, news of the German sweep had spread throughout the region. Everyone was agitated and had his or her own story to tell. We learned that the Germans had killed a woman with two of her sons, poor people who had made a poor living making charcoal. Almost all of the partisans who had been killed were from the neighboring village of Montefortino, where they had openly cele-brated the First of May (Worker's Day). We also learned that our Jewish friends who had been interned in Palazzo had escaped just before the Germans arrived.

The day after the German sweep, Don Domenico climbed Monte Sant'Angelo to inspect the scene of the massacre. He then descended to our house to learn what had become of us. He told us that the corpses of the partisans had been left lying where they had been riddled beyond recognition by machine-gun blasts. It appeared that the Germans had surprised them in the stupor of sleep induced by drugged wine. My father told the priest how we had fared, and, with tears in his eyes, Don Domenico said, *"Il Signore ha allontanato i loro sguardi da noi."* (God has diverted their attention away from us.) At that moment, my father ceased to be an atheist and became a man of religion, because he was convinced that only a miraculous power could have saved us when so many others perished nearby.

Not many days after the German attack on the partisans on Monte Sant'Angelo, the Fascist authorities issued a public declaration that all classes of the citizenry born after 1914 were to be drafted into the army. Since we now had Italian documents, this concerned me, too. I remained hidden inside Attilio's house every night, but during the days I would usually slip away into the woods to a ravine that a mountain stream had sliced deeply into the earth. There, bathed in the cool humidity that rose from the gently flowing waters, I would hide amid the dense foliage that clothed the steep banks. I began to carve a large chunk of wood into a Madonna and Child to avoid going crazy, listening all day to the babble of the brook. When people in the area asked for me, Attilio told them that I had left for the south, hoping to cross the front to go over to the Allies. And so was life to continue for three months—I spent my days hidden on the bank of the brook, always alert to Friano's barking, and at night I crept to Attilio's room, ready to squeeze into my hiding place if necessary—until August 1944.

The entire month of May was an exciting and painful time. Although the Germans had delivered a blow to the partisans on May 4, we could feel the Fascist regime collapsing around us, even while its last thugs were still in circulation. Armed to the teeth, Fascists from Cabernardi roamed around the countryside, looting small farms for provisions and sometimes making arrests. But they made no real effort to systematically enforce the public declaration of the military draft or any other official program. Any pretense of a central government had broken down. The only authority that the Fascists had came at the point of their guns. They surely had no popular support. They were merely gangsters whose time was running out. Around the middle of May, we learned that the Allies had launched a massive offensive on the German Gustav line to the south. A week later, we heard that the linchpin of the German line—Montecassino—had fallen. Still another week passed, and everyone understood that the Germans were in full retreat. The Allies entered Rome on June 5, raising our hopes that the Germans would soon be swept out of Italy altogether.

In those exhilarating days of June, as the Germans retreated to the north, and the fighting came closer to our region, our situation became even more uncertain and dangerous. I remained in hiding, moving cautiously from my streamside hiding place to the shelter of Attilio's home at night, but I spent time with Father, Mother, and Buena in the twilights of those beautiful days of late spring. Throughout the month of June, the weather was seductively fair. Our nearest neighbor was a peasant named Possetti, the father of ten children. Possetti had kept his distance from us, but he came to the door of our little house one day early in the month. My father asked him if the Allies had really entered Rome. Possetti confirmed that it was true, but, he added, in confidence, that the next day the Germans and Fascists would launch new raids to collect young people for the army. Possetti told Father that I should be very careful, or I would be captured. Father answered that I had gone to Milan, to the university. But Possetti was smarter than that. He knew about me.

The morning after Possetti's visit, the Caudino road was choked with a convoy of trucks filled with the black-uniformed soldiers of Mussolini's puppet Fascist regime, the so-called Republic of Salò. These taciturn and brutal soldiers were the scum of the country—the remnants of Mussolini's lingering power. Most of them were armed with machine guns. They looted houses and farms along the road, but they found no one to conscript into the army. Fortunately, they didn't venture up the cart track to the Caverni homestead, and Santino, Antonio, and their families were unharmed. Vilma, Maurina, and Attilio were all hidden in carefully chosen positions to watch for any Fascist patrols, but none

of Mussolini's thugs approached our little community. At noon, the entire convoy concentrated near Caudino. Everyone had worried that the
Fascists would plunder Palazzo and burn it to the ground—it was
known to be a center of the partisan Resistance—but the convoy
passed through the village a few hours later without stopping, and
headed north. After their appearance that day, we saw no more concen-
trations of Mussolini's henchmen in the region, although small groups
of Fascists based in the towns continued to mount scattered raids into
the countryside, and German troops moved through the valley toward
the nearby front.

We remained extremely tense after the departure of the Fascist convoy. We couldn't believe that we had not been attacked, that the danger had passed. Our mountainside settlement slowly came to life late
in the afternoon, as people came out of hiding and gathered on the
path between the houses to exchange anxious appraisals of the situation. The worst had not happened. What could they expect tomorrow?
The peasants just wanted to be left in peace. After exhausting their
rumors and fears in anxious talk with their neighbors, they turned
back to their normal occupations. What else could they do? Maurina
was soon at work in her kitchen. The fear and tension of the day—and
the fact that we had not eaten since morning—had famished us. I de-
voured the *pasta asciuta* that Maurina prepared for us that evening.

By the end of June, the Germans had taken strong positions along
a new line across Italy, anchored along the Arno River, about 150
miles north of Rome, and the Allied advance ground to a halt. British
bomber squadrons had become a common sight in the skies above us.
We heard bombs exploding in the valley beyond Caudino. The British
dropped leaflets telling the peasants to disperse when they heard
planes coming—from high above, their pilots could not distinguish
between peasants and hostile forces—but in late June, bombs fell
around Caudino, killing thirty peasants working in the fields there. We
heard the constant rumble of artillery to the south. We saw very little
of Don Domenico during this period. He could visit us only rarely,
because he was under suspicion, and Fascist agents were closely
shadowing his movements. With liberation so frustratingly close at
hand, we all the more feared the threat of capture.

With little news from Don Domenico, and with most of the neighboring peasants fearful to go far from their homes, we were almost completely isolated. No one in our community had a radio, but we did learn that the Allies had successfully landed in Normandy, and were advancing. Through a doctor who lived in the nearby village of Palazzo, we heard that a fierce battle had taken place at Caen. We saw more of Attilio's neighbor and friend Possetti—we had abandoned any effort to conceal from him that I was still living on the property—and we also often saw another neighbor and friend, Gino Moncarelli, who went by the name Spazzone. Possetti and Spazzone had their own reasons to hide from the Germans, and they often took shelter in the forest that reached down the mountainside behind our house. Spazzone was an old and experienced peasant. He liked to talk, and in the weeks of late spring and early summer, he often kept company with my father, who enjoyed speaking with him about a variety of topics of interest to them both. Only one peasant gave us cause to be afraid. This nettlesome character's name was Lumacca. He threatened Attilio that he was considering notifying the police about us. When Attilio told him that our documents were in order, Lumacca began to circulate the rumor that we were Fascists. Absurd as such talk was, this rumor frightened Spazzone, who then kept away from us. We begged Don Domenico to speak to Lumacca. We wanted to be on good terms with everybody.

Happily, nothing came of Lumacca's threats, and we continued to live quietly on the side of the mountain. Despite the tension and fear that infected our days, there were moments of relaxed humor. One evening, I decided to prepare spaghetti in the way we had made it in Belgrade—with sugar and crushed walnuts. Attilio and his household could not believe that I could commit such a sacrilege, and watched incredulously while I concocted this alien dish. As soon as it was ready, and I asked them to taste it, I saw immediately that they didn't like it at all. When Attilio mournfully commented, "What a waste of raw materials!" I laughed like crazy. But I couldn't laugh when I heard that the Germans had executed peasants in the town of Montefortino. And Maurina's constant talk of Fascist spies alarmed us, although we saw no one passing in the village. We were saddened when we heard the news that Aldo Filinić, who was called "Signor Angelo," had been arrested. We didn't learn until later that he had managed to escape from prison. I was shocked when I learned that the Fascists had arrested Angelo Anav. Angelo was the husband of Signor Camerini's eldest daughter. He was a close friend. I was intensely worried that Vittoria and her family were in danger. But I could do nothing. I didn't even know where Vittoria had found refuge. So, despite our isolation in our mountain retreat, we did receive some news in the currents of rumor—some of it malicious—that came to us each day. We did not know what to believe anymore. We could only wait, and hope.

18

Liberation

DESPITE THEIR FEARS OF BOMBARDMENT AND OF MARAUDING FASCISTS and Nazis, the peasants around us did their best to tend their animals and raise their crops as the last days of a beautiful, but tumultuous, spring ripened into summer. Throughout the month of July, we heard the continuous rumbling of artillery in the distance, day and night. The sky was constantly filled with Allied warplanes, which strafed roads and railways and dropped bombs on every site of any strategic importance—bridges, railway stations, depots. The town of Fabriano came under especially heavy attack. Amid all of this violence and destruction, the peasants struggled to make their first harvest of corn, which they gathered in the traditional manner, into neat piles equally distributed in their open fields. There was no gasoline to run tractors and other farm machinery, so all of this work had to be done with the brute force of animals or by hand, and much of the harvest could not be collected. Reports of looting and wanton destruction circulated wildly. Everyone feared that the Germans would pursue a scorched earth policy as they retreated, destroying all the livestock and crops, vehicles, and everything else of value that they could not take with them.

The peasants suffered terribly. There were many instances of looting and wanton destruction at the hands of the Nazis, but none of these horrors touched us directly, and the Nazis had neither the strength nor the will to carry out any systematic plan of total annihilation. As they were driven northward, they blew up the few bridges that had not already been destroyed by Allied bombardment, and they also blew up what was left of the region's electric transmission and telephone facilities. The Nazis detonated huge explosions at the two major sulfur mines at Cabernardi and Volatica, utterly destroying the mines and spreading thick clouds of sulfurous smoke that poisoned vast tracts of

land around them. Well before the end of July, we learned that the
Allied forces had advanced to Sassoferrato, where their forward movement was slowed because the important bridge there had been destroyed. Our isolated community was not on the main line of the Nazi
retreat, but we did see a few famished German stragglers fleeing the
front. Some of these stopped to demand something to eat or drink.
They were isolated and vulnerable, but they were armed, and we
feared them. A commissary unit of Austrian soldiers was stationed in
Caudino to supply the Nazi fighting forces that were still in the area.
We could hear them yodeling Tyrolean songs at night. A German artillery unit had taken up a position at Caudino as well.

With the Allies so close, some of the peasants set out to try to seek
safety behind their lines. Many of these souls turned back, however,
unwilling to confront the dangers of crossing the front. Imbued with a
sense of fatality, most of the peasants remained close to their homes,
hoping that the fighting would somehow bypass their lands and wash
over them without bringing any more death and destruction than they
had already suffered. Insecure within their own homes, some peasants
set to digging shelters for themselves and their families. Our village
was sufficiently far from the Caudino road to be under any immediate
threat, but I also thought it would be wise to dig a shelter. Attilio was
not convinced that this would provide any more security for any of
us—he told Father that he would never on his own initiative have
begun work on a shelter—but he agreed to help. We began digging
into a spur of Monte Sant'Angelo, at a site concealed within the forest
about three hundred yards away from our house. Because the sulfur
mine at Cabernardi had been destroyed, and Attilio no longer had
work there, and because he felt insecure tending his garden and fields
in the open, he had time for the work. Attilio was a hard worker by
habit and by nature. Despite his initial reservations, he threw himself
enthusiastically into the project as the shelter took shape. Maurina
and Vilma helped also, hauling planks from the house to the site and
gathering wood in the forest to shore up the sides and support the
ceiling of the tunnel. Gino and several other neighbors soon joined us,
digging a shelter into the other side of the spur.

Fighting continued in the valley and beyond, while we worked on
the tunnel. We hoped that the Nazi lines would soon break, and the

Germans would be swept out of the region, but day after day passed with no change in the situation. Wild rumors of all kinds circulated among the peasants, whose worst fear was that the Nazis would round up the men at gunpoint and force-march them to labor camps to the north. Everyone was prepared to flee to the cover of the mountain forest at any sign of the Nazis. Even the local priests had to go into hiding. False alarms of approaching Nazi soldiers several times interrupted the frustratingly slow progress on our shelter. Attilio, my father, and I scrambled up the mountain to hide among dense vegetation in the most unapproachable places, often for an entire day. Attilio, poor man, had to drag my old father up the mountain, even though Attilio and my father were of the same age. Nevertheless, despite these interruptions, after almost three weeks of work we had joined our tunnels and hollowed out a gallery where they met. Everyone was satisfied with the results of our efforts, and the distraction of our work was of inestimable psychological value during what otherwise would have been an excruciating period of enforced inactivity and waiting—either for disaster to fall upon us, or for our liberation. As it turned out, the shelter proved to be very useful.

In early August, soon after we had completed work on our mountain shelter, the bombardment intensified in the valley, and around Caudino and Palazzo. British artillery pounded continuously at the German positions. Many shells overshot their targets and landed not far from us. Since beginning work on the tunnel, I had altogether abandoned my hiding place by the stream in the ravine beside the house. I remained with Attilio and our families, either inside our houses, or in our new shelter, where we went when the shelling became too intense. All of the peasants in the region did the same. Nobody went far from their homes—except when news spread that food was being distributed in Arcevia or at some other center. We ate whatever Maurina had to sell to us. She baked bread for us. She also permitted us to dig for potatoes in her garden. Attilio provided us with wine that he had pressed from his own grapes. Because Maurina had very little to spare, we purchased eggs and lard from our peasant neighbors. We carefully rationed the last remnants of a large ham. We spent about 4,000 lire each month for everything, including our rent. Our money was quickly vanishing, but that was not too great a worry for us, since it seemed to us that liberation was just around the corner.

The first Allied soldier we encountered was an American pilot who appeared at our door a week before our liberation. He knew only how to say, *"Aqua, aqua!"* (Water, water!). When I first saw him approach, I thought he was a German straggler, so I hoarsely called out to my family, "The Germans are here!" before darting behind the house and running to hide in the ravine. My father opened the door to the strange soldier, and tried to speak to him, first in Italian, then in German, but he got no answer. Only when my father started to speak English to him did the pilot explain that he was an American pilot whose plane had been downed near Rimini. When it became clear that the pilot was a friend, Buena ran to call me from hiding and I rejoined the family. The pilot had traveled a great distance in his effort to reach Allied lines. He was filthy. His uniform was in tatters, and he walked with a painful limp. Fresh blood stained the dirty bandage tied around his forehead. He accepted our help with gratitude and relief. We settled him on my bed in the kitchen and administered first aid, applying iodine to his wound and freshly bandaging it. Buena brought him a hand cloth and a pot of steaming water. Mother prepared a hearty meal for him, the best that our home had to offer—bread, eggs, and sausage. The pilot asked Father if he was Italian. Father explained that we were refugees, but did not offer any more details about who we were. As grateful as the pilot was, it was clear that he did not trust us completely. He left almost immediately after eating. But he trusted us enough to heed our advice to avoid the Nazi troops stationed at Palazzo and Caudino, and in the valley beyond these hill towns. He headed up Monte Sant'Angelo. I hope that he found his way safely to his destination.

The appearance of the American pilot sharpened my impatience to see Allied troops. All of us were desperate to be liberated, to be released from the strange and dangerous no-man's-land in which we had been living since the Allied forces had surged forward in June, only to see their advance grind to a halt not far from us a few weeks later. We knew that the Nazis would be beaten back, but when? I certainly did not want to be captured or killed on the eve of liberation, but the dangers remained very real. If the Nazis questioned me and I failed to present my false papers, I would be shipped off to a concentration camp. If I did present these papers, I risked being drafted into the army. I considered following the route toward Arcevia that we had indicated to the pilot. In that direction, there were only scattered Nazi patrols between our position and the Allies. But the real danger had nothing to do with documents of any kind. The Nazis were capable of killing without asking questions. And this was a threat that all of us lived under. In the end, I decided to remain with my family. How could I leave them?

The sounds of battle came closer and closer, as the Allied and German artillery continued their endless dueling. I had, weeks ago, abandoned my refuge in the ravine, but was ready to run into hiding at the first sign of trouble. With Attilio's little dog, Friano, at my side to alert me to any approaching danger—Friano and I had developed a real attachment—I surveyed the scene with my binoculars from a position on the high ground at the edge of the woods near our house. With Monte Sant'Angelo at my back, I could see the hilltop villages of Caudino and Palazzo, and the valley beyond, in an arc of more than two hundred degrees, and could catch glimpses of the Germans retreating along the Caudino-Palazzo road. I couldn't monitor what was happening on the other side of the mountain, but Attilio had heard that the Allies had pushed forward there, as far as Montefortino, barely twenty-five miles away.

Several nights after the pilot had appeared at our door, the pounding of heavy artillery intensified to a constant roar. The exploding shells illumined the entire night sky in a lurid, red light. Attilio, Maurina, and their son and daughters had gathered with Mother, Father, Buena, and me on the higher ground at the edge of the forest near our house, when a stray shell exploded with a shattering scream less than one hundred yards away. Everyone immediately scattered and ran through the trees toward our shelter. Poor Friano was left abandoned, whimpering in fear at the end of his long leash behind Attilio's house—until Attilio remembered to go back and release the little dog. Friano scampered after us to our shelter, where he leaped into my arms, beside himself with joy to be with us. We later learned that the Allies had laid down the heavy artillery barrage that night to discourage Nazi counterattacks, while the Allied forces struggled to consolidate their hold on ground that they had just gained. We couldn't judge what was going on at the time, but it was clear that we would be safest in the refuge of the tunnel that we had excavated into the spur of Monte Sant'Angelo. We stayed there throughout the night. Many of our neighbors joined us, and found safety with us in our vigil of hope in the several nights that followed.

We had become inured to the thump of artillery. No more shells had struck nearby, but we continued to gather each night in our mountainside shelter—Father, Mother, Buena, and I, with Attilio and his family and at least two dozen of our neighbors. Attilio and the other peasants cautiously dispersed to their homes during the day, always alert to any approaching danger. Although all but a few had abandoned work in their gardens and their fields, the peasants had to care for their animals, gather food, and attend to other tasks. Father, Mother, and Buena did not sleep well in the tunnel, so they were happy to return to our house, where they tried to rest. Four nights had passed since the heavy nighttime bombardment had first driven us to our shelter. I continued to keep watch, Friano at my side, from the vantage point close to our house. We had heard that the Allies had begun to move forward from Sassoferrato, and that advance elements had already reached Arcevia, but I had seen no sign of the Allied forces, and the Nazis posted on the nearby hill towns of Caudino and Palazzo were strangely quiet. I wondered if the German artillery unit at Caudino had withdrawn during the night. I observed a few German vehicles on the Caudino-Palazzo road, then nothing. The artillery had quieted on our side of Monte Sant'Angelo, and the hot summer day was calm and filled with expectation. Apart from the thump of artillery in the direction of Montefortino on the other side of the mountain, the only threat seemed to be a heavy line of clouds building up over the valley.

Having slept only fitfully for many days, I was exhausted. I was lulled to sleep, almost hypnotized, by the buzzing of bees in the mountain meadow and the occasional bursting into song of birds, who seemed to be tentatively testing their music against the rare peace of the day. Friano was gamboling about, chasing butterflies in the tall grass. But Friano came to attention when I suddenly pulled myself alert. I had spotted a patrol of three men in khaki uniforms cautiously advancing along the path toward Attilio's house. Inspecting them with my binoculars, I could tell that they were not Germans. Sweeping the horizon with my glasses for other signs of movement, I focused on a German patrol of four men descending the hill behind Caudino. The Nazis were moving in our direction, toward the three men whom I had just spotted. I was certain that the Germans had observed the three khaki-clad soldiers from their lookout on the Caudino hill, and had sent out the four-man patrol to ambush them—not far from Attilio's house. Despite the danger of being noticed by the Germans as well, I shouted and gestured wildly to attract the attention of the friendly patrol, waving them up the slope to my position so I could alert them to the danger. But was it a friendly patrol? I couldn't know for certain, nor can I evaluate to this day if I had assumed too great a risk in calling out to them. Was their appearance the first sign that the war had ended for us? Was this the moment of our liberation? Or were we to be killed in these last hours of the war?

The three-man patrol saw me and approached, their weapons ready at their sides. Before I could speak, the youngest of them demanded, *"Chi siete?—Siete Tedesco?"* (Who are you—are you German?). I smiled at this, answering—of course not. Another demanded to see my papers. His name was Marinelli. Although Marinelli and the soldier who had first spoken were wearing Allied uniforms, I could tell from their Italian dialect that they were local partisans. The third soldier had not spoken, but he carried himself with such an air of authority, that I quickly understood that he was the ranking officer. *"Venite dentro e vi dirrò chi siamo"* (Come inside and I will tell you who we are.), I said. After a moment's hesitation, the leader of the patrol nodded his assent, and the three men followed me into our house, where I turned and told them, "We are Yugoslav Jews." I waved toward Father, Mother, and Buena, who were gathered timidly at their bedroom door. The leader then spoke, explaining that he and his men were a scouting patrol from the "Maiella" Brigade of the Polish Legion, which was attached to the British army.

Attilio appeared at our door. He recognized Marinelli. Attilio and Marinelli were both amazed when the leader of the patrol and I embraced each other. I then told the soldiers that I had spotted four Germans heading out of Caudino toward them. The youngest soldier, a bold fellow, immediately exclaimed, *"Dore sono? Gli ammazzerò"* *(Where are they? I'll shoot them!)* Looking to the leader of the patrol, then back to the youngster, I told them not to act rashly, not to draw reprisals down on our little community. Many lives could be put at risk. I urged them to take cover and wait. But I don't know what they decided to do. The soldiers left our house as soon as I told them about the Germans.

Only minutes later the sky darkened, and a terrible wind began to howl, as a violent summer storm that had gathered in the valley pushed suddenly up against Monte Sant'Angelo, and released torrents of hail and rain with terrifying bursts of lightning and thunder, as if God were tearing open the black canopy of sky. Attilio, my family, and I, and little Friano remained huddled in the shelter of our house, expecting the "Maiella" soldiers to return to seek shelter with us. A half hour later, the storm suddenly expired into a gentle rainfall, and the clouds quickly dissipated, revealing a dazzlingly blue sky. When I cautiously stepped outside to regain my lookout, I could find no trace of either the Germans or of our new friends. Attilio followed me. His curiosity perhaps renewed by the excitement of the moment—and the surprising fraternal embrace I had exchanged with the Italian leader of the patrol—he repeated the comment that he had made a few months earlier, when we had first come to stay with him and his family: "I don't know who you people are, and I haven't wanted to know, but the time perhaps will come soon that you can tell me. I will be very sorry if you don't." I looked at my friend with a smile, as if to say that that time indeed showed promise of coming soon.

The landscape, bathed in the rich golden light of a late summer afternoon, was eerily peaceful and deserted. Even the occasional rumble of the artillery on the other side of the mountain sounded like the last claps of thunder of a distant, fading storm. The birds were singing joyfully. There were no signs of Nazis at Caudino or Palazzo. It was as if the storm had washed all danger away. But no one stirred from their homes, apart from crusty old Possetti, who plodded down the path with his sons in tow to inspect the pig that he kept at Attilio's, and to check for any storm damage to the ripening summer wheat that he had planted in a field beyond Attilio's house. Attilio came to our house later that evening, to tell us that the Germans had gone, adding that British troops had occupied Palazzo and the hill above it. No one stirred from their houses that evening, and no one took refuge in the mountainside shelter. We really could consider ourselves liberated as of that day!

When we awoke the next morning, Father was determined to visit Don Domenico. I scanned the surrounding countryside to assure myself that we would be safe, and decided to go along with him. My father had not left Attilio's since we had arrived there five months before. Unfortunately, we did not find the priest in the war-scarred village of Caudino, where we learned that he had gone off with the partisan Marinelli to help improvise repairs on a bridge on the Caudino-Palazzo road that the Nazis had destroyed in their retreat. We also encountered two soldiers from the "Maiella" Brigade. They told us about the terrible destruction that the Nazis had left in their trail. The soldiers were encouraging to us. They assured us that our sufferings would very soon come to an end. Father and I discussed whether we should go on and try to find Don Domenico, but we decided that it would be wiser to return to our house.

We had just reached Attilio's when Vilma came running with the terrible news that the British had abandoned Palazzo. Her report shook me. I wondered again whether I should make my way over Monte Sant'Angelo, to Arcevia, where I knew the Allies had established a strong presence. Maurina told us that Attilio had left after us that morning, to join in the effort to repair the bridge on the Caudino-Palazzo road. We were worried about Attilio, Don Domenico, and others among our neighbors, but could not decide what we should do. Soon afterward, we saw the deacon of the church at Caudino calmly approaching us, his fiancée at his side, on the path in front of Attilio's house. A familiar figure in our community, the deacon soothed our fears, assuring us that the Germans had retreated from the area, and that the British had been at Palazzo that morning. Only minutes later, we were relieved to see Attilio returning home. Our anxieties were completely allayed when he happily confirmed that the Nazis had left, and a British advance guard had occupied Palazzo. More troops, he told us knowingly, were on the way.

Attilio, Father, and I decided to set out for Palazzo immediately, to inspect the situation there directly. We were eager to visit with the doctor there—the doctor who had so fearfully come to diagnose Bue-

na's appendicitis—and we also wanted to see if Signor Scandellari
and the brothers Spurle—who had left Pergola to seek shelter in the
town—had survived the ordeal of German occupation. On our way to
Palazzo, Father finally revealed to Attilio who we were. Poor Attilio
was clearly disappointed that my father was not, as he had surmised,
an important senator who had been in hiding from the Fascists, but he
was happy at last to know who we were, and pressed us for more details of the odyssey that had brought us to his door. Father promised
to tell him the entire story, but asked Attilio to be patient for a just a
little while more.

After a brisk walk, we arrived at Palazzo, less than half an hour
after setting out from Attilio's house. The few British soldiers and partisans who had reached the hill town were only an advance unit, but
they had no thoughts of abandoning their posts, nor did they seem to
expect any German counterattack. We learned that they were expecting reinforcements the next day. Palazzo was a shambles, although the
damage from artillery shells was not as severe as I had thought it
would be, and the town's citizens were already busy making repairs
and restoring order. We found the doctor in his clinic. He relayed to
us what he had learned from a British officer: that the Germans were
pulling back along the entire front to a new line that they had prepared far to the north. The doctor also relayed other news of the war
to us. The British soldiers had told him that morning that the Allies
had broken out of Normandy and were driving the Nazis back across
France, and that the Russians had shattered the Nazis in Central Russia, and had advanced hundreds of miles.

Despite all this good news, the doctor was more nervous than optimistic about the immediate future—doubtless due to the stress and
terror of the recent Nazi occupation. The Germans would surely
launch a counterattack, he told us. He advised us to go to the south.
He said that he was prepared to flee at the first sign of fresh danger.
Our friend Spurle had gone to Arcevia the day before. Scandellari
then appeared with Attilio, and Father and I decided to join them at a
café to discuss the situation over a glass of wine. That fine summer
day in mid-August of 1944 was like a dream. We were all exhilarated
to be able to openly share the simple pleasures of wine and conversation. Later that afternoon, Scandellari and his wife visited Attilio's

house, where Maurina greeted all of us with refreshments. Scandellari and I decided to go to Arcevia the next day to speak with the authorities. Madame Scandellari assured us that we would get plenty of food and clothing from Allied stores, so we would not starve. Amen! Food was in shorter and shorter supply and was becoming more and more expensive, and our funds were almost exhausted.

Scandellari and I set out for Arcevia early the next morning, leaving his wife to stay with Father, Mother, and Buena in our little house. It was a hot, humid day, but we traveled the twenty miles openly on mostly deserted roads and reached the town early in the afternoon. As we approached Arcevia, we saw more and more British and Polish soldiers. They did not detain or question us, so we entered the town without delay, where we witnessed an incredible bustle and confusion. The Allied authorities were preoccupied with the conduct of the war. They were just beginning to set up a civil liaison office, so we could find no one to speak with immediately. After lingering for an hour in the crowd milling in front of the Allied command center, Scandellari and I decided that it was futile at that point to try to clarify our situation with the authorities. We found a table at a local café—again we were pleased to see how quickly the essentials of life were being restored—and took in the scene with the same exhilarating sense of liberty that we had felt the day before in Palazzo. We decided that I would stay in Arcevia to continue to try to speak with officials, while Scandellari returned to Attilio's to report on the situation, and to bring his wife back to the town.

Achille Caverni came to visit us late in the morning of the very day on which Scandellari and I had departed for Arcevia. He—with his sister, brother-in-law, and two other friends—had escaped from Pergola to avoid being seized by the Nazis, who were rounding up young people in the last days of occupation. Achille had led his small band to the refuge of the Caverni homestead, where he had arranged shelter for my family during the long, cruel winter months. Achille spent three happy hours with my family in our little house at the edge of the woods. When Father later shared the details of this reunion, I was sorry to have missed it.

Above the noise of all the activity at Arcevia, I could still discern the thump of artillery in the distance, as the Allies pounded at the tail of the Nazi retreat. After exchanging farewells with Scandellari, I remained at our table, surveying the fascinating scene around me. I learned from my neighbors in the café that Allied troops had pushed forward to Sterletto. There was even talk that they had occupied Pergola. The owner of the café told me that I could stay there that night. I very much appreciated this kindness, when it was volunteered to me. I had nowhere else to go. My thoughts turned to my family and all that we had survived, especially as the night advanced into the hours of early morning, and the activity quieted around me. I wondered whether I should have returned with Scandellari to my family at Attilio's. I had accomplished nothing in remaining behind. But the peace of sleep finally overcame me—an exhausted sleep, undisturbed, at my café table.

I felt surprisingly refreshed when the strong August sun awoke me the next morning, and was grateful to wash up and take a simple breakfast. As the morning went by, the scene in Arcevia became even busier than the day before, as regiment after regiment of the Allied main force moved through the town. There was even a unit of tanks. My five bitter years of war had not jaded me. I observed this parade of military might with a boyish enthusiasm. This really was the end of our suffering. But I hardly had time to reflect on this. I was simply caught up in the joy of the moment, as were all the people of the town. I caught a glimpse of my friend Arthur Spurle later in the morning, and managed to catch his attention and call him to my table, where he joined me.

By early afternoon, the scene had become joyfully riotous. The streets and cafés were bursting with celebration, music, and singing. I reflected on the first heady days after my own country had declared war on Germany. Did I still have a country that I could call my own? The war was ending for us, just as it had begun—with celebration. Arthur didn't understand when my spirit suddenly darkened. I couldn't help myself. I was struck with the madness of it all, and bitter memories of all the waste, and destruction, the sorrow, and the loss that we had survived. Was this really the end of our suffering? What difficulties lay before us? And I wondered if it would not have been better if I had remained with my family in the little house between the shade of the mountain forest and the sun-drenched hills and valley. I could only hope that this madness would soon truly reach its end; that my family would be safe; that Vittoria and her family would be safe; that everyone would be safe; that I might recover the happiness that I had found with Vittoria; and that we might all find a way to survive and live happy and productive lives. There was no certainty, even in those moments of celebration. I could only hope, and rejoin the shouting and the singing, which is exactly what I did.

Scandellari had managed to reach Attilio's the prior night. He returned to Arcevia late the following afternoon with his wife, and with my father, who had been determined to join them in the journey. I was alarmed to see Father looking so old and frail. The long, hot journey had utterly exhausted him. I immediately asked the café owner if there was a room that we could rent. Miraculously, he was able to offer one to us, at a steep nightly rate. After an uneasy night of sleep, Father pulled himself together the next morning, and marched off with me to the town hall to see if we could gain an audience with the appropriate authorities, whoever they might be. We took our places standing in a long queue, and waited the entire morning in the reception hall, but the line had hardly moved, so we abandoned our place, hoping for better luck the next day. Arcevia was crowded with people in our situation. And the troops passed by continuously.

Two mornings later, we finally found ourselves gratefully standing before the military governor of the town, a burly, good-natured Scotsman—a true gentleman. We were somewhat startled when he received us with open cordiality. He looked on kindly as my father mustered all his dignity and read to him in a quavering voice a statement that he had prepared in English describing our situation and our needs. If the Scottish officer's kind and respectful disposition toward us had been startling, we were astounded when he called in the mayor of Arcevia and sharply ordered him to provide us with transportation and the best lodging and the best food in town—all at the expense of the Allied Military Government. We were incredulous, but we could not have been happier than we were at that moment. My father bowed, and I sharply returned the military salute with which the Scot dismissed us.

So, less than an hour later, it was in an automobile that we returned to Caudino, where we found Don Domenico, who smiled warmly at the news of our good fortune, and embraced us. He told us that he was happy that God had answered his prayers for us, and that he hoped to see us in the better days that were before us all. He then hurried us on our way, knowing how eager we were to rejoin Mother and Buena. We directed our driver to the point in the Palazzo-Caudino road closest to the path that led up to Attilio's house and raced up to reunite with our family and to bid our farewells to Maurina and Attilio, their daughters and son, and our neighbors, with promises to meet them again very soon under much better circumstances. Mother and Buena had already prepared our baggage. I was almost reluctant to leave, but after pausing briefly to take in our home with the lens of my heart, I hurried down to Attilio's for a final good-bye. Little Friano followed at my heels, as we made our way down the path, and I had to stop several times to tell him to heed Attilio's calls to come back to the house. This simple country dog had become my best friend. I was saddened to say good-bye to him. We finally arrived at the road. Mother and Buena were amazed to see the car waiting for us there. We hoped that it would take us to a life renewed.

After pausing briefly—well, not so briefly—at the Caverni homestead, where we had a joyful reunion with Santino and Antonio and their families, we went on to Arcevia. On orders from the Allied Military Government, the mayor's office had designated two rooms for us in the town's principal hotel—all at the expense of the Allied Military Government. Exhausted, Father immediately took to his bed, while Mother and Buena arranged our few possessions and began tentatively exploring our new surroundings, although neither dared at first to leave the hotel. The endless columns of Allied troops continued to parade down the town's main thoroughfare, which ran directly past our hotel. I spent all that remained of our first day there, and all of the next, sitting on the curb in front, watching the marvelous procession go by: British, Polish, American, and even Italian units, artillery, armor, and infantry, endlessly marching toward the defeat of the Nazis. I felt as happy as a clam, and was already thinking about how to get back to Pergola to see Vittoria.

After having waited so long—and, when the end finally came, waiting longer still, unsure that we had truly been liberated—now everything around us seemed to be happening with a dizzying speed. For our part, we were content to remain motionless, at least for a time, while the world spun around us. After three days of rest and plentiful food, we had recovered some of our strength. No longer troubled with any dark thoughts of the futility of war, I watched the unending parade of Allied strength with increasing satisfaction. Father and I voraciously read every newspaper we could obtain. We discussed in their most minute details every new report of progress toward the ultimate defeat of the Nazis. We had been starved for news. I gave in completely to the pleasure of following the chronicle of the defeat of our evil enemies. Yet unaware of the worst of their evil, I relished my hatred for them.

And so things could have continued—could I have objected? But new complications soon arose, and once again we had to make adjustments. With the advance of the Allies, command jurisdictions naturally changed, and our status was to come under review in less than a week—as soon as the bills began to accumulate. My family, Scandellari and his wife, and others in the town's swollen refugee population were called in groups to audiences before an American officer, who had been named the new military governor of the town—relieving the Scottish gentleman who had received us so cordially and had treated us with such exceptional kindness and respect. It was not difficult to discern that the American's attitude would be less forthcoming.

"Who is going to pay for your expenses?" he asked sharply, waving a clutch of papers and looking directly at me.

"The Allied Military Government," I replied, simply.

"Why do you think that?" the American snapped back.

"The previous military governor so ordered it, Sir," I said, carefully underlining with "sir" the respect that I felt toward my interrogator.

Then he asked, "Do you have anything in writing?"

"No, Sir," I admitted, "but is not the word of an English gentleman always honored?"

The new governor replied, again shaking the bills in my face, "I don't know anything about the word of a British gentleman. I am an American, and I don't have any budget for this."

Feeling threatened, and my skills as a diplomat somewhat rusty, I answered, "Well then, Sir, I suppose that the previous governor may have made a mistake, but, even if he did, that changes nothing, as far as we are concerned. An officer of the Allied Military Government made a commitment to us, and the Allied Military Government should honor that commitment!"

"You will have to pay," the American said, showing no inclination to yield.

"But, Sir, we have no money at all," I answered.

"That is not my concern," he answered, unmoved.

No longer able to contain her anxiety and outrage, Madame Scandellari screamed fiercely at the officer, "You have to help us! We have been waiting five years for you to come to liberate us. You cannot allow us to die of hunger!"

In a very restrained voice, the American said, "We are fighting a war here. We are not set up to provide for refugees, not in this fashion." He wearily set the papers down on his desk and looked back at us.

Father finally stepped in. He explained to the officer that the war had forced all of us far from our homes and driven us from our livelihoods. He added that the Italian government had granted us a stipend while we were under *confino libero,* but that Mussolini's puppet Fascist regime, the Republic of Salò, had ended these payments in November of the prior year when it issued the order that all Jews and foreigners should gather at collection points to be sent to concentration camps. We could handle our own affairs without the help of the Allied Military Government, if these stipends could be renewed, and if the back payments due to us were made. Seeing the sense of this, the American officer agreed to order the local Italian authorities to take care of the matter.

But our troubles had only just begun. We soon learned that the local authorities—willing though they were—did not have the funds to make the payments to us, but with this came assurances that we would be paid. They requested a loan from the local prefecture. We simply had to wait until their request was processed. Happily, this was done in a relatively short time. We were paid the weekly stipends that were due to us from early December 1943 through the second week of August, but were told that we would receive no additional payments. The war was over, at least in our region, the officials insisted, and the government would assume no further responsibility for us. After Father paid our hotel bill, there was little left. We didn't know what to do, but it was clear that we could not continue to live at the hotel.

However unclear and troubled our future, our problems seemed insignificant relative to the progress of the war. Frontline troops continued to pour through Arcevia—infantry regiments, heavy tank battalions, engineering units with entire bridges loaded on the backs of trucks, and artillery units with their heavy ordnance in tow. Ordnance heavier still was being moved to the north on the railroads, which the Allies repaired with unbelievable speed. The sheer volume of these movements was awe-inspiring, the long lines of ammunition trucks and supply vehicles no less so when the flow of troops finally tailed off. Only after I had witnessed this endless procession of men and material did I really understand what an incredibly massive enterprise the war had been, and my admiration of the United States soared. That one country, even a continental country, could have produced so much and shipped it all across an ocean, amazed me. When I considered that we were just one small section of a secondary front in a three-front struggle for the control of Europe, and that the United States was fighting in the Pacific as well, I could understand that it had taken the Americans a year or two to reach us! I relished the daily bulletins of fresh victories on other fronts.

We very soon left our rooms at the hotel for less expensive accommodations in a private apartment with two rooms and a kitchen. Over the following two weeks, life in Arcevia gradually calmed down to the natural pace of a small mountain town, a self-contained life within the massive medieval walls and ramparts that were the crumbling witnesses of past conflicts. After the excitement of the massive troop movements through the town, everyone turned to the grim realities of getting on with their lives in the backwash of war. Mother and Father organized card games with the Scandellaris, but we had few other friends. Although Buena did her best to maintain a cheerful disposition, I could tell that she was weary with the new insecurities of our situation—even more so, in a sense, than she had suffered while we were in hiding from the Nazis. Food prices soared. We felt trapped. Our meager resources were dwindling. We couldn't blame the town officials. They had done all that they could. Everyone was suffering. Everyone was hungry. An American doctor from the Red Cross advised us all—my family, Signor and Signora Scandellari, and others in our situation—to move to a refugee center near Rome, at Cinecittà, a town that had been so-named because in better days it had been a center for the production of motion pictures. But the very idea of this repelled us. We had had quite enough of camps and refugee centers.

Everyone in the family felt a poignant nostalgia for our little house at Attilio's. I miss it to this day. It would have been pleasant to spend the last ripe days of summer there, and to linger there to see the autumn in. It would have been better to be that much closer to Caudino and Don Domenico, to Santino and Antonio and their families. It would have been much better for me to remain more closely tied, in those days of passage, to my good friend Achille, and to all of our friends in Pergola, and to Vittoria, above all to Vittoria, and her family. But we had had ample reason to seek shelter in Arcevia, even if we had been wrong in our expectations of more support from the liberators for whom we had waited so long. The very length of our vigil of hope for liberation had magnified our expectations of what liberation would mean. What else could we have done but to seek help from our liberators? But yes, they had a war to fight, and we had our own struggles. I blamed myself for the downward spiral of my family's situation, and fell into a depressed state of inertia for several days. This depression was only broken when Otta Levi, a local vegetable seller, offered to take me to Pergola in the back of the battered truck that he shuttled back and forth between the towns. I leaped at this opportunity. I was very anxious to see Vittoria. I wanted to see my other friends there. And I wanted to find a more viable situation for my family.

As soon as we arrived in Pergola, I ran directly to the Camerini Palazzo to see Vittoria. She was there. She had returned with her family at the end of August. Of course, Vittoria was happy to see me, but our meeting was awkward. Although other members of the Camerini family were at home that day, Vittoria and I met alone, perhaps for an hour. I could tell immediately that the months of our separation had weakened the bond between us. Vittoria told me that she and her sister Helena had been sheltered among nuns in a nearby convent for nine months after their family's flight from Pergola, in early December. We exchanged stories of our lives in hiding, but Vittoria seemed embarrassed and reserved with me, and she revealed few details of

her exile, apart from telling me that she and her sister had been completely isolated throughout the period and had seen nothing at all of
the Germans. She inquired about my parents and sister. I related how
they were, and sketched in the salient features of our flight and hiding,
of the last days before liberation, and what had since transpired.
When I told Vittoria that I was hoping to bring my family back to Pergola, the embarrassment between us became even more acute. My
family and I clearly needed help. I did not ask for help, and Vittoria,
who herself could offer no assistance to us, simply looked at me sadly
and then turned her eyes away. I rose from the chair she had offered
to me, explaining that I had much to do, embraced her in parting as I
had in arriving, and left the palazzo, happy that she was well, but
deeply troubled that my reunion with her had not been more joyful.

I set out immediately to see our friend and former neighbor Capanoni, the town druggist who had kindly agreed to care for the belongings that we had been forced to leave behind when we fled from
Pergola that December night so long ago. I made my way slowly to
his door, passing unrecognized among all the familiar faces of that
Pergola—*"Pergola, paese di felicità!"*—that I had come to love so
well during the many months that we had spent there in *confino libero*.
By outward appearances, the town was unchanged, apart from the
happy absence of the few Nazi soldiers and the more numerous black-
shirted Fascists that had haunted its streets. It was the same, beautiful, medieval town. The impressive palazzi, the cathedral, the old town
gates were all intact. The monumental colonnaded town hall was un-
touched. But the streets were not as animated as I remembered them,
and, despite the beautiful late summer day, there was a depressed and
sullen cast over everything. I saw fewer children at play, and fewer
adults engaged in idle conversation. I saw many empty tables at the
café on the town square. When I finally arrived at Capanoni's door, I
looked sadly across the street at the modest house that my family and
I had occupied. Someone else was living there. I was relieved when
Capanoni answered my knock, and when he greeted me with happy
laughter and a warm embrace, "How good to see you, Alberto! Yes,
your possessions are secure. Have you and your family decided to return to Pergola?"

Capanoni and I had a long talk that afternoon. He explained to me how difficult life had been in Pergola in the final months before liberation. The town had not suffered from the bombardment, and the fighting had not touched it. Pergola was too isolated. But the Fascists and the Germans had terrorized the townspeople, and had stripped the town of anything that was useful to them—trucks and automobiles, gasoline stores, provisions—before they had fled to the north. The Fascists had even taken his medicines, Capanoni told me. Food prices had gone up dramatically that past winter. Many people had had very little to eat. Even coal had been hard to come by. The winter had been severe. Most of the townspeople had been forced to cut down trees and to gather wood for heat. The fighting in the region that summer had interrupted the harvests, and had destroyed what was left of the distribution system. Food prices had shot up even more. What could people expect in the coming months of winter? When liberation came, of course, the people were happy. There was some celebration. But liberation did nothing to improve their dire situation. For anyone of the few who had any money, there were one hundred relations and friends clamoring for help. What good was money anyway, with prices the way they were?

I listened carefully to Capanoni's sad account, and understood for the first time how fortunate we had been during most of our exile in the countryside—despite all the suffering that we had endured. I thought of my parents and sister in Arcevia, where after the first heady days of liberation, life had become so hard. I understood that our life would be no easier in Pergola, but I decided that afternoon that we would at least be among friends there, and would somehow find our way. So, I asked Capanoni if he knew where we could find an apartment, or at least a couple of rooms in the town. He had no certain answer to this, but suggested a few places where I could look, and told me that I could stay with his family for a few days while I searched. Two days later, I sent a letter to my family through the vegetable monger, Otta Levi. I had found rooms for us—very modest and only temporary—but a home, and a new start. Several days later Father, Mother, and Buena arrived—on the back of Otta's truck.

The weather was fair through the end of October. We were able to renew many friendships. We were safe from arrest and transport to a concentration camp. Otherwise, our lives were terribly difficult during the first weeks of our return to Pergola, and our hopes for the future were almost extinguished. Many others were in the same difficulty, or worse. Of course, those who had their own roofs over their heads were better off. Unable to pay any rent, we had to move several times. But Father had a small reserve of money, and for a time we could buy food—cornmeal for polenta, the occasional tomato, olives, and pasta. The town authorities gave us 200 pounds of flour. As winter approached, food shortages became more and more grave, prices spiraled out of control, and our money was almost entirely exhausted. Malnourished, our strength spent, we were in terrible shape. We knew that we would not be able to survive the coming winter without help. But what could we do to better our situation? That question was tormenting me day and night. It was an incredible irony to me that we were in greater danger now than ever before.

Everyone was in need. Everyone was hungry. The Italian authorities could do little for us. They simply told us that we were now free to do as we wished. We could leave. We could appeal to the Allied authorities for help. But the military authorities sent us back to the Italians, always repeating what the American officer had told us in Arcevia: "We have no time for civilians; we are fighting a war." My father wrote to the Embassy of Yugoslavia at the Vatican, but he received no reply. Our troubles accumulated. Buena had another attack of appendicitis. Doctor Melletti—the father of my friend Lucia—operated on her successfully. While Buena was still recovering from her operation, Mother began hemorrhaging again. Father was distraught and exhausted, but he remained strong, and once again saw Mother through the worst of her illness. Winter was upon us.

We survived that winter. I can hardly bear the memory of it. We were destitute, but somehow Father always found a few lire to sustain us. Like many others, we lived mostly on boiled cabbage. Father sought help wherever he could. He wrote to the regional headquarters of the Allied Military Government in Urbino, but his pleas for support yielded nothing. He even requested that my family be transferred to the refugee camp at Cinecittà. Again, no response came. When he could, Achille brought us a little food that he managed to forage in the countryside, but this was rare—his own family was suffering. The Camerini had nothing to spare, but the Camerini sons-in-law, my friends Angelo Anav and Luigi Tagliacozzo, were deeply concerned about us and tried to find help for us. Angelo wrote from Rome that he had told the American consul there about our plight, and that the consul had noted our address, but I knew as soon as I read Angelo's letter that we could expect nothing from the American consul in Rome. Nevertheless, I appreciated Angelo's initiative. The very fact that he had spoken on our behalf sustained my hopes. Luigi Tagliacozzo also wrote from Rome with a report that a relief agency there—DELASEM (Delegazione Assistenza Emigrati Ebrei—Delegation for Aid to Jewish Immigrants)—granted refugees 4,000 lire per month. Father continued to write his appeals. I continued to search for ways that we could improve our situation. Starving and cold, we had little more than hope to nourish and warm us.

We greeted the New Year of 1945 with the little cheer that we could muster. Our fortunes had reached their nadir. Once again, we were told that we would have to move. At that point, we were living in a single room, in a squalid, overcrowded apartment. Buena had recovered from her surgery, but she was weak. Mother was still bedridden, in the wake of the recent recurrence of her hemorrhaging. My father was a shadow of himself. He had managed to maintain his strength and dignity only by the force of his will. We had no money for rent. We had no money for food. No one had any money. My friend Lucia Melletti—the daughter of the surgeon who had removed Buena's appendix—told me about an empty apartment in her building, on the floor above her family's. It belonged to the Ginevri family, who had left Pergola to live in their country house. The beautiful, large apartment was sitting vacant. Our need was so great that I had no scruples about taking it and led my family there. I didn't bother to clear this with the authorities, but Father did write a letter to the Ginevri family. Father naturally had reservations about our "requisitioning" the apartment without authorization of any kind, but he advanced no arguments against the action. We had to move. Mother and Buena would be much more comfortable. If we had to starve, then at least we could starve in the dignity of decent surroundings. It was a comfort to be close to Lucia during this difficult period. We were often together.

Just after we had moved to the Ginevri apartment, we received a letter from Arthur Spurle, who had decided to take his chances at Cinecittà. Arthur reported that the conditions were terribly crowded and unsanitary in the refugee camp there, but that there was at least plenty of food. He wrote that he had met no one from Belgrade in the camp, or any other Yugoslavs. My father sent a letter to DELASEM through Angelo Anav in Rome. Angelo was still doing his best to find help for us. He had contacted the newly reopened Yugoslav consulate in Rome on our behalf, but the responses that he had received were confusing. We received a bewildering letter from him at the end of January, telling us that the Yugoslav consulate had changed, and promising us that Mother and Father would get some help, but also reporting that Buena and I were ineligible, because we had to be repatriated first. We couldn't make heads or tails out of that. We were happy to read in his postscript that Angelo planned to come to Pergola to explain everything to us. A few days later, Angelo and Luigi came to visit us together. They explained that we would not be getting any help from the Yugoslav government after all, because Marshal Tito had seized control. We still did not understand, but we realized that it was futile to press for any clarity. What could anyone do?

Signora Ginevri returned from the country with her daughter in late January. Given the circumstances, she greeted us pleasantly enough. She was clearly relieved to find the apartment in good order, but she made it clear that she wanted us to leave as soon as possible, and that she expected payment of a thousand lire for January, and an additional payment for any time that we were to remain. Applying the most pragmatic Marxist reasoning, I politely told the Signora that we had no intention of paying, that we had no *money* anyway. I did have some success in reconciling the matter by making a portrait of her daughter, and inviting Signora Ginevri to choose one of my paintings. We were not thieves and squatters, after all. We had suffered enormously, and Mother and Buena had been very ill. Signora Ginevri relented and seemed happy to take one of my paintings and to leave the matter to her husband, who proved more difficult to placate when he retuned, several days later, and angrily took the matter directly to his friend, the mayor of Pergola. If he had to receive refugees in his home, then he had the right to demand compensation for it! Let the mayor decide the rate! But Signor Ginevri's anger made us no richer. We had no money for food, let alone rent. The mayor understood this reality immediately, and dismissed Signor Ginevri's claim against us, but he told us that we would have to move, this time into a house that the city had officially requisitioned from Signora Barbanti, who at the time was staying in Rome. And so, in early February, we moved once again. The Barbanti house was as pleasantly appointed a home in which to go hungry as one could wish! We were happy to have a hearth where we could warm ourselves in front of a wood fire. The weather had turned bitterly cold.

Of course, our move to Signora Barbanti's house did not end our troubles. Less than two weeks later, the Signora appeared with her young son and daughter and maid. Because our presence in her home was officially sanctioned—if more as a result of the mayor's exasperation than due to any organized humane policy—Signora Barbanti couldn't order us to leave, but she did demand that we move into her cold, humid pantry. This alteration was completely unacceptable to us and provoked a real quarrel. Once again, the issue went to the mayor's office for resolution. This time we were determined to remain where we were. Weary of such disputes, and because there was ample room in her home for us as well as Signora Barbanti, her children, and her servant, the city officials who treated the matter—the mayor declined direct involvement—set aside the case "for later review." We kept our two bedrooms and shared the kitchen and a bathroom. Happily, the Signora accepted this decision and determined to make the best of it. We soon observed in her an inclination to regard us with compassion. When she understood that we were people of culture, she showed more interest in us. We became good friends.

As it did with almost all of our fellow refugees, and with so many native Italians, the harsh winter months took a dramatic toll on my family and me. Famished, and in the wake of their illnesses, Mother and Buena were weakened and housebound. I don't know how Father and I continued. Vittoria knew how much we were suffering. She was horrified that we were starving. I believe she risked raising her Father's temper in speaking to him about our real situation. I didn't ask her to do this. I had long ago resolved not to do so; I knew that many people were in our situation, and that Signor Camerini was beset on all sides with requests for help that even he could not satisfy. We were completely destitute. By the middle of February, when I had almost become too weak with hunger to do the hard work of gathering wood, and all that we had had to eat for more than a week were a few vegetables that we had boiled in water, Father finally approached Signor Camerini to ask him for a loan. Signor Camerini respected my father. To the extent that it was possible for him, he regarded Father as his equal. But he told Father plainly that he would not give him a loan. What good was there in a loan, he protested, when the value of money had declined so sharply? Father did not press the desperation of our situation on Signor Camerini, and left his palazzo with dignity and grace. He was successful later that day in his appeal to Signor Caverni, who lent him a small sum of money, although the situation of his own family had become extremely difficult. And Signor Camerini relented, promising us half a pig that he was preparing to slaughter in the coming days. I did not display my anxiety, and concealed the outrage that I felt inwardly at how absurd it was, after surviving five years of war, exile, internment, and flight into hiding, that liberation should have brought us freedom and liberty, but only freedom and liberty to perish from hunger!

We survived. Looking back at those bleak days, I realize that our darkest hours fell over us just before the brightening light of hope finally dawned late in the winter of 1945. Although Signor Caverni could only loan us a sum barely sufficient to purchase some little food for one or two weeks, his kindness and sacrifice helped us bridge our most desperate moments. Although Signora Barbanti's return to her home in mid-February at first posed a real threat to us, to which we reacted with the fierceness of weakened souls unwilling to relax our last grip on life, our conflict with the Signora was soon resolved, and by the end of the month she had all but adopted us into her family. We thought ourselves enormously wealthy when, toward the end of the month, Signor Camerini finally sent us half the slaughtered pig, as he had promised. This was, after all, a priceless treasure that money at the time could not buy. In return for a few precious cuts of meat, we engaged a butcher to carve the carcass and transform it into hams, salami, sausage, and lard—provisions most welcome at the Barbanti-Alcalay household. They amply sustained us in the weeks that followed.

As a new spring approached in the brightening days of a surprisingly fair March, the shift in our fortunes buoyed my own energies and interest in life. Food in my belly certainly helped me along in this. With Signora Barbanti's encouragement, I resumed work on my painting, when I could. And I found that I could make a little money, working freelance as a porter at the town's bus station. The bus service on which the isolated town depended for its connection to the outside world had fitfully resumed in the course of the winter. By March, there was quite a bustling of coming and going at the station, and no lack of parcels that needed to be loaded and unloaded. For the first time, we began to see a considerable number of Allied military personnel—mostly officers on leave from the front, and Allied administrative officials who were working with the local authorities to establish government services and in liaison capacities that most of us really didn't understand. There was certainly a great deal of ambiguity about who was running the country. Suffice it to say, the Allied officials, no longer exclusively preoccupied with prosecuting the war, were beginning to show more interest in civic affairs. Apart from a few local officials and their friends, who were naturally jealous of our prerogatives and beginning to joust with new political realities, no one really minded the increased Allied presence. Everyone certainly welcomed the flow of humanitarian aid that was beginning to reach the community, especially the appearance of American military rations, which, for many months, were to become a welcome complement to the local cuisine, and, in some quarters, supplant it altogether. And everyone appreciated the money that began to circulate—American dollars!

With the first stirrings of a revived local economy, renewed cultural life also began to surface in Pergola. Among the brightest stars of this little renaissance was Professor Marcello Camilucci, who arrived that March from Rome. A writer and a translator of Romanian, and a devout Catholic, he was an impressively knowledgeable man. Professor Camilucci organized gatherings every Saturday afternoon, during which he would expound on the political situation, and stimulate discussions. He sometimes organized literary afternoons. We became very good friends that spring, and we remained so for decades afterward. I was thrilled to exchange ideas on an equal footing with a man of his caliber. We spent many happy hours walking together and discussing all kinds of things. Because my worldview was still very much influenced by a Marxist materialism that was so much at odds with Christian spirituality, I was surprised that I could enjoy such a good relationship with a devout Catholic. But I had matured, and my mind was more liberally open to other points of view. The professor was startled and pleased with the depth of my knowledge of Christian theology and church history, knowledge that I owed to my discussions with Don Domenico, and the many books that he had provided me with in the winter of the prior year.

Apart from my contributions to Professor Camilucci's Saturday seminars, I did not involve myself in local politics. Although we had many friends in the local community, I didn't feel that I had any direct role to play in the awakening debate over how the townspeople wished to arrange their affairs as the war drew to an end. But I observed, with intense interest, the revival of political life and the fresh organization of political parties in the town, and my confirmed progressive orientation certainly inclined me to sympathize with the socialists, who were the most active among the new factions. I was most concerned with the welfare of my family, and, of course, with progress in my relationship with Vittoria. Although we had pulled back from the abyss of starvation, at best our situation remained uncertain, if no longer desperate, and most of my time was absorbed in my efforts to earn money from tips as a porter at the bus station, and the resumption of my work as a painter. The revival of trade in the town stirred an entrepreneurial spirit in me. To supplement my meager earnings in my work as a porter at the bus station, I arranged wherever I could to display my paintings and drawings—at butcher shops, vegetable stands, and stationers—offering my work for fifty or seventy-five cents. My art attracted some admiration and comments, but, unfortunately, the market for fine art was still weak in Pergola, and I had little success. I began to think that I might have better luck if I set my prices higher.

From the onset of winter, I don't believe there had been a single day in which Vittoria and I had not spent at least some time together. We had reestablished a real relationship, and my love for her had deepened, but I knew within myself that we no longer shared the same strong bond that had made us inseparable a year before. The nine months that she had spent sequestered in the convent had not changed her. No, it wasn't that. It was more that she was a young woman coming to terms with her own identity, and that she was deeply insistent that she should accomplish this independently. In the far-away first months of our romance, Vittoria had relied on me as she struggled to come to terms with her Jewish identity amid the terrible anxieties of that time. Now, free of those anxieties, and having fully explored her Jewish identity and resolved what it meant to her, much of our relationship had to be reestablished on a new foundation. Yes, Vittoria was deeply attached to me. She admired me and was deeply attentive to me. She was loyal to that questing passion that had united us so strongly. Since my return to Pergola, tenderness—more mature than any feelings we had earlier experienced—did gradually grow between us. But it had become a requirement for Vittoria—and she was determined in this—that she should stand on her own. In short, Vittoria was not prepared to make a long-standing commitment to our relationship. I accepted this, even as I struggled to understand it, and I knew not to push beyond the limits of the boundary that Vittoria had set.

But Vittoria and I did love each other, and we cherished the time that we had for each other through the terrible winter of 1945 and in the brighter, more hopeful days of the following spring. As Pergola again came to life, as the weather grew fairer with each passing day, Vittoria was willing in an instant to step outside her palazzo to stroll with me through the streets of her town, quick to comment on everything, even the tiniest details of life, which her nuanced observation captured, and joyful to see the fresh cut flowers again on sale, and the miracle of Mediterranean oranges at the greengrocer's. Innocent of politics, and by nature not inclined to be involved with such matters, she was nevertheless eager to hear my views on the changing political landscape in the town, and the competing interests of the various factions that were jousting for influence and power. We often visited our friends, especially Lucia, whom we both liked very much.

I often thought about a future with Vittoria. I seriously considered proposing marriage to her—when she was ready to accept this. Her family seemed unconcerned about her continuing her studies. They did want to see her happily married, and I knew that they would prefer that she marry into prosperity. But who was prosperous in the closing days of the war? I could never be sure how they evaluated me as a prospective husband to their youngest daughter. I did know that they would never have tolerated my continual presence in her company if they had altogether ruled out that possibility. I was unsure how or when my family would be able to reestablish our fortunes. The first step would be to go to Rome to normalize our situation. For myself, I was certain that I would never return to Yugoslavia, and though I had been educated as a Zionist to make my life in Palestine, I now doubted that I would ever live there. I had become too invested in working on my painting, and I had not abandoned the idea of completing my studies in architecture.

As April approached, and the end of the war drew near, my family's survival was assured, but our future, of course, was still unclear. I was overjoyed to see that Mother and Buena had by then recovered their health. Although we were all still concerned about Mother, and Buena as well, they were both at least under the care of a fine physician, Doctor Melletti, and, with an adequate diet, had regained much of their strength. Father was feeling much better, but he was burdened with our financial worries. He wanted to repay Signor Caverni as soon as possible. We even tried to sell our watches—for a high price—but without success. Perhaps we were too ambitious in asking so much for them, but we didn't want to part with them for anything less than their real value. I badly wanted to find a way to repay Signor Camerini as well. I had done everything that I could. There was something else that I fervently desired—the basket of figs that was displayed in the window of the greengrocer's shop. I passed by that window every day to admire the figs, but I never had the twenty lire or so that I needed to purchase them. They assumed a symbolic importance that grew more intense each day. Not being able to have that basket of figs tore my insides apart.

In the days following, I continued to work at the bus station. I gathered tips each day, but never enough to buy the figs, nor nearly enough to begin to repay Signor Caverni, or even Signor Camerini for the half pig that he had given to us. Father and I were both extremely worried about our future. My paintings and drawings were still displayed in the shops, but I was completely discouraged, because no one had expressed any interest in buying even one of them. But our luck turned when two American Air Force colonels arrived at the bus station in early April. Their luggage was so heavy that I could not carry it all. They began to laugh, and asked me what kind of porter I was.

"I am a painter, not a porter!" I retorted.

The American officers immediately showed great interest. They asked me to show my paintings to them. Naturally, this surprised me, but, after helping them get their luggage to their quarters, I led them to Signora Barbanti's immediately. I was pleased that they "very much" admired my work. To my amazement, they selected five paintings and six drawings—small paintings on plywood, and figure drawings and portraits of peasants in pencil—and offered to buy them. I didn't know what to ask, but I knew very well that my family needed as much as I could get for my work, so I asked the officers for seven hundred dollars—seven hundred dollars! I didn't dream they would accept this price. I was thinking that we would bargain down from it. However, one of the gentlemen casually drew a thick wad of money out of his pocket and counted out seven hundred dollars—all in ten-dollar bills! I fainted from emotion. Mother had to dowse me with a bucket of water to bring me back to consciousness. The officers were alarmed about me, but they laughed when they saw me get up to my feet, and left, quite happy with their acquisitions. As for me, I immediately set off for the greengrocer's shop—to buy the basket of figs that I had been hungrily coveting for so many days. I then rushed off to see Vittoria.

Later that very day, Father and I were out walking and discussing our brighter situation, when Buena arrived at a run with a letter in her hand. The letter had been addressed to us through Signor Camerini, who had personally brought it to us at Signora Barbanti's house. The letter was from our close friend Dr. Amodaj. He wrote that he, Ergas, and other friends from the camp at Kavaja were all safely in Rome. They had all feared that we had perished, and had only recently learned that we were living in Pergola. We learned from Dr. Amodaj's letter that some of our friends had already left for America. Others had returned to Belgrade. Dr. Amodaj also wrote that he had sent 5000 lire to us in the care of Signor Camerini, and that he was sending his son Armand to bring us to them in Rome.

The letter that brought us such welcome news ended with a report that we had long feared—we had not heard from anyone in Belgrade for a very long time now. Dr. Amodaj wrote that the Nazis had killed all of our family and friends who had remained in Belgrade— everyone. My father cried like a child for his dead brothers, for all of our relatives and friends, for everyone who had been executed or had died in concentration camps. We had begun to hear about the worst, but we still did not fully understand the horrors from which we had been able to shelter ourselves in Italy. My father wept for the dead, and he wept in gratitude for all who had been saved. I tried to comfort my father, but there was nothing that I could do to assuage his grief.

Grief did not overwhelm me, as it had Father. That would come to me later, although without tears, and generally in the deep of the night. I felt first a hollowness, and then I felt that hollowness fill with the bitter bile of my hatred for the Nazis. I tried to comfort Father, and led him home. The next morning we set out together for the Camerini palazzo to speak with Signor Camerini, who had received the funds that Dr. Amodaj had sent to us in his care. Father insisted that Signor Astore keep half of the money, as repayment for the meat that he had given to us, but the Signor refused to consider this, and inquired of our news with a tenderness that I had never before seen in him. Father replied to his friend with restraint, but thanked Signor Astore with all the warmth that he could express through the screen of the grief that had deeply affected him. Father and I then visited our friends the Caverni family. Signor Caverni gratefully accepted repayment of what we owed him, gently silencing Father's apologies that we could not repay him in gold, and graciously accepting our thanks for all that he and his family had risked and done for us—a debt that could never be repaid.

We waited anxiously for Armand to arrive from Rome, until a few days later, when we received another letter from Dr. Amodaj, again through Signor Camerini, explaining that his son Armand would not be able to come to Pergola. Our good friend the doctor had sent another 20,000 lire, with instructions that we were to come to Rome as soon as possible. The following day, we received still another infusion of funds, 30,000 lire from our friend Ergas, with a note saying that he, too, was eagerly awaiting our arrival. We quickened our arrangements to leave Pergola. Our friend Signora Barbanti had decided to accompany us, and would not hear of our staying elsewhere than at her home on the outskirts of the Eternal City.

The entire family was overjoyed at the prospect of rejoining our friends in Rome, and the relief of again having the means to assure our survival. Now we had considerable capital, certainly enough with which to begin the process of reestablishing our lives. And, miraculously, we had dollars! That night we discussed how we would travel to Rome. Because we wanted to bring our belongings with us, we really could not take the bus. I knew well just how much passengers could take with them—quite a lot! But there were limits! I considered buying a truck with a portion of my new wealth, if I could find one. The next morning, however, I found a truck for hire, whose peasant driver would be very happy to take us all the way to Rome for twenty dollars. Father arranged for our travel permits. He had already been working on that problem for a few days, but I still don't know how he managed to obtain the required documents so quickly. Everyone had time to say their good-byes. After I collected my paintings and drawings from the shops, I visited Achille and his family, and Lucia and Dr. Melletti, and Capanoni, among other friends. I had time to see and kiss Vittoria, who promised that she would soon follow us to Rome, where she would stay at the home of her sister and brother-in-law Luigi. Vittoria and I would soon be together again.

We departed at first light of the following day: Mother, Father, Buena, and I, with Madame Barbanti, her two children, and her maid, all in the back of the truck, on a beautiful April day. We had purchased ample provisions, including two sacks of flour, a case of soap, sugar, tea, coffee, and we brought all the salami that was left from our pig! It was a bouncy, joyous, sunny bright, all-day ride. We breezed through all the checkpoints, our driver having no difficulty proudly explaining that he was driving "Allied people." He delivered us with our cargo directly to Signora Barbanti's house in Città-Giardino, just a little bit outside Rome.

And so, that evening, we had arrived at an end, and at a new beginning. We were able to telephone Dr. Amodaj from Signora Barbanti's house that night. We were joyful to learn from the good doctor that three of my father's brothers had survived—my uncles David, Isaac, and Aron, who spent almost all of the war in German POW camps.

They had recently returned to Belgrade. But our joy was darkened with the grief that we felt for our three civilian uncles, Bukus, Nisim, and Rudi Alcalay. They had been sent to Auschwitz. We knew about Auschwitz now. We knew that these brothers, and so many others, had not survived the war that was finally coming to an end. Would Rome be the end of our wandering and suffering? Our hearts filled with hope.

Epilogue

Soon after my family and I had settled in Rome, I was invited to participate in an exhibition at the University of Rome, and one of my works was acquired by the University for its permanent collection. The community of artists of Rome welcomed me wholeheartedly as one of them. I had managed to somehow escape from Belgrade, the first city in Europe declared *Judenrein* (Jew-free) by the Nazis, and begin a new life in a center of creativity, Rome.

After the sequence of events that befell all Jews from the barbarism of the Nazis, I realized that I had always been driven to achieve by a need to redeem the destructiveness that terrible period had introduced into the world. The Nazis, who emerged from the cultural heartland of Europe, had methodically organized the slaughter of the most culturally prolific sectors of the Continent. As a victim of that brutality, I incorporated an instinctual force that sought to restore a balance toward creativity and the value of life. In biblical or philosophical terms, this might be viewed as a push for redemption, but in my case it was a very psychologically understandable need to continue living as a person who could make sense of the world, and not to succumb to a view in which meticulously planned yet senseless and destructive violence went unchallenged.

Six years following the official cessation of hostilities, I arrived in the United States of America, the beneficiary of a bill offered by President Truman to repatriate displaced persons, with my wife, my parents, my sister, and $200 in my pocket, of which I spent half on food, and the other half on an FM radio. Thus began my new life in my third country and language, in the United States—a life of family, teaching, artistic creativity, and friendships, which has lasted a bit longer than the actual years of Hitler's thousand-year Reich. Although I did not experience the horrors of the extermination camps, after children, grandchildren, many one-man shows and several retrospectives as an

315

artist, decades teaching visual thinking at Harvard, and a rich career as a teacher of painting, I realize it was the tenacity of a common Jewish family, the goodwill, humanity, and bravery of good Italians, and others, and perhaps some luck, my resourcefulness, serendipity, or divine intervention that enabled us to rebuild our lives in our newly adopted home in the United States. Most of all, I have enjoyed sharing with my family, friends, and students the wisdom acquired through my life experiences.

Index

Page numbers in **bold** refer to illustrations.

317